THE LONDON
UNITED TRAMWAYS

Volume Two, 1913 to 1933

This posed photograph taken at Hounslow Heath terminus, with the motorman carrying out a "watching brief" from inside the car, shows the potential danger involved when the youth of the day attempted to obtain a "whippy" on the back of a tramcar.

(Courtesy National Tramway Museum)

COVER PHOTOGRAPH

The company invested in new cars to be as Type UCC, but more commonly called "Feltham". One of these is seen here, soon after completion.   (Courtesy National Tramway Museum)
Photo M.J.O'Connor.

The London United Tramways

Volume Two, 1913 to 1933

by
C. S. Smeeton

Published in London by

THE LIGHT RAIL TRANSIT ASSOCIATION
13A The Precinct, Broxbourne, Herts EN10 7HY
in association with
THE TRAMWAY AND LIGHT RAILWAY SOCIETY

2000

———

Printed and bound in the UK by
MPG Information Division, Unwin Brothers Limited,
The Gresham Press, Old Woking, Surrey, GU22 9LH.

ISBN 0 948106 24 7

CONTENTS

INTRODUCTION TO VOLUME TWO

This volume continues the story of the London United Tramways from 1913 when the company, still part of the Underground Electric Railways of London Ltd. group, was brought under the management of a holding company, the London & Suburban Traction Company Ltd., in which the British Electric Traction Company Ltd., owners of the Metropolitan Electric Tramways Ltd. held a large interest. The smaller BET-owned South Metropolitan Tramways & Lighting Company Ltd. was also brought into the BET group, as was the MET-owned Tramways (MET) Omnibus Company Ltd. This placed day-to-day management and operation of all three tramway companies in the hands of the senior BET directors and officers, chief among which were James Devonshire and Arthur Henry Pott, managing director and general manager and engineer respectively of the Metropolitan Electric Tramways.

The arrangement of this volume varies from that of Volume One in being largely chronological, covering the extensive financial and administrative aspects of the company, its financial reconstruction in 1918, and initial post-war attempts to rehabilitate the company's undertaking, culminating in the introduction of the "Feltham" trams and the trolleybuses in 1931. Chapter and page numbering are continued in sequence from Volume One.

The company's relations with the London County Council have been touched upon in Volume One; the present volume relates Clifton Robinson's abortive attempts to secure through running powers over the LCC lines to central London and the final settlement of the disputed sale of the LUT lines in Hammersmith to that body in 1922.

It has been possible to deal with rolling stock comprehensively following the discovery of records of the acquisition of the car fleet, its equipment and subsequent history. Fares and tickets and the allied subject of routes and services are also dealt with in detail, as are the financial difficulties faced by the company, which quickly followed the sale by the White family of Bristol and their associates' majority interest in the company to Charles Tyson Yerkes' newly formed Underground Electric Railways of London Ltd.

The main narrative in this work ends at 30 June 1933 but an additional section has been added, taking the story forward to the closure of the last LUT routes in 1937, for which the author is indebted to Mr.Geoffrey E.Baddeley.

Much of the material in this volume has been obtained from the Sir George White archive which became available at Bristol Record Office by the time work on this volume had commenced. This invaluable collection also includes many of James Clifton Robinson's papers relating to his period as managing director and engineer of the LUT and to his life and times generally. The author is indebted to Bristol Record Office staff for the help given during extensive research carried out there and is grateful for the encouragement given by Sir George White's great grandson, the fourth baronet.

Spring 1999.   C.S.Smeeton.

ACKNOWLEDGEMENTS

Compilation of this work has been made possible only through help received from many sources, both private and official. The complexity of the subject necessitated lengthy research at many institutions, and to all those who have helped I extend grateful thanks and appreciation.

Reorganisation of London local government in 1965 lightened the task somewhat when the formation of the Greater London boroughs brought records of twenty-one of the old urban districts and boroughs together in seven centres, the reference libraries and local history departments of the London Boroughs of Ealing, Hammersmith and Fulham, Hillingdon, Hounslow, Kingston upon Thames, Merton and Richmond upon Thames. Mrs.Christine Bayliss and Mrs.Anna Manthorpe of the Hammersmith & Fulham Local History Archives are specially thanked for their assistance during protracted research into the early horse tramways in the West London area which metamorphosed into the London United Tramways in 1894.

Records of the London County Council and Middlesex County Council, now located at the City Corporation & Metropolitan Record Office (formerly the Greater London Record Office) at 40 Northampton Road, Clerkenwell in company with the Minute Books of London United Tramways Ltd. (from November 1901) and those of the constituent companies of the Underground Electric Railways of London Ltd. and the London & Suburban Traction Company Ltd. have been invaluable sources. I am most grateful for the help given me by the staff there over a long period, as I am for assistance given by those at the Surrey County Council Record Office.

Ms.Patricia Austin, Librarian and Archivist at the London Transport Museum and Miss Sheila Taylor, Photographic Archivist at the Museum have given invaluable assistance in their respective fields during the research period and their contribution is acknowledged with thanks.

Other sources at which research has been conducted are the House of Lords Record Office, the Institutions of Electrical, Civil and Mechanical Engineers, H.M.Patent Office and the British Library (at the time of writing in the process of transferring from Bloomsbury to the new complex adjoining St.Pancras Station).

Minute books and other records of the 1894-1901 London United Company have not survived but as mentioned in Volume One the extensive collection of material on Sir George White and Sir Clifton Robinson became available at Bristol Record Office shortly after work on this book commenced. This valuable archive enabled me to provide a much more detailed history of the early years of the LUT than would otherwise have been the case and I extend grateful thanks to the staff at the Record Office for the help given me during that time. I also acknowledge the assistance given by Mr.Geoffrey Baddeley with the chapters dealing with the LUT trolleybuses and operation of the LUT system by the London Passenger Transport Board from 1 July 1933.

I am indebted to Mr.Bryan Woodriff for the loan of material from the Bryan Woodriff Industrial Archaeological Collection and to Mr.K.C.Blacker for copies of reports on results of trials with new electrical equipment from 1923 and technical data on the 1931 trolleybuses. Mr.C.L.Withey has kindly provided details of the withdrawal and disposal of ex-LUT cars following the LPTB merger.

Many others have provided information as individuals; these include Messrs.P.Broadley, R.Brook, D.F.Croome, E.C.Dawes, W.Fuller, F.P.Groves, G.B.Hammond, J.D.Markham, J.H.Meredith, and G.W.Purton. The late G.L.Gundry, C.W.Herbert, Philip Pugh, J.H.Price, R.E.Tustin and M.N.A.Walker all made valuable contributions to the work during their lifetimes. In particular I am especially grateful to the late Frank Thornton-Jones for the encouragement he gave me during the lengthy research period, and his help with the subject of independent omnibus competition in the 1920s.

Photographic coverage is extensive; this has been possible through the loan of many rare views from several sources, which include the Sir George White Collection at Bristol Record Office, the London Transport Museum and the National Tramway Museum, whose Photographic Curator, Mr.Glynn Wilton has given invaluable assistance in selecting suitable illustrations.

Track and depot plans in both volumes have been prepared by E.R.Oakley from originals by the late B.Connelly, and are based upon the company's official mileage diagrams, the Ordnance Survey maps and later alterations and additions to the track and buildings recorded by the late F.Merton Atkins.

Mention has been made in Volume One of the special contribution made to this work by E.R.Oakley and the late J.H.Price; I again express gratitude for their assistance, and join with their names that of the Rev.P.S.G.Lidgett, custodian of the Omnibus Society's ticket collection for his contribution to the chapter dealing with fares and tickets.

Last, but by no means least among the many institutions mentioned in these paragraphs is the Library and Archives at the National Tramway Museum. I am most grateful to Mrs.Rosemary Thacker, the Librarian and Archivist there, for the help she has given me, especially her unfailing patience in seeking out answers to the many difficult questions encountered during the research for this work.

Finally, the work of the printers is acknowledged, and that of their binders, and my thanks go to my wife, who has endured the past years of absences and burning of midnight oil so entailed.

To any whose name I have omitted and who has helped in any way, my apologies and sincere thanks.

Ambergate, Spring 1999.   Cyril S. Smeeton

BIBLIOGRAPHY

Official publications

Applications to the Board of Trade under the Light Railways Act 1896 and to the Ministry of Transport for a Provisional Order.
Parliamentary Bills and Acts.
Provisional Orders.
Accident Reports of the Board of Trade and the Ministry of Transport.
Files of the Companies Registry.
Minutes of the London Traffic Advisory Committee and the London and Home Counties Traffic Advisory Committee.
Board of Trade (later Ministry of Transport) Returns on Tramways and Light Railways.

Local Authority Minutes

Minutes of the councils and committees of London County Council, Middlesex CC, Surrey CC, Acton Urban District Council, Barnes UDC, Brentford UDC, Chiswick UDC, Ealing UDC, Hampton UDC, Hampton Wick UDC, Hanwell UDC, Hayes UDC, Heston & Isleworth UDC and Hillingdon East and Hillingdon West Parish Councils, The Maldens & Coombe UDC, Merton & Morden UDC, Mitcham UDC, Southall-Norwood UDC, Staines UDC, Surbiton UDC, Teddington UDC, Twickenham UDC, Fulham Vestry (later Fulham Metropolitan Borough Council), Hammersmith Vestry (later Hammersmith MBC), Richmond Vestry (later Richmond Borough Council) and the Council of the Royal Borough of Kingston upon Thames.

Minutes and Reports of Companies and other Bodies

Minutes of the London United Tramways (1901) Ltd., the London & Suburban Traction Co. Ltd., The London General Omnibus Co. Ltd., the Metropolitan Electric Tramways Ltd., the Underground Electric Railways of London Ltd., the Union Construction Co. Ltd. (later Union Construction & Finance Co. Ltd.) and Annual Reports of these companies.

Annual Reports of the West Metropolitan Tramways Company and its successor from 1881 the West Metropolitan Tramways Co. Ltd.

Reports of the Proceedings of the Tramways & Light Railways Association and of the Municipal Tramways Association. Reports of the Proceedings of the Institution of Electrical Engineers.

Note: *Under the Local Government Act 1929 some adjacent smaller urban districts were amalgamated and most urban districts received charters of incorporation as municipal boroughs by the 1930s, an example being the urban districts of Brentford and Chiswick which became the municipal borough of Brentford and Chiswick.*

National Newspapers

The Times; Daily Telegraph; Morning Post; Daily Mail; Daily Chronicle.

Local Newspapers

The Acton Gazette
Brentford Times
Chiswick Gazette
Ealing Times
Middlesex Chronicle
Middlesex County Times
Richmond & Twickenham Times

Surrey Comet
Uxbridge Gazette
West London Observer
West Middlesex Gazette
Willesden Chronicle
Wimbledon Borough News

Technical and Trade Journals

The Architect's Journal
B.E.T. Gazette
Contract Journal
Engineering
Electrical Engineer
Electrical Review
Electrical Times
Electrician
Engineer

Light Railway & Tramway Journal
Municipal Journal
Modern Tramway
Railways & Tramways
Railway News
Street Railway Journal (USA)
T.O.T. Magazine
Tramway & Railway World
Tramway Review

Printed Books

Acton, Middlesex: W.King Baker, 1912
Electric Traction: A.T.Dover, various editions
The British Electric Car Company Limited: J.H.Price, 1978
The Dick, Kerr Story: J.H.Price, 1993
The Evolution of the British Electric Tramcar Truck: A.M.Goodwyn, 1976
The Feltham Car: Underground Group, 1931
Five Decades of B.E.T.: Roger Fulford, 1946
Great British Tramway Networks, 4th ed.: W.H.Bett & J.C.Gillham, 1962
Hurst Nelson Tramcars: J.H.Price, 1977
The London County Council Tramways (Vols.1 & 2): E.R.Oakley, 1989 & 1991
Manual of Electrical Undertakings: Garcke, various editions
Middlesex: Jubilee of the County Council 1889-1939: C.W.Radcliffe, 1939
Semi-detached London: A.A.Jackson, 1973
Souvenir of Inauguration of the Company's Electric Tramways: LUT, 1901
Tramlines to the Stars (George White of Bristol):   Sir George White, Bt., 1995

ABBREVIATIONS IN THE TEXT

ac	alternating current
BC	Borough Council
BEC	British Electric Car Co. Ltd.
BoT	Board of Trade
BET	British Electric Traction Co. Ltd.
BTH	British Thomson-Houston Co. Ltd.
BWEC	British Westinghouse Electric & Mfg. Co. Ltd.
CLR	Central London Railway
cwt	hundredweight (20 cwts equals one ton)
dc	direct current
EMB	Electro-Mechanical Brake Co. Ltd.
f.	furlong (length: 8f. equals 1 mile)
ft.	foot (feet) (length: 12 inches equals one foot)
GE	General Electric Company, Schenectady, USA
GEC	General Electric Company Ltd., Witton, Birmingham
GWR	Great Western Railway
hp.	horse power
ITC	Imperial Tramways Co. Ltd.
in.	inch(es) (units of length)
Kw	Kilowatt(s) (unit of power)
lb.	pounds (units of weight)
lb²	pounds per square inch
LRTJ	Light Railway & Tramway Journal
LSWR	London & South Western Railway
L&ST	London & Suburban Traction Co. Ltd.
LCC	London County Council
LER	London Electric Railway Co.
LGOC	London General Omnibus Co. Ltd.
LHCTAC*	London & Home Counties Traffic Advisory Committee
LPTB	London Passenger Transport Board
£sd	Pounds, shillings, pence (UK currency to February 1971)
LTAC*	London Traffic Advisory Committee
LTE	London Transport Executive
LUT	London United Tramways
MBC	Metropolitan Borough Council
MDR	Metropolitan District Railway
MET	Metropolitan Electric Tramways
MIEE	Member, Institution of Electrical Engineers
MCC	Middlesex County Council
mile/h	miles per hour (mph)
ml.	mile
MoT	Ministry of Transport
MV	Metropolitan-Vickers Electrical Co. Ltd.
RE	Royal Engineers
SCC	Surrey County Council
SMET	South Metropolitan Electric Tramways & Lighting Co. Ltd.
T&LRA	Tramways & Light Railways Association
T&RW	Tramway & Railway World
TMOC	Tramsways (MET) Omnibus Co. Ltd.
TOT	Train, Omnibus, Tram
UCC§	Union, Construction & Finance Co. Ltd.
UEC	United Electric Car Co. Ltd.
UDC	Urban District Council
UERL	Underground Electric Railways of London Ltd.
WMT	West Metropolitan Tramways Co.
yd.	yard (length: three feet equals one yard)

*   The London Traffic Advsory Committee appointed by the Minister of Transport was renamed London & Home Counties Traffic Advisory Committee on 1 January 1925

§   Union Construction Co.: name changed 4 February 1929

CHAPTER SIXTEEN

FINANCE AND ADMINISTRATION

The original London United Tramways company was formed on 19 July 1894 and registered as a joint stock limited company with authorised share capital of £50,000, half in Ordinary shares and half in 6% Cumulative Preference shares, all of ten pounds each. The holders of the £32,000 debenture stock of the West Metropolitan Tramways Company, having recovered their investment through the efforts of the WMT Receiver, George White, re-invested their money in 4% First Mortgage Debenture Stock of the LUT for repayment ten years from 1 July 1894. Details of the events leading to the formation of the company and the personalities involved are recorded in the first volume of this book.

Following an extraordinary general meeting of the shareholders held on 7 October 1895 the directors resolved to increase the company's share capital to £100,000 by the issue of a further 5,000 ten-pound shares, again half in Ordinary and half 6% Preference. On 11 February 1897 another 15,000 ten-pound Ordinary shares were agreed to, bringing the authorised share capital to £250,000. By 21 November 1898 the company had brought the erstwhile WMT lines to an excellent state of repair and was about to embark upon a long-delayed programme of electrification of the original lines, construction of the power station and extensions to the existing lines. On the same date, the shareholders agreed to a new issue of 15,000 ten-pound Preference shares, bringing the total authorised share capital to £400,000.

On 4 July 1900, with this extensive programme under way, a further issue was formally approved. This consisted of 20,000 ten-pound shares, half of which were Ordinary, and half 6% Preference, to bring the total share capital to £600,000. On 3 October 1900 the directors voted to issue 4% First Mortgage Debenture Stock equal to the company's paid-up share capital, of which £350,000 was immediately taken up. The trustees for this were George White and Joseph Wethered, the latter a business associate of White with wide interests in mining and railways in Wales and the West Country. A further £100,000 of this stock was issued on 16 August 1901.

By this time the electrification of the old West Metropolitan lines, together with extensions to Southall and Hounslow had been completed, with the formal opening of the system taking place on 10 July 1901. Powers for further extensions were obtained by the Acts of 1901 and 1902. A section in the 1901 Act also empowered the company to sell or to transfer to a reconstituted or new company the undertaking authorised by the Acts of 1873 to 1901 and the Light Railway Order of 1898. Obligations under these enactments were incumbent upon any new or reconstructed company created under the 1901 Act.

This power was sought after the directors and shareholders had considered the financial and other implications arising from the rapid development taking place, and in September 1901 a decision was taken by the shareholders to reconstruct the company in order to strengthen its position and broaden its financial base. Up to this time the shares and stock of the company was almost wholly owned by the White family, who had bought the assets of the West Metropolitan Tramways in

1894, and this was considered an opportune moment to make a public share offer. The company was also considering extending its transport interests to the London underground electric railways, while large sums were about to be spent on the extension of the tramways to Hampton Court.

A prospectus was published on 18 November 1901 under the terms of which the "old" company, i.e., the existing company, would be sold to a "new" company for £1,650,000. Part of this sum was to be satisfied by an exchange of shares, nominees of the "old" company receiving £360,000 in ten-pound 5% Cumulative Preference shares in the "new" company in exchange for £300,000 in ten-pound 6% Cumulative Preference shares in the "old" company. In adddition £600,000 in Ordinary shares in the "new" company was offered to holders of the same amount in Ordinary shares of the "old" company. £450,000 in new 4% First Mortgage Debenture Stock of the "new" company and £240,000 in cash were also offered to the "old" company shareholders. In the prospectus it was stated that the "old", or 1894, company had spent £1,050,000 to acquire, establish and build up its undertaking, and outstanding liabilities under this heading had been discharged. The difference between this sum and the purchase price amounted to £600,000, regarded as "goodwill" but not so described in the sale agreement. (The "old" company paid annual dividends of 8% from 1895 to 1898 and 10% thereafter).

Incorporation of the "new" company as London United Tramways (1901) Ltd. took place on 11 November 1901. The authorised share capital of £1,650,000 was divided into 82,500 each of ten-pound 5% Cumulative Preference and ten-pound Ordinary shares. An issue of £825,000 4% First Mortgage Debenture Stock was authorised, the share and stock issues being managed by Baring Brothers & Co. Ltd. The trustees for the debenture stock were George White, Joseph Wethered and Lord Revelstoke of Baring Brothers & Co. and the balances of this, amounting to £375,000 together with the 5% Cumulative Preference shares amounting to £465,000 were offered to investors at par. Thᵉ remaining 22,500 ten-pound Ordinary shares were reserved for future issue. It was anticipated that the surplus capital (in cash) available would suffice to complete the lines from Isleworth and Richmond Bridge to Twickenham and Hampton Court respectively, with the remaining authorised lines being financed by raising additional capital as and when required.

The directors' statement anticipated receipts from the existing 20 miles of electric lines of £11,150 per mile annually, based upon 10d per car mile run, or £312,200 less operating expenses of £165,905. From this a profit of £146,295 was expected to be sufficient to pay annual interest of £33,000 on the 4% Debenture Stock and £89,250 in dividends to the Ordinary and Preference shareholders, leaving a surplus of £26,045 for contingencies. The statement indicated that renewals were fully provided for in the estimated working expenditure. Demand for the new issues was strong and the subscription lists were closed early.

First directors of the new company were George White, Edward Everard, Hugh C. Godfray, James Clifton Robinson and Samuel White, who had been Secretary of the 1894 company. Secretary of the new company was William George Verdon Smith, who also held posts with the Imperial Tramways Company and the Bristol Tramways and Carriage Company. George White, Everard, Godfray and Robinson were also directors of the original company. It should be noted that the London United Tramways Ltd. as founded in 1894 was a true family business, with George White at the centre and, apart from Robinson and Godfray, all the others mentioned were related in some way to him. Several other members of the family held posts or owned holdings in the company, together with several of White's business associates in Bristol.

Ownership of the undertaking passed formally to the 1901 company on 31 December and its management was vested in the new company on 1 January 1902.

The conveyance of the assets was sealed on 26 February 1902. The first major transactions of the new company were the placing, on the same day, of large contracts for provision of additional plant at Chiswick power station, rolling stock and extensive public works in connection with the tramway extensions to Hampton Court, described in Volume 1. The financial arrangements for these contracts had been provided for by the 1894 company. The success of the November 1901 share offer led to a further issue of 17,500 ten-pound 5% Preference and the same number of ten-pound Ordinary shares. On 18 December 1902 the directors resolved to allot these shares *pro rata* to the Ordinary shareholders, subject to payment of one pound per share on or before 9 February 1903.

At an extraordinary meeting of the 1894 company's shareholders held on 12 April 1902 a special resolution, "that the undertaking's tramways and light railways property and assets of the company having been purchased by London United Tramways (1901) Ltd. the company be voluntarily wound up", was passed and Samuel White was appointed as liquidator. On the same day, the allotment of 60,000 fully-paid Ordinary shares of the 1894 company to the new company was approved, together with the balance of the company's capital, i.e., 22,493 ten-pound Ordinary shares; 4,500 of these were allocated to the Imperial Tramways Company and 17,993 to George and Samuel White.

The £600,000 remaining from the sale of the 1894 company was distributed in varying sums to George and Samuel White, Hugh C. Godfray, H.G.Doggett, W.G.Verdon Smith and Henry White Smith. This "goodwill" payment was made "in recognition of their having transformed the decrepit and loss-making West Metropolitan Tramways Company's system into an efficient and profitable undertaking". Smaller sums, up to £939 each were paid to a number of individuals who were among the original subscribers of the 1894 company.

The abortive underground electric railway scheme in 1902 (described in Volume 1) had a profound effect upon the future of the London United Tramways. Differences between George White and the American joint promoters resulted in both parties withdrawing from the scheme, and a decision by White in the summer of 1902 to dispose of his majority interest in the LUT and to withdraw from London traffic schemes generally. His shares were offered to an unnamed American electric railway promoter who did not complete the transaction, but were ultimately purchased by another American, Charles Tyson Yerkes, who in April 1902 had formed the Underground Electric Railways Company of London Ltd. (UERL) and was interested in a proposed "tube" railway linking Hammersmith, the City and the northern suburbs. Yerkes was financed at the outset by American interests. Later, when the UERL was building its power station at Lots Road, Chelsea, large additional sums were required to complete its schemes. These were supplied mainly by the Frankfurt financial house of Lazard Speyer Ellissen.

Discussions between Edgar Speyer, the senior partner of Speyer Brothers (the London branch of Lazard Speyer Ellissen) and Yerkes resulted in a decision being taken on 4 November 1902 by the UERL directors to buy 50,000 LUT ten-pound Ordinary shares "in accordance with Speyer Brothers' offer in their letter of 10 September 1902 to George White & Co". In addition to these fully paid-up shares, Yerkes also bought 22,493 of the one-pound paid Ordinary shares.

On 19 March 1903, with the UERL having gained the controlling interest, the London United directors met, with Clifton Robinson in the Chair. At this meeting George White, Edward Everard and Hugh Godfray resigned their seats on the board. They were replaced by Yerkes (who was appointed Chairman), Charles Ainsworth Spofford and Walter Abbot, all UERL directors. Samuel White remained on the board as the sole representative of the old regime, reflecting the still large interest of the White family and the Imperial Tramways Company in the

1901 company. Robinson remained as managing director without voting powers, while W.G.Verdon Smith retained office as Secretary. The final liquidation of the 1894 LUT company took place on 31 October 1903.

The last construction project carried out by the LUT with finance provided by the White interests through the Imperial Tramways Company were the lines at Hampton Court. The completion of the line from Southall to Uxbridge and the construction of the Acton-Hammersmith link in 1904, the Surrey lines and the Boston Road link between Hanwell and Brentford in 1905-7 all took place under the new regime as described in Volume 1. On 14 July 1903, following a request by Clifton Robinson to Edgar Speyer for finance to continue the authorised construction programme, the UERL directors approved a loan of £50,000. This was repayable when £200,000 of LUT debenture stock was realised.

Yerkes did not remain for long as Chairman of the LUT. He was in poor health and wished to devote his time to the completion of the UERL's own construction programme. He resigned as Chairman on 2 August 1905 but retained his seat on the board. Charles James Cater Scott, one of the original directors of the Underground Company and Chairman of the London and India Docks Company was elected to the LUT board and appointed Chairman. At the same time Samuel White resigned his seat and was replaced by another UERL director, William H. Brown, leaving Clifton Robinson as the sole remaining member of the original Bristol syndicate on the board.

American influence on the administration of the company made itself felt at an early date. At the request of Yerkes a New York firm of public accountants, Niles & Niles, carried out an investigation into the administrative procedures of the LUT, but details are unavailable. A later report, dated 28 November 1906 (much of which has not survived) was produced by C.S.Sergeant, sometime General Manager of the Boston West End Street Railway. This touched upon the need for closer interworking between the officers of the various companies within the sphere of the UERL, for more advertising on the cars, and the recommendation that a flat fare system be introduced. Sergeant also said that services were too frequent and that through fares with "the Tube" would not pay.

By this time the UERL was finding that the huge costs of its electric railway schemes were becoming a strain on resources, and the position was causing concern at Speyer Brothers' head office. As a result, the LUT became embroiled in a search for economies. In an effort to ease the difficulties being faced, the Underground management went to the LCC with a plan for that authority to provide finance in exchange for the County Council being able, after a statutory period, to take over the entire railway assets of the company, in much the same way that the Council had dealt with the acquisition of the tramways in their area. Due, however, to a change in the make-up of the majority of the Council membership from "Progressive" to "Moderate" at this time, the proposal was rejected, with the result that the company had to look elsewhere, as is mentioned later in this chapter.

The Position Of J.Clifton Robinson

One victim of this crisis was Clifton Robinson, whose salary as managing director and fees as engineer had been confirmed by the directors on 14 February 1902, and followed arrangements made in 1898 at the start of electrification of the old lines. Robinson had been re-appointed as managing director and engineer to the 1901 company on 14 November 1901 on "such terms as the directors might determine thereafter in respect of his fees as engineer". His salary as managing director was fixed at £2,000 per annum, and it was agreed that in lieu of this sum he should have the use of the LUT-owned Garrick's Villa at Hampton as his personal residence. On 14 April 1902 the directors and Robinson agreed to his fees as engineer being fixed at 5% of the costs of Parliamentary promotions and construction of the lines, whether or not fully carried out. This proposal, by Robinson, was accepted by the board and the agreement countersigned on that day by George White and the Secretary, W.G.Verdon Smith.

On 2 December 1903 the subject of the engineer's fees was again raised, and it was resolved that the agreement of 14 April 1902 should be modified and not apply to the schemes for the 1903 and ensuing Parliamentary Sessions, and that Robinson should receive "such remuneration for work involved in these schemes as may be decided by the directors". Costs arising from the promotion of the two very large Bills of 1904 would be borne directly by the company. These two Bills, if passed in entirety, would have entailed expenditure of £1,282,000, but in the event only a small section of the 1904 tramways Bill was passed and even this was not built, while the Bill for a tramway beneath the Thames at Hammersmith was totally rejected.

In 1905 a disagreement arose over the interpretation of the terms. Robinson disputed the board's decision, contending that he was entitled to commission on land acquisitions for widenings and other purposes, at 5% of expenditure. Agreement could not be reached and both sides took the advice of Counsel. Frank Dawes, for the UERL, submitted that there was no commission entitlement in respect of land acquisitions, saying that "works and equipment" only was meant. He also maintained that no commission entitlement existed in respect of parts of authorised lines subsequently abandoned.

J.H.Balfour Browne, KC, advising Robinson, said that in December 1905 his client was entitled to 5% commission on all expenditure on an estimate of capital which would have been spent if all the lines had been built, and that "works" should include land acquisitions as had been the case in previous settlements. Estimated costs of works to be completed amounted to £501,634, and those to be abandoned, £660,605.

Proposals by the directors for a settlement varied between £19,000 and £39,000. Robinson suggested a payment of £25,000 in respect of schemes in progress and of £20,000 covering those to be abandoned. A compromise was agreed on 20 March 1906 and Robinson accepted £24,882 in full settlement of his claims, and the engineer's future remuneration would be on the basis of a fixed annual salary. Robinson expressed his appreciation of Balfour Browne's help in negotiating the settlement and to Cater Scott and his fellow directors for "the courteous manner in which the discussions were conducted".

Continuation Of The Crisis

A grandiose scheme for a light railway from the authorised line at Cranford on to Reading, and a plan to extend the line from Uxbridge to High Wycombe were briefly discussed by the directors in December 1904, but not taken further. Also, while the Surrey lines as far as Raynes Park were built in 1906, continuation of those through Wimbledon and on to Tooting and Summerstown were delayed. When work did start it was slow, and for a time it appeared that it might not be completed. Wimbledon Corporation pressed Robinson on the matter and he asked for their forbearance, saying that money markets were working against the company and financial difficulties were delaying completion of the work.

Meanwhile, the LUT was the subject of unfavourable comment in *The Economist* on 11 March 1905. This centred upon the small percentage of money set aside for repairs and renewals. The article pointed out that the company had spent 1.39% of capital expenditure on maintenance in 1903/4 and dividends paid were 3.84%. This was compared unfavourably with other systems, including Bristol, Bradford and Manchester, which had allotted respectable sums for these purposes, but did not feature in the LUT accounts. Yerkes replied to this criticism, saying that large sums under these headings were utilised out of revenue, that the whole undertaking was maintained to the highest standards and thus depreciation was a negligible quantity. *The Economist* reported that the percentage of receipts to capital was "wretched" and could not provide suitable depreciation and large dividends, at least until traffic greatly increased.

That there were some grounds for these strictures became clear later in 1905 when the track, first in Ealing and soon followed elsewhere on the system, began to deteriorate, bringing serious complaints from the local authorities. Poor track led to increased wear and tear on the cars, and from this time heavy expenditure became necessary on track and rolling stock which, however, did not keep pace with a worsening situation. The excellent financial results under the erstwhile Bristol management did not continue under the UERL regime, and dividends declined to the point when nothing was paid on the Ordinary shares and only occasional small percentages on the Preferences.

Further Changes

Yerkes died in New York on 29 December 1905. He was replaced as Chairman of the UERL by Edgar Speyer on 29 December 1906. The LUT was now even more under the direct control of Speyer Brothers, and with the UERL heavily committed to their own construction programme, together with other financial problems, Speyers were finding it difficult to provide additional finance to carry the LUT programme through. However, all parties were committed to the completion of their respective works, and the comparatively small amount of money required for the LUT Surrey scheme was found, the line to Tooting completed and the Summerstown branch constructed. By this time also, the UERL owned £765,000 of the LUT share capital, and was its largest shareholder.

A minor alteration to the company's style took place in 1907 when the Board of Trade sanctioned the removal of (1901) from the title, which reverted to "London United Tramways Limited". In November 1906 a Bill was deposited in Parliament for the 1907 Session which, however, did not have any financial provisions, but contained an important clause which, if passed, would have conferred valuable benefits upon the company.

In November 1907 a further Bill was deposited for the 1908 Session, containing a clause which had a disturbing effect upon the White interests in

Car No.240 in final condition and still with its original motors, awaiting departure from the "Red Lion" at Tolworth for Richmond Park Gates.   (Photographer unknown)

Bristol. This sought powers (which had been the subject of earlier Bills) to reconstruct the line in Kew Road, Richmond for electric traction, and to connect this line with the electrified line on the north side of Kew Bridge. The company, however, was unable to obtain the consent of Richmond Corporation to the use of overhead electric traction in Kew Road, and of Middlesex County Council to cross Kew Bridge. The directors therefore resolved, on 16 June 1908, to withdraw the bridge crossing clause from the Bill if agreement could not be reached. This was not forthcoming, but upon hearing of this, Sir George White and his colleagues at the Imperial Tramways Company became alarmed. The Bristol interest in the LUT was still considerable, amounting to nearly £500,000 in the Preference shares, ranking as the second largest shareholder after the UERL.

Sir George wrote to C.J.Cater Scott on 13 July 1908, expressing his concern at the decision. He asked that a special board meeting be called for the next day and for Edgar Speyer (who, by now, had received a baronetcy) to be present. At this meeting the ITC representative said that the proposal to withdraw the Kew Bridge clause from the Bill was "fraught with danger for the LUT" and suggested that his company might offer to assist with financing, specifically, the bridge crossing. A conference was arranged at which Sir Edgar Speyer with Sir George Gibb (UERL), and C.J.Cater Scott (LUT) attended, resulting in the ITC making an offer to supply the capital to construct the track on the bridge and its equipment for electric traction. The clause was reinstated in the Bill, which received Royal Assent on 1 August, with the bridge crossing sanctioned. On 12 August details of a proposed loan agreement were discussed for submission to the parties after the summer vacation.

On 18 December the LUT board learned of the terms for a loan by the ITC. £15,000 was offered for five years at 5% interest per annum, subject to payment of a 1.25% dividend on the Preference shares for the half-year to 31 December 1908. Evidently these were not acceptable to the LUT side as the matter was not discussed again until 31 March 1909, but even then, no decision was reached. Meanwhile a financial crisis was developing, and on 22 June the LUT board, still having made no decision on the ITC offer, was told that repayment of a £20,000 loan from the company's bankers was overdue and, to help clear this, some American railway bonds, bought for £75,000, had been sold for £14,831.3s.

Discussion on the financial position subsequently took place at a further conference, at which Speyer and representatives of the three parties were involved, the outcome of which was reported to the LUT board on 4 August 1909, although no details are rcorded. Following this the board decided to accept the Imperial Tramways' loan offer, but meanwhile there had been a change of heart in Bristol. On 13 October 1909, Hugh C.Godfray of ITC, wrote to the LUT solicitors in reply to their decision, referring to the failure by the London United to pay a dividend on the Preference shares for the half-year to 30 June 1909, and went on "... the whole course of the affairs of the LUT ... has had so disastrous an effect upon both companies as to make it quite impossible for the Imperial Tramways Company to raise any further capital for assistance of the LUT, however much the ITC board might desire to do so". The LUT Secretary, W.G.Verdon Smith, on receipt of this letter, sent copies to Cater Scott, Robinson and Speyer.

By June 1909 the company's position had deteriorated further, both financially and materially, resulting in Cater Scott, on 3 June, commissioning the American firm of J.G.White & Co, (not related in any way to the White family of Bristol) to investigate and report upon the state of the company and its assets. White's had a branch in London and had been involved in the formation of the UERL, had interests in tramway and railway construction, shipping and manufacturing, and were responsible for building the LUT line between Kingston and Wimbledon.

Their report, submitted to Cater Scott early in October 1909, concentrated mainly upon the track, was very detailed and contained recommendations for extensive renewals, most of which were hotly disputed by Robinson, who countered with his own report and recommendations. A brief supplementary report from White dated 11 October covered rolling stock, power plant, cabling and the overhead installation and presented a more satisfactory general picture, but was critical of the cars' trucks and electrical equipment, saying that the use of heavier trucks and better motors would have been a worthwhile investment. If all of White's recommendations for track renewals had been implemented, expenditure of £904,936 would have been required.

The J.G.White report also underlined the fact that Speyer, Cater Scott and their respective fellow directors were faced with hard decisions. The loss of the 1909 LUT Bill seeking running powers over the London County Council tramways and postponement of the Council's power to purchase the company's Hammersmith lines, together with the Board of Trade's failure to support the company's case, placed Sir Clifton Robinson in a dangerous position. Speyer and his colleagues saw no alternative to taking radical steps in a desperate attempt to retrieve the situation, and a decision was taken, possibly unilaterally by Speyer, to replace Sir Clifton as managing director and engineer.

On 14 January 1910 Speyer and Robinson visited Cater Scott at his residence at 37, Courtfield Road, South Kensington. There, Robinson agreed to resign his posts as managing director and engineer, writing his letter of resignation to Cater Scott at the meeting and in the following terms: "Referring to my interview with Sir Edgar Speyer and yourself I now write formally to resign my appointments as managing director and engineer and my seat on the board of London United Tramways Ltd. I shall be pleased to consult the convenience of the board as to the date of carrying out the contemplated change, and to afford Mr.Stanley every assistance upon his taking over the management. Believe me, very faithfully yours, James Clifton Robinson". After the private meeting, the LUT directors entered the room and the resignation was formally accepted at a special board meeting at which the directors voted him an honorarium of one year's salary and expressed their appreciation of his many years' work on behalf of the company.

Under New Management

The man chosen to fill the post of managing director was Albert Henry Stanley. With his family, he had left England in 1885 at the age of eleven years to settle in America and, after further education in that country, entered the transport industry as a stable lad with the Detroit City Street Railways Company, eventually attaining the position of general superintendent. In 1903 he joined the Street Railway Department of the Public Service Department of New Jersey where he became general manager. He returned to England in 1907 to take up work with the UERL, becoming a director in 1910.

The departure of Robinson left W.G.Verdon Smith, the Secretary, as the sole remaining representative of the Bristol interests in the LUT management and he continued in that office under the new regime. Stanley appointed as his assistant Zac Ellis Knapp, an American who, like Stanley, had arrived in England earlier to take up a post with the UERL. In 1910 he was appointed general manager and engineer of the LUT. The outward sign of these changes was the replacement of Robinson's name on the trams' rocker panels with that of William George Verdon Smith, and the gradual replacement of the ornate fleet-name lettering LONDON UNITED ELECTRIC TRAMWAYS (never a company title, but adopted in 1901 as a fleet name) by "The London United Tramways Ltd." in one-inch high characters in the bottom left-hand corners of the rocker panels.

Stanley's first task as managing director was to tell the board that large sums were required for urgent renewal of much of the track and for rolling stock repairs. In his first year in office £28,435.7s.7d was spent on the rolling stock, £23,559.6s.10d on the track and £5,505.5s.1d on overhead and cabling. Special expenditure amounted to a further £36,120.9s. on rolling stock and plant and another £23,348.10s on the track.

Falling revenues combined with heavy costs found the company in a critical position by the mid-1910 and the directors sought a large loan from the Union of London and Smith's Bank, who were bankers to the UERL. Albert Stanley met Sir George White, a trustee for the LUT debenture stock and discussed possible terms. The amount of the loan was not specified, but it was agreed that it would be secured on the proceeds of the sale of the Hammersmith lines to the London County Council, which had not at that time been finally agreed, but in the event amounted to £235,000. Sir George concurred with this proposal and Stanley was authorised by the directors to make the necessary arrangements with the bank.

Despite management changes and heavy expenditure on track and cars in 1910 and 1911, local authorities and other bodies continued to complain about noise. No dividends were paid, all available funds being devoted to the refurbishment programme. More cash was borrowed from the banks to pay debenture interest and one half-year's interest in 1911 was satisfied by a loan from the Imperial Tramways Company. Parr's Bank, who had dealt with company business, discontinued banking facilities, the account being transferred to the Union of London and Smith's Bank.

Omnibus competition intensified from 1905. Speyer continued to express concern over this and, in 1908 pointed out that the LUT was restricted to an average speed of 8½ mile/h, while omnibuses, particularly on the Uxbridge Road route were working at anything between 12 and 20 mile/h, and without the restrictions imposed upon the tramway (see also Chapter 29). A decision was eventually taken in 1910, to attract increased traffic by fitting top covers to 100 cars. These, to a spartan pattern, cost £12,750, the work being completed during 1911. Total special expenditure of £27,642 was incurred in that year on repairs to rolling stock, track and power plant, in addition to routine maintenance costs.

Throughout 1910, 1911 and the first half of 1912 the company continued to battle against falling revenues, increasing costs and unrelenting omnibus competition, especially from the London General Omnibus Company, which intensified in 1911 when that company introduced its new B-type vehicle, the first really reliable motor omnibus, which came on the streets in large numbers. The recently electrified London & South Western Railway made heavy inroads into the LUT share of the traffic in the Surrey suburbs. The other two company-owned tramway systems in London, the Metropolitan Electric Tramways and the South Metropolitan Electric Tramways and Lighting Company were experiencing similar difficulties, and it was becoming clear that some form of co-ordination of passenger traffic services, as envisaged in the report of the 1905 Royal Commission on London Traffic, was becoming a vital necessity.

Speyer's concern about competition had previously crystallised in the autumn of 1909 when exploratory talks were held between senior members of the UERL, LUT and London General Omnibus Company managements, seeking a basis for a pooling arrangement. A tentative proposal was put before the LGOC board for the amalgamation of road transport operators in London, with the possibility of the underground railways also becoming involved. These talks did not bear fruit immediately, but early in 1911 senior members of the three undertakings together with those of the Metropolitan Railway Company met to discuss the situation. On 10 May the UERL and LGOC directors met and a joint advisory committee was formed to devise a scheme for through ticketing between the Underground railways, London General omnibuses and London United trams, and the re-routing of omnibuses where competition was damaging, to areas where they could be best used as feeders to the electric railways, mainly the north and north-western suburbs.

High Street, Acton seen c.1908, with No.335 bound for Hammersmith and No.148 heading towards Uxbridge. No.148's history is described elsewhere in this book; it was the longest surviving vehicle of the original LUT fleet.

(Commercial view)

Bound for Uxbridge, Type Y car No.28 passes through Southall. This view was taken shortly after the end of the Great War. The conductor is wearing "mufti".

(Courtesy National Tramway Museum)

This conflicted with the interests of the Metropolitan Electric Tramways (owned by the British Electric Traction Company), the operator in those areas, on whose routes five Underground stations were located. The MET directors met on 13 October 1911 when their managing director, James Devonshire, advised his colleagues to create their own omnibus undertaking in connection with their trams. Their board accepted his advice, and on 4 December 1911 Emile Garcke, the MET and BET Chairman, promised the latter's support for the new company, which was incorporated on 13 January 1912 as the Tramways (MET) Omnibus Company with £20,000 authorised share capital.

This brought the UERL and LGOC closer together, and at a special meeting of the omnibus company board on 1 November 1911, they agreed to receive an amalgamation proposal from Edgar Speyer. Agreement between Speyer, Stanley and the LGOC directors was reached on 22 December 1911, despite strong opposition to the proposal by two of the General's board members. The UERL offer was finally approved on 15 January 1912 and the omnibus company chairman, Henry Hicks, was replaced by Cater Scott, while Albert Stanley was appointed as managing director. At the same time as these events were taking place it was announced, on 19 November, that the UERL was about to acquire full control of the City & South London and the Central London railway companies. The "London traffic combine" was becoming a reality, and criticisms were levelled against Sir Edgar Speyer alleging that he was attempting to set himself up as "a *de facto* traffic authority for London".

Also in 1911, as part of an economy programme, the services of several long-serving staff members' were dispensed with. Among them were William Nairn, the overhead, cabling and sub-station engineer, who had been with the company since the start of electrification, Fritz Rogers, the traffic superintendent and C.D.Braidwood, divisional inspector. Nairn returned to the Bristol Tramways & Carriage Company, while Braidwood was re-engaged or retained, as his name appears on notices in the 1920s as the traffic superintendent. There were also numerous staff reductions at the power station, workshops and sub-stations and among the engineeering and office staff.

The London and Suburban Traction Company Ltd.

While the merger with the LGOC was taking place Albert Stanley approached the boards of the Metropolitan Electric Tramways and their parent company, the British Electric Traction Company, the immediate objective being an amalgamation between their undertaking and the LUT in a holding company. Emile Garcke and James Devonshire followed up Stanley's suggestion and the MET board accepted the proposed draft merger terms. A provisional agreement was approved by the parties in September 1912. The London and Suburban Traction Company was promoted by the MET and incorporated on 19 November 1912 with initial nominal capital of £3,250,000 in one-pound shares, 1,500,000 of which were 5% Cumulative Preference and 1,750,000 Ordinary. The issue of £550,000 Debenture Stock was also authorised.

The first directors of the new company, nominated by their respective boards were Emile Garcke and James Devonshire (MET); E.R.Soames (T(M)OC); William Mitchell Acworth and Albert H.Stanley (LUT). James Devonshire was appointed managing director, and Arthur Lea Barber, secretary of the MET was appointed secretary. The company's constitution provided for the appointment of an independent chairman, pending which Emile Garcke acted in that capacity at the initial board meetings. The registered office was at the BET and Electrical Federation offices at 1, Kingsway, London, W.C.

The chief objective of the new company was the acquisition of the shareholdings in the two companies taken over. In the case of the LUT this meant that each £10 LUT 5% Preference share was exchanged for £5 in LST 5%

Cumulative Preference and £4.12s. Ordinary shares, while each £10 LUT Ordinary share was exchanged for a £7 LST Ordinary share. The LUT debenture stock was not affected. The British Electric Traction Company held £859,314 of the LST capital.

A special meeting of the London United Tramways shareholders was held on 4 December 1912 with William Acworth as chairman. He told them that the position of the company was grave. Dividends on the Preference shares were £233,000 in arrear, and gross receipts in the current nearly-ended year were no more than £13,000. Heavy increases in maintenance costs were expected as the lines and their equipment aged. The shareholders were strongly advised to accept the LST scheme as the best opportunity to restore financial stability and the meeting voted to accept the proposal.

Sir George White still owned a large proportion of the LUT Preference shares and had earlier given his consent to the proposed scheme conditional upon the new company purchasing from him, for cash, 25,000 LUT £10 Preference shares at the price of £7 a share. The directors of the new and associated companies agreed to this on the basis of the UERL and the MET taking 15,000 and 10,000 of the shares respectively.

The MET shareholders accepted the London & Suburban Traction Co. scheme without hesitation and on 18 December the first major management changes took place. Albert Stanley resigned as LUT managing director and was replaced by James Devonshire. W.G.Verdon Smith, the last remaining member of the original Bristol management, resigned as Secretary "by arrangement" and his place was taken by Arthur Lea Barber. The directors recorded their appreciation of Verdon Smith's long service to the company since its inception and voted him an honorarium of £1,500. He took up senior posts in Bristol as managing director of the Imperial and Bristol Tramways & Carriage companies. Under the exchange of shares the Imperial Tramways holding in the LUT was exchanged for 125,000 one-pound 5% Preference and 118,382 one-pound Ordinary LST shares.

Another change in the LUT directorate took place on 11 February 1913 when Captain Felix Schuster replaced William H.Brown of the UERL, and at the same time Arthur Henry Pott, general manager and engineer of the MET, who had been with the company since its inception in 1902, was appointed to a similar post with the LUT, replacing Zac Ellis Knapp, who moved to a senior engineering position with UERL. These changes meant that the day to day administration of the LUT was firmly in the hands of members of the BET management, notwithstanding that the UERL still retained a large holding in it. At the same time as these changes were taking place the LUT registered office was transferred from Electric Railway House, Broadway, Westminster to the British Electrical Federation offices at 1, Kingsway, the "umbrella" organisation to which all British Electric Traction companies were affiliated, and where LUT directors' meetings were henceforth held. The LUT engineer's, accountant's and traffic manager's offices were transferred to the MET head offices at Manor House, Finsbury Park, but local facilities for these departments were retained at Chiswick. The Rt.Hon.Charles B.Stuart-Wortley, KC. MP., was elected to the LST board and appointed Chairman on 25 April 1913.

The financial arrangements between London & Suburban Traction and the tramway companies, to which the UERL was a party were, in broad terms, on the basis of loans made to them by the LST through its bankers at agreed rates of interest, and in some cases taking loans direct from the UERL on the companies' behalf and guaranteeing repayment. This meant that the UERL remained the dominant partner in the group and in the final analysis all advances came from it and its bankers. One of the first loans, made in May 1913 to the LUT by the LST, was £100,000 "urgently required to maintain services". The Union of London & Smith's Bank offered this sum, at unspecified interest, to be repaid by 30 June

1914 against the security of £300,000 LUT Second Mortgage Debenture Stock, repayment to be guaranteed by the LST and that company's obligation also to be guaranteed. On 18 June the terms were modified and it was agreed that the UERL should, in this case be sole guarantor. Such loans were taken regularly and renewed from time to time, continuing on the same basis throughout the remaining life of the company.

On 14 June 1913 the third tramway system, the BET-owned South Metropolitan Electric Tramways and Lighting Company, was brought into the LST scheme, under similar arrangements to those covering the LUT and MET. Their general manager, Archibald Victor Mason, remained in his post until December 1918, when he became assistant manager and engineer to the three companies. This formed the last link in what became "the London Traffic Combine", popularly known (and sometimes vilified) as "the combine". About this time the companies adopted a symbol composed of the letters T-O-T (Train-Omnibus-Tram) for use on timetables and other publicity material. Steps were taken to standardise office procedures and stationery, uniforms and where possible, equipment, although it was some considerable time before a measure of standardisation was achieved, the Great War of 1914-18 intervening to halt the process.

The LST management then asked the LUT board to arrange with the MET for the use of the latter's facilities at their Hendon Car Works in anticipation of the Chiswick complex passing to the London County Council, when that body purchased the Hammersmith lines. An 80-yard gap between the LUT line in High Street, Acton, and the southern terminus of the MET at the end of Horn Lane could only be closed by taking a single line through King Street. As described elsewhere in this volume the link did not materialise until 1915, when wartime conditions overcame the objections.

On 13 May 1914, the LST directors were told that continuing decreasing revenues were creating a serious situation, and a conference was arranged between the managements of the three tramway companies and the LGOC to discuss reduction of tram services, the LUT being in the most serious position. The "General" expressed willingness to accept the principle of repaying the tramway companies the value of traffic lost to competition, and it was agreed to proceed on this basis without delay. (See also Chapter 29).

At the same meeting James Devonshire said that the tramway staff were seeking a large wages increase which, if granted, would cost the LUT £30,000 annually. 48% of the men were non-union and Devonshire said he had made it clear that the company would resist the unions' threat to force them to discharge all non-union men. This stand was approved and supported by all present, and the strike threat was averted.

The Great War brought continuing and intensified problems to the LUT. Pleasure traffic, upon which it relied heavily, was eventually drastically reduced, costs increased and the company became ever more dependent upon its bankers and financiers to keep its services operating, while the shareholders were receiving no return on their investments.

Notwithstanding the large British Electric Traction Co. holding in the LST and the fact that BET men held most senior posts in the tramway companies, the management of Underground Electric still held the controlling interest. This became evident on 14 April 1915 when the LUT directors were advised that the registered office of their company was to be transferred, "as soon as convenient", back to Electric Railway House, Broadway, Westminster, where it was to remain for the rest of the company's existence.

No payments were made in 1916 by the LUT to London & Suburban Traction, whose board concluded that a second reconstruction of London United capital was inevitable. They asked that the LUT directors commission J.G.White & Co. to conduct an investigation into the current financial standing and future prospects of the company. This report has not been seen and nothing of its content is known, but it evidently presented a picture that caused the directors of the LUT, UERL and LST to take far-reaching decisions. As matters stood, in order to continue operations, loans of £68,000 and £33,000 were obtained from the LST and UERL respectively, under agreements sealed on 6 March 1917, security for which debentures were allocated to the lenders. Such loans became larger and more frequent from this time on.

Because LUT fares were fixed by statute, at very low levels, the Board of Trade was unable to sanction desperately needed increases. Working profits in 1916 were insufficient to meet revenue liabilities, and net results to June 1917 were even less favourable. Once again, maintenance arrears had built up and large sums were required to put the undertaking into a proper state of repair. Meanwhile wartime traffic had to be kept running, although services in non-industrial districts were heavily reduced. Lack of confidence in the future of the company was underlined when the auditors, Deloitte, Plender Griffiths & Co., declined to offer their services for the year 1917, their place being taken by Price, Waterhouse & Co., joint auditors to the LST.

Continued operation of the undertaking hung in the balance. On 5 June 1917 the debenture stockholders obtained the appointment of a Receiver in the High Court, pending submission of a scheme for reorganization of the LUT capital. F.S.Price, of Price, Waterhouse & Co. was duly appointed and a committee of investigation formed. From this time the LUT operated under severe handicaps. There were occasions when suppliers could not be paid and materials necessary to maintain services could not be obtained. The debenture holders asked for a seat on the LUT board, to which the directors would not accede. A number of capital re-organisation schemes were proposed. One, by C.G.Tegetmeier, was submitted to the debenture holders' committee, and was subject to a satisfactory agreement for pooling receipts of the three tramway companies and the LGOC, or alternatively an equivalent arrangement being made between the companies and the UERL.

Low fares remained an intractable problem and on 17 October 1917 the LST board advised the LUT directors to go to Parliament for authority to make increases. The necessary Bill was deposited in November 1917 for the 1918 Session and in addition to fare increases it sought sanction for a capital re-organization, abolition of the wayleaves payable to the local authorities and provisions for abandonment of the lines between Southall and Uxbridge, in Richmond Road, Kingston, between King's Road and Ham Boundary and in London Road and Kingston Hill between Cambridge Road and Kingston Hill terminus. The Bill also sought postponement of the local authorities' power to purchase the lines until 1960. The provisions regarding fares are described elsewhere in this volume.

The Parliamentary Agents, Lees & Co., on behalf of the company, asked Alfred Baker, general manager of Birmingham Corporation Tramways, to report on the condition of the system and advise what expenditure would be required to place the track and rolling stock of the undertaking upon a sound footing, and annually thereafter to maintain the system in such a condition. Baker estimated that track reconstruction would involve costs of £406,000, repairs to paving, £45,000 and renovation of the rolling stock, £90,000. Baker also estimated that £31,750 should be set aside annually for reconstruction purposes, to be regarded as a minimum figure, and provided that ordinary repairs and renewals chargeable against revenue were not neglected. These figures were accepted by the Parliamentary committee and formed the basis of financial conditions enshrined in the 1918 Act. Further details of Baker's report on the track are given in Chapter 14 (Volume 1) and in the rolling stock Chapter 21 of the present volume.

Delay in securing agreement to some of the clauses in the Bill held up its passage through Parliament, but it was finally passed and received Royal Assent on 21 November 1918. The financial provisions were largely unaltered and the resulting Act directed that the company should obtain the sanction of the High Court for a scheme of reduction of capital to a total of £2,623,000, to consist of a maximum of £1,000,000 of debenture stock, £963,000 of 5% Preference and £660,000 of Ordinary shares. Dividends on the existing Preference shares were to be cancelled, and for five years from the end of the war dividends on the Preference shares in any one year would be paid only from the revenue of that year. A right to create further capital was retained. The clause referring to abandonments, however, had been withdrawn from the Bill.

Except in the case of the London County Council, the local authorities' power to purchase the lines was postponed by the Act until within six months of 1 January 1950, instead of 1960 as requested, and in like manner every seven years thereafter. An obligation was placed upon the company to put the undertaking into good repair as soon as possible, and until £400,000 was spent on reconstruction no dividend was payable on either class of the shares. The £235,000 to be received from the LCC on completion of the sale of the Hammersmith lines was to be applied to the £400,000 to be spent on reconstruction.

The Act also called upon the company to establish a Special Reserve Fund by setting aside £60,000 per year for five years, £40,000 per year for the next four years and £30,000 annually from 1 January 1928, after paying loan and debenture interest. A deficiency in one year did not have to be made good in a succeeding year. This reserve was to be devoted to reconstruction and renewals, but no part of it was to be used for these purposes until the £400,000 previously mentioned had been spent. The target was, in fact reached and exceeded by 31 December 1925, and by the same date £76,452.7s.11d. had been placed in the Special Reserve Fund at which figure, owing to continued heavy interest payments and other costs, it remained until 30 June 1933.

On 8 April 1919 the scheme was sanctioned by the High Court. The whole of the issued Ordinary shares were cancelled, £4.15s written off the Preference shares and the remaining £5.5s per share sub-divided and converted to 21 new fully-paid 5s Ordinary shares. Of the 963,000 new 5% Preference £1 shares, 962,841 were issued together with the whole of the 656,250 Ordinary 5s shares. £857,841 of the authorised £1,000,000 First Mortgage Debenture Stock was also issued. At the directors' meeting on 25 April 1919, W.M.Acworth was re-elected as Chairman and two new directors were appointed to the board. These were George Balfour, MP., Chairman of Balfour, Beatty & Co. and a director of a number of tramway and power companies throughout the country and abroad, and Sir Lewis Coward, KC., Recorder of Folkestone. George Balfour's appointment came immediately prior to the commencement of the post-war reconstruction programme, and his extensive experience in the electrical and traction industries was invaluable during the period up to 1930, when he resigned from the board. Sir Lewis Coward remained on the board for one year, his legal experience essential for implementing the complexities of the 1918 Act.

On 17 July 1919 William Corwin Burton, a director of the UERL and of J.G.White & Co. was appointed managing director, succeeding James Devonshire. This, however, was short-lived, Burton relinquishing office and his seat on the board from 30 September. Meanwhile James Devonshire continued to carry out the duties of managing director but without that title until major administrative changes took place on 7 March 1929. On this date the office was revived, when Frank Pick was appointed to the post, in addition to that of managing director of the LGOC and all the other UERL companies. The High Court having sanctioned the capital re-organisation scheme on 8 April 1919, the company was able to ask for the discharge of the Receiver appointed on 15 June 1917. The application was

The top-cover on Type Y 27 was built to higher standards than the main batch. This July 1929 view also portrays Motorman Gower, the oldest driver then in the company's service.

(Hugh Nicol. Courtesy D.W.K.Jones)

granted and the Receiver was discharged on 21 July 1919, allowing the company freedom to resume managing its own affairs.

A.H.Stanley, who was knighted in 1914, remained a director of the LUT until 1916, when he was appointed to a senior government position, eventually to become a Member of Parliament following a by-election at Ashton-under-Lyne, at which he was returned unopposed. At the invitation of the Prime Minister, David Lloyd George, he also became the President of the Board of Trade, and later, a Privy Counsellor.

After relinquishing government service in 1919, he returned to the UERL as Chairman and managing director, but not to the tramway companies as a director. On 14 November 1919 he was installed as Chairman of the London & Suburban Traction Co., with C.B.Stuart-Wortley (by then Lord Stuart of Wortley) as Deputy Chairman. The LST directors then asked the London United Tramways board to vest in Stanley the powers of managing director, "including in particular, power to appoint, discharge and fix remuneration of the operating officials of the LUT, who shall act in accordance with his instructions".

The LUT reconstruction programme began at this time, albeit with setbacks owing to shortages of money and materials. Recently granted fare increases were insufficient to make up shortfalls of income and additional legislation was introduced in 1920.

The Ministry of Transport had been formed in 1919, taking over responsibilities for tramways hitherto the province of the Board of Trade. One of the new ministry's first actions was the formation of the London Traffic Advisory Committee, to inform the minister on all aspects of road traffic in the capital, including passenger transport. Shortly afterwards this body was renamed the London and Home Counties Traffic Advisory Committee, the name change reflecting the widening of its remit. Each major traffic undertaking was represented on the committee, with Frank Pick being appointed on behalf of the LUT.

At a Ministry inquiry into an application for a fare increase in 1920, the manager, C.J.Spencer, who had succeeded A.H.Pott in November 1918, said that the company's reconstruction programme for three years from 1921 was expected to cost £521,000, and therefore the £400,000 for reconstruction called for in the 1918 Act would be insufficient to cover the costs. Money was being borrowed from the banks against the security of the £235,000 payable by the London County Council upon completion of the sale of the LUT Hammersmith lines. It was estimated that a further £383,000 would be required to complete the reconstruction programme, envisaging, *inter alia*, replacement of the rolling stock with a fleet of cars built to the latest design. However, it was ten years before new cars materialised, and then in partial replacement only of the old fleet. A fare increase was granted under the London United Tramways (Temporary Increase of Charges) Order of 18 November 1920.

Throughout the 1920s the company struggled with the need to continue and complete the reconstruction programme laid down in the 1918 Act, and to pay the interest on bank loans and the debenture stock. In addition, falling revenues coupled with the heavy costs of operating the ageing car fleet added to the company's burden. The original LST holdings in the LUT were 68 Third Mortgage Debentures of £1,000 each, and 97,987 Ordinary shares of £10 each, but as at 19 May 1920 they consisted of 70,693 new 5% Cumulative Preference shares which replaced £68,000 in Third Mortgage Debenture Stock, and 2,285,295 Ordinary shares of 5s. each. No income was received from the LUT up to 1919 and very little thereafter.

By 1922 the three tramway companies, together with their associated undertaking, the LGOC, were again facing fierce competition from large numbers of small "independent" or "pirate" omnibus operators, many of whom had half a dozen vehicles or less. The proprietors of these undertakings were able to buy, at very low prices, surplus lorry and other chassis which came on the market after the Great War, for which bodies could be built at comparatively low cost. This made heavy inroads into the tramways' share of the market. In 1921 and 1922 tramway traffic had improved, but by 1923 the position had reversed. The LGOC, as a constituent part of the LST group of companies, had exercised "friendly restraint" in its workings on and near tramway routes, but felt that this could not continue if it meant only that other operators could enter the vacated sections and cream off both theirs and the tramways' share of the available traffic. Poor returns in 1923 also resulted in wage cuts being imposed from 27 July of one shilling per week for men and 6d for those under 18 years of age. These were reinstated as from 26 October but were reimposed from time to time when traffic returns were bad.

The improvements made in the 1920s to the condition of some of the cars by replacing the electrical equipments in 130 of them and, at the same time providing better seating, lighting and interior decotation, was reflected in enhanced traffic figures for 1924 and 1926-1928 and later years. There were, however, deficiencies on the Revenue Account in all these years, that for 1925 being £29,149, the Preference shares then being quoted at 1½d. These were carried forward resulting in arrears of dividend payments for the Preference shareholders who continued to receive nothing on their investments. In the same year the LST had advanced £22,228 to the LUT "to enable the company to continue operating until relief becomes available under the 1924 London Traffic Act". This, in turn, affected the LST which, by March 1926 paid no dividends, and whose shareholders were, by this time, voicing criticism of the "combine" financial arrangements, suggesting that the assets were not being managed in the best interests of the shareholders.

Sir Albert Stanley, who had become Lord Ashfield in 1920, told the LST shareholders at their 1926 meeting that despite the tramway companies' difficulties, they were striving to maintain and improve their services, saying "tramways can and do, do better, and still give good service". Later in 1926 the LUT found it necessary to obtain a loan of £77,000 from the Westminster Bank, which was guaranteed by the LST and the UERL. This was in addition to the regular loans of £35,000 to cover payments to the debenture holders.

While the LUT continued to make improvements to the rolling stock, by 1927 no substantial improvement in the traffic situation had materialised, the 1924 Traffic Act so far having done little to curb the activities of the "pirate" omnibus operators. The company Chairman, H.A.Vernet, told the shareholders at their 1927 meeting that the London and Home Counties Traffic Advisory Committee had formulated proposals for the establishment of a common fund and common management to cover passenger transport undertakings within the London Traffic Area, and that their board had accepted these proposals in principle.

On 7 June 1928 the LUT Secretary, A.C.Ingram, informed the directors that "a serious cash crisis" had arisen. There was an undischarged balance of authorised capital and extraordinary expenditure amounting to £71,000, in addition to £14,000 outstanding debenture interest. It was stated firmly that "no cash resources" existed and the directors decided to place the matter in the hands of Lord Ashfield. By 5 July, Ashfield had succeeded in putting the LST in funds, and the sums in question were covered by loans from that body at 6% per annum.

During November 1928 the British Electric Traction Co. sold its holdings in the London & Suburban Traction Co. and Metropolitan Electric Tramways, amounting to £896,881 at that time, to the Underground Group. These realised £850,000, and in internal correspondence it was remarked that the BET had obtained a low price for them, but the sale was concluded "to keep them from falling into unfriendly hands".

The disposal of these shares resulted in important changes being made in the LST directorate. Emile Garke's place as Chairman of the MET was taken by Lord Ashfield, who also, on 7 March 1929, became Chairman of the LUT, following this by being elected Chairman of the LST in succession to Lord Stuart of Wortley. H.A.Vernet, who had been Chairman of the LUT, then became its Deputy Chairman, while Frank Pick was appointed as managing director of all UERL companies.

A "Common Pool" proposal was under discussion at the Ministry of Transport throughout 1928, with these talks culminating in the publication of two Bills in November for the 1929 Parliamentary Session, by the Underground Group and the London County Council respectively. These sought powers to authorise the setting up of a Common Pool arrangement, each Bill seeking a dominant position for its respective sponsor. In the event, neither were proceeded with. At the same time the MET and Middlesex County Council were involved in negotiations regarding the renewal of the lease to the company of the Council's system of light railways.

Serious consideration was also again being given by the UERL and LST to the future of the LUT system, which was in urgent need of new rolling stock. As mentioned elsewhere, some improvements had been made, such as re-motoring of the cars working on the Uxbridge Road route. The scheme for complete renewal of the fleet however, was shelved, to allow the available resources to be devoted to completing the more immediately pressing track reconstruction programme.

In 1929 the question was brought to the fore after discussions had taken place between UERL officers and the Traffic Advisory Committee. This resulted in the submission, on 24 July, of a detailed report by C.J.Spencer, on the general state of the system accompanied by estimates for a programme of "regeneration of the London United Tramways". In it, he pointed out that part of the rolling stock had been greatly improved in comfort, lighting and speed. Revenue had increased once the omnibus competition, rampant for several years, was eventually curbed by the operation of the London Road Traffic Act 1924. Financial resources, however, were virtually non-existent, the outlook not entirely clear, and despite large sums spent on track reconstruction, new motors and other improvements, much more money was required to modernise the undertaking completely.

The proposals involved replacement of the 189 then-existing trams, partially by 126 new cars to work the lines north of Twickenham and by 65 trolleybuses to work southward into Surrey. The tramway part of this scheme, which included reconstruction of the Uxbridge line between Hanwell and Uxbridge as a "high-speed light railway" was estimated at £534,590, and the trolleybus scheme, including the 65 vehicles, Parliamentary and abandonment costs, at £164,250. Extensions to Hanwell Depot and additions to the power supply were costed at £15,000, bringing the grand total for the whole scheme to £713,840.

Such a large scheme could not have been contemplated in the light of the financial position, not only of the LUT but the whole UERL undertaking. As discussed in Chapter 14, consideration was made possible by new legislation, the Development (Loan, Guarantees and Grants) Act of 1929, which, in approved cases, authorised Treasury grants to cover interest payments on such schemes of public utility.

The plan was modified several times, especially the tramway portion which was much reduced in scale, largely on the advice of Sir Ernest Clark, financial adviser to Lord Ashfield, and by an application by Leeds City Council for assistance with its proposal to purchase 150 new tramcars having failed, resulting in Leeds reducing its order. This resulted in the LUT application not being proceeded with. However, part of the scheme was carried out in 1931, as described elsewhere.

From mid-1931 the directors and officers of the LUT and associate companies considered variants on the revised proposals. Financial considerations were overseen by Sir Ernest Clark who, more than once, advised caution on investment in tramways. As each revised scheme was submitted to him he suggested reductions which were opposed by Spencer. The delays thus occasioned brought the passing of the London Passenger Traffic Bill closer, which effectively halted further progress with the Spencer scheme.

At this time much thought was being given to replacement of the South Metropolitan Electric Tramways & Lighting Company's tramway system with trolleybuses, and the UERL group of companies were treading carefully on all expenditure connected with tramway development in view of the possibility of a new Transport Authority being formed.

On 11 June 1932 Sir Ernest sent a memorandum to Lord Ashfield commenting unfavourably on the SMET proposal, saying that "... in view of the financial results being shown by the MET and LUT the question of modernising the SMET might well be deferred until more prosperous times. Indeed, I would suggest that, as a general principle ... no further capital expenditure should be authorised in connection with tramway development and improvement, because the return from ... this type of transport is of so speculative a character that any further expenditure must inveitably weaken the financial position of the Group". In the face of this blunt advice Spencer had no defence; the LUT proposals went no further, part only of an extensive programme of improvements to the MET system was carried out and the SMET scheme was dropped in its entirety.

From this date the London United continued to be financed by further loans from the LST, their bankers and the UERL, all of which were, in the final analysis underwritten by the Underground Group. These had increased in frequency from the mid-1920s, and by November 1932 outstanding loans from the LST stood at £167,000, which had increased to £265,000 by 5 January 1933, although a long-standing £77,000 loan by the Westminster Bank had been reduced to £56,000.

With the passing of the LUT and all associated companies to the new London Passenger Transport Board, the joint liquidators of the company, Lord Ashfield, H.A.Vernet, James Devonshire and C.G.Tegetmeier appointed J.C.Mitchell as their Secretary on 3 July 1933. Holders of each £100 of 4% LUT First Mortgage Debenture Stock received £50 of 5% "B" Transport Stock and £25 of "C" Transport Stock, and holders of each £1 LUT 5% Cumulative Preference Stock received six shillings of Transport "C" Stock. Each five-shilling LUT Ordinary Share was exchanged for 7½d of Transport "C" Stock.

CHAPTER SEVENTEEN

RELATIONS WITH THE LONDON COUNTY COUNCIL

Differences between the LUT and the London County Council centred, initially, upon the insistence by the latter on the adoption of the underground conduit system for electrification of the former West Metropolitan Tramways in what later became the Metropolitan Borough of Hammersmith in the County of London. This phase in the LUT history is chronicled in the first volume of this book, as is the acquisition by the company of the powers and assets of the West Metropolitan Tramways Company and its predecessors in Hammersmith and the effect the formation of the administrative county of London in 1889 had upon both companies.

The new body lost no time in stating that one of its main objects was ownership of all tramways within the county, as empowered by Section 43 of the 1870 Tramways Act. A reconstruction clause in the West Metropolitan Tramways Act of 1889 was confirmed to the LUT in its 1895 Tramways Provisional Orders Confirmation Act, and in return for the company carrying out obligations under this clause the county council postponed their purchase rights for 6 years until 6 July 1909.

On 4 April 1901 the lines in Hammersmith were electrified together with those in Acton and Chiswick, and in 1902 the company obtained powers to link the line in central Hammersmith with the one in Acton by way of Paddenswick Road and Askew Road, meeting Uxbridge Road at the "Askew Arms" at the London-Middlesex boundary. The LCC consented to this link on the understanding that it would fall in for purchase at the same time as the earlier lines.

In 1908 the proposed purchase date by the LCC was drawing near, and on 1 September Sir Edgar Speyer and Sir Clifton Robinson conferred and concluded that the company's case for postponement of the sale relied upon the detrimental effect that this would have upon services to the public. Robinson also reminded Speyer of the low fares fixed by statute, and especially those for workmen who could travel the 5.34 miles between Hanwell and Shepherds Bush for one penny; of the possible necessity for passengers to change cars at boundary points, with the accompanying inconvenience and fares increases; and the arrangement of through bookings between the LUT, the Underground Electric Railways and Metropolitan District Railway, as sanctioned by Parliament in 1902. Given these, Robinson contended that it would ensure that the Board of Trade must refuse to consent to the "dismemberment" of the LUT system, or at the very least, impose upon the LCC conditions which might give that body some financial participation but leave the lines in the company's hands.

Speyer had requested this information in preparation for a confidential meeting with Sir Francis Hopwood, formerly Permanent Secretary at the Board of Trade, who had recently transferred to the Colonial Office. He wished to obtain the latter's views on the likelihood of success of a Bill for the 1909 Parliamentary Session seeking postponement of the LCC rights of purchase. Meanwhile,

Robinson attempted to obtain the support of Acton and Chiswick UDCs and petitions were raised and presented to the BoT asking for the Hammersmith lines to be retained in LUT hands. At this stage the company suggested that they would accept a postponement of the purchase until such dates as the contiguous lines at Young's Corner and the "Askew Arms" became purchaseable.

A second letter to Speyer reinforced, presumably, by the view of Sir Francis Hopwood, convinced him that the matter might be resolved in the company's favour through Parliament, and a Bill was deposited in November 1908 for the 1909 Session. This sought postponement of the LCC power to purchase the 5.37 miles of LUT route in Hammersmith outward from the Shepherds Bush and Hammersmith termini to the boundary at Young's Corner until 1919, and to the "Askew Arms" until 1924.

Powers were also sought for mutual joint through running for both bodies via the London and Surrey boundaries at Tooting and Summerstown, to enable LCC cars from London to continue across the boundaries through to Wimbledon and Hampton Court, and LUT cars to cross the boundary points to reach the London termini at Blackfriars and Westminster bridges respectively. The shareholders approved of the Bill at an extraordinary general meeting held on 16 March 1909.

The LUT Bill went before a House of Lords Select Committe between 5 May 1909 and 14 May and was fiercely opposed by the LCC legal advisers, the LUT mounting an equally vigorous case presented by J.H.Balfour Browne, KC., who was assisted by the Hon.J.D.Fitzgerald, Lewis Coward, KC., the Hon. Evan Charteris and Lyndon Macassey. The LCC side was led by Erskine Pollock, KC., who stood firm on their right and intention to purchase the lines, and insisted that, once in possession, some arrangement to maintain through traffic could be made, but declined to offer a specific proposal.

On the question of joint through working over the London-Surrey boundaries at Tooting and Summerstown, Counsel for the LCC submitted that no great demand for such facilities existed, and the large difference between the traffic carried by the two systems would make such arrangements detrimental to the LCC. It was also alleged that the LUT cars were unsuitable for operation over the lines in London. Apart from Clifton Robinson, the chief witnesses on behalf of the LUT were Alfred Baker, who had been tramways manager of the LCC until 1903 and J.B.Hamilton, general managers respectively of the Birmingham and Leeds Corporation Tramways.

Baker stated that the LCC had obtained powers in 1903 to connect their line in Garratt Lane, Wandsworth into Wimbledon Road to meet the authorised LUT tramway at the end of Plough Lane, Summerstown. The LUT line was built but the County Council had never made the connection. He also said that the powers were obtained in fulfilment of a pledge given to the Select Committee in the previous year, again pointing out the value of mutual interchange of running powers there, and said that he had not changed his views. He then described the extensive through running arrangements in Birmingham and said he saw no difficulty to similar arrangements in London. J.B.Hamilton also supported the LUT Bill, quoting the Leeds-Bradford dual gauge system of through working at Stanningley as evidence of his authority's commitment to such a principle.

The proposal that LCC cars should work via Tooting and Summerstown to Wimbledon and Hampton Court was opposed by the Maldens & Coombe UDC however, on the grounds of increased traffic through their district. Their representative told the Committee that the operation of LCC cars through the district would double the number of trams working on their roads, and Counsel for the LUT had some difficulty in convincing him that, with joint through running, the number of cars passing a given point did not increase. Conversely, members of the public spoke in favour of through running and of eliminating the need to change cars at boundary points.

Despite the evidence given in support of the Bill the Select Committee upheld the LCC petition against it; the Board of Trade was free to approve the purchase, and had indicated that they would like to see certain conditions met. Consent, however could be given without any conditions, and the County Council had an entirely free hand. The Chairman of the Select Committee, Lord Ludlow, said it was for the Board of Trade to act in the public interest. The Committee found that the preamble to the Bill was not proved and it was accordingly struck out on 14 May.

The company now relied upon the BoT refusing to consent to the purchase. Speyer had previously discussed the matter with Sir Francis Hopwood, and on 21 June 1909 Sir Francis wrote to Winston Churchill, the President of the Board of Trade, asking him to ensure that the lines would not be taken over without safeguards to continue existing through services and bookings. Earlier, on 17 June, Col.Yorke, the BoT Chief Inspecting Officer, said that he was sure that the LCC would arrange through running on "mutual principles", and insisted that these should be upheld.

On 15 October the company submitted a statement to the Board of Trade, describing the Hammersmith lines in detail, their relation to the electric railway stations at Shepherds Bush and Hammersmith, with tables indicating the numbers of ordinary passengers and workmen carried each year from 1902 to 1908, showing that traffic had increased from 36,209,737 to 59,255,919 passsengers per annum over that period. Of those conveyed in 1908, 40,000,000 were carried on the cars arriving at and departing from the electric railway stations. Of these, 974,915 passengers had used the through booking arrangements at Hammersmith and Shepherds Bush in 1908.

Tables of fares were presented, showing that ordinary fares averaged less than one halfpenny per mile, workmen's fares under a farthing a mile and a workmen's 2d return ticket over some of the routes covered 16½ miles. The statement showed concern at the loss of the through routes to the London termini and the disruption of the established through fares over the electric railways to the City, reducing a great trunk route to a line for merely local purposes.

Heavy expenditure involved in the establishment of the power station, works and depot at Chiswick, in Middlesex but properly applicable to the Hammersmith lines in the County of London were described, and practical objections to the LCC proposal were tabulated. Sale of the lines would nullify much of what Parliament had sanctioned in the public interest, and similarly affect the company's many agreements with the local authorities, especially those of Acton, Chiswick and Hammersmith, to carry passengers to and from the existing stage points at the established fares. The company asked the Board of Trade to hold a full public inquiry to decide the matter fairly and completely upon its merits. The statement concluded by saying that the directors were prepared to consider financial participation by the LCC from continued LUT ownership and operation of the lines in Hammersmith.

Meanwhile, the County Council remained adamant that they would proceed with the purchase, but offered no proposals for the future of the lines when bought. Winston Churchill then brought the opposing sides together at a meeting at the Board of Trade on 25 November 1909, when Clifton Robinson and Albert Stanley of the UERL represented the LUT, with Sir Llewellyn Smith and A.Shirley Benn speaking for the LCC. The company side were suspicious of the LCC's motives, reminding those present of harsh terms imposed upon the MET after the purchase of the Harrow Road tramway. A.S.Benn was non-committal, but suggested that matters might be resolved by arbitration. W.F.Marwood noted that it was almost impossible to persuade the LCC to come foward with reasonable terms. Matters stood thus until 21 December 1909, when the BOT finally consented to the purchase, saying that a public inquiry would serve no useful purpose.

On the following day, 22 December, the LCC served formal notice upon the LUT to sell the lines. The company insisted that Chiswick Depot, the power station and some cabling between the county boundary at Young's Corner and the depot, properly formed part of the 5.37 miles of lines in Hammersmith, and fixed their price for the whole at £414,234. At the same time the implications of the inclusion of the depot and power station in the sale became clear to the County Council, who could draw upon their generating station at Greenwich to supply the lines, and had earlier built a depot in Hammersmith with space for later extension.

Discussion on these and other matters were protracted, resulting in the purchase date, six months from 6 July 1909, expiring on 5 February 1910, being missed, the next purchase date arising on 6 February 1917. Meanwhile, Clifton Robinson resigned his posts with the company on 14 January 1910, leaving matters in the hands of Albert Stanley as the new managing director.

Attempts to reconcile differences between the parties over Chiswick Depot and what part of the plant there, together with the number of cars to be taken by the LCC as sufficient to work the Hammersmith lines, at what constituted a fair price for the whole were fruitless. After negotiations conducted intermittently through 1910 and the spring of 1911, the parties agreed to submit the matter to arbitration, and on 26 July 1911 the Board of Trade appointed Robert Elliott-Cooper as Referee.

The hearing commenced on 26 October, continuing for five days. The LUT was represented by J.H.Balfour Browne, KC. and the LCC by C.C.Hutchinson, KC., together with their respective assistants. Technical evidence for the company was given by Stephen Sellon and Lyndon Macassey. The company's claim of £414,234, which included £236,789 for Chiswick Depot, the power station, workshops and contents, and £177,445 for permanent way, ducts, cables, overhead wire equipment, cars and Parliamentary expenditure was contested by the LCC valuer, who stated positively that the whole package was worth no more than £198,582. The depot and its associated facilities were of little use to the LCC and were the subject of hard bargaining, with every item being fought over.

On 27 October the referee, the parties and their advisers visited Hammersmith to view operations. From there they went on to inspect the depot and power station, which were assessed at £127,249, including lands, buildings, permanent way and overhead equipment within the complex, generating plant and workshop machinery. From these, a number of major items were excluded from the award, consisting of the power station switchboard panels relating to the Middlesex lines, i.e. the Kew booster panel, the Kew Bridge, Gunnersbury and "Packhorse" (High Road, Chiswick) feeder panels, two 1,000Kw machine panels, three high-tension Hanwell feeder panels, and two each Hounslow and Fulwell high-tension feeder panels. Two main steam generating sets, seven Babcock & Wilcox boilers, seven Vicars mechanical stokers and three-fifths of the coal bunkers were also excluded, together with about half of the workshop tools and equipment, which the LCC convinced the Referee were not applicable to the working of the Hammersmith lines.

The track in Hammersmith was valued at £33,964, the overhead equipment at £2,803, cables, ducts and manholes at £8,941, acquisitions of lands for widenings £35,462, and paving, £4,500, Parliamentary costs £15,500, and a number of miscellaneous items at £911, making a grand total of £248,653.

A major bone of contention was the number of cars required to work the Hammersmith lines. The company insisted that 48 vehicles were necessary, which they wanted to be taken from the Nos.101-150 batch built in 1901. The Council maintained that 40 was sufficient, but they wished to choose these for themselves.

This group of cars had been the subject of considerable controversy some years earlier, as described in Volume One of this work. The LCC representatives said the cars had been inspected and were found to have rotten roofs, mentioning specifically Nos. 103, 107, 108, 111, 123 and 141. In evidence, Stephen Sellon said that up to 1909 the cars had been in regular use, and since then had been allocated to reserve, going into service only at holiday times. All had been passed by the Metropolitan Police for service by the time of the hearing. He also said that the company wished to eliminate one complete batch of 50 cars for standardisation purposes.

Counsel for the LCC explained that his clients did not want "any old car covered in"; they wanted new ones. Sellon said that the 101-150 batch were stored in Fulwell Depot and had been at Chiswick until January 1911. He again stated that they had been painted, varnished and "stamped by the Police Commissioner" in that month and that the cars were in sound repair and fit to work in 1912. Hutchinson compromised; he would take 48 cars, but six had to be "of a different type", which he wished to choose for himself, and he accepted 42 cars from Nos.101-150 without further discussion. The LCC offered £323.1s. each for them, and it was agreed that the Refereee should examine the cars, test them for himself and say which would be taken and "which should be sold for summerhouses". In the event the cars chosen were Nos.101-106, 109-116, 119-124, 126-136, 139-147 and 319-323, the last five from the 1906 batch of 40 open-balcony top-covered cars, Elliott-Cooper having ruled a reduction from 48 to 45 cars in the LCC's favour, the price for the whole batch to be £21,125, or £469.9s each.

Details of the award were published on 15 February 1912, following which negotiations began upon numerous seemingly irreconcilable differences between the parties which continued until events were overtaken by the outbreak of the Great War. Litigation between the parties had begun after the award was announced, but was suspended by agreement at Easter 1915, and it was later agreed it should stand out of the Court List until 14 February 1916. On 15 May 1917 the LCC Highways Committee reported that agreement had been reached on the main points at issue.

The purchase price for the tramways, Chiswick Depot, the workshops and the power station with the plant there was agreed at £235,000, and the LCC undertook to pay £12,000 towards the company's costs of the arbitration and later proceedings. The LUT, then in the process of negotiating with the UERL for all its power requirements to be supplied from Lots Road power station, was granted use of part of the power station to accommodate a sub-station for the Middlesex lines and the purchased Hammersmith lines. The agreement provided for the LCC to have perpetual access over the company's tracks to Chiswick Depot, and for the LUT to have free access to the cables for 21 years.

When giving consent to the transaction, the Board of Trade had noted the LCC's statement that arrangements had been made for the company to run through cars to and from Shepherds Bush and Hammersmith, and these facilities would be continued. In return, the 1917 agreement provided for the Council to run cars over the company's Middlesex lines. The LCC Tramways and Improvements Act of 1914 had already sanctioned these arrangements, and each party was given power to fix fares for stages wholly within its own area, subject to existing statutory fares provided for in the company's Acts. The company undertook to supply at no charge, for 21 years, the direct current used by the LCC cars working over the Hammersmith and other lines of the company to a maximum of 1,800,000 units per annum, any excess to be paid for on terms to be agreed between the respective tramway managers. The agreement was signed on 6 December 1917, but its provisions were not to be implemented until a date within one year after the end of the war.

Wartime conditions compelled both parties to concentrate their resources upon maintaining services in the face of enemy action, labour and materials shortages, and rapidly rising costs, resulting in further discussions being shelved. The official end of the Great War was delayed until 31 August 1921, when the last of the peace treaties were signed. On 31 January 1922 the LCC served notice upon the company to complete the transaction, which was carried out largely under the terms of the December 1917 agreement.

Physical transfer of the assets to the LCC became effective on 2 May 1922, and the company continued to work the services as hitherto, although several differences still existed between the parties. The LUT board were told on 27 April that the final conveyance could not be completed on 2 May as planned, but the LCC was making the connection at Hammersmith Broadway between their Harlesden-Putney line and the LUT line in readiness for through running by County Council cars from the inner London terminus at the Hop Exchange via Hammersmith and Chiswick to Kew Bridge. This service duly started on 2 May as arranged, and on the same day LUT trams between Wimbledon and the London boundary at Tooting were withdrawn and replaced by an extension of LCC cars on the Westminster and Blackfriars services.

Completion of the Hammersmith conveyance remained outstanding on 28 July 1922. Spencer then advised his directors to give up a right to use some cables, ducts and manholes in Hammersmith at the end of 1943 if the LCC agreed to waive a dilapidations clause in the 1917 agreement. Spencer and the solicitor were authorised to bring the matter to a conclusion; sealing of the conveyance was agreed to on 12 October, becoming fully effective on 7 November. A supplementary agreement to the main one of 6 December 1917, confirming final details of the sale and the arrangements made for through running by the LCC at Tooting, was signed on 8 November 1922.

To enable the trams from London to transfer from the conduit system at the LCC boundary at Tooting to the LUT overhead trolley line, a conduit change point was inserted there by the LCC, and the overhead equipment extended to meet it, while the 30-yard gap between the two ends was closed. Power for the line from Tooting to Wimbledon continued to be supplied by the LUT.

The London-Surrey county boundary at Tooting was subsequently re-arranged at Longley Road about 82 yards south of its original line, this small area becoming part of the Metropolitan Borough of Wandsworth. Sale of the track to the LCC was authorised by the LUT 1918 Act, but this was not proceeded with, remaining in LUT ownership throughout the remainder of the existence of the company.

When the County Council took over the working of the line to Wimbledon, it was operating trailer cars from London to Tooting. The LUT had also obtained powers in 1914 to operate trailers and coupled cars, subject to Board of Trade and local authority approval. The LCC wished to extend the use of these to Wimbledon, and asked the company to seek Wimbledon Corporation's consent to their use in the borough, but this was refused. In the event, trailer operation on the Tooting services was short-lived, ceasing on 20 November 1922.

None of the LUT cars sold to the LCC under the 1912 arbitration award left the possession of the company, remaining in Fulwell Depot pending their removal, or disposal, by the LCC, who could not make use of them. Towards the end of 1921 tenders were sought for their purchase. On 11 May 1922, A.L.C.Fell, told the LCC Highways Committee that no tenders had been received, and he was authorised to approach the managers of provincial systems. Fell again advised the Committee on 19 July that he had received no offers and it was agreed to consider breaking the cars up or selling them for scrap. Later, on 27 October, the LUT general manager, C.J.Spencer, who had advised his directors that the cars would provide a useful source of spare parts for the remaining fleet, was authorised "to re-purchase, if possible, the 45 cars upon the terms that he had suggested", i.e. for £2,000 for the lot.

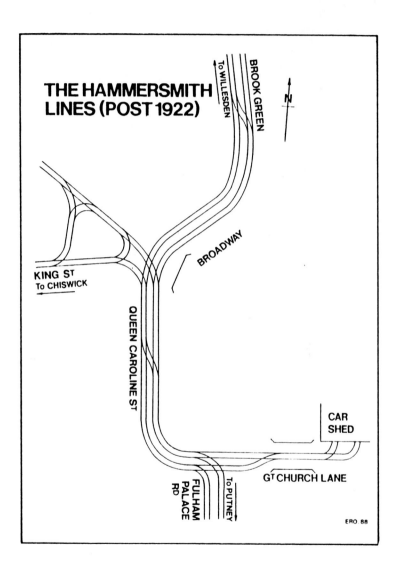

THE HAMMERSMITH
LINES (POST 1922)

N

To WILLESDEN

BROOK GREEN

BROADWAY

KING ST
To CHISWICK

QUEEN CAROLINE ST

CAR
SHED

FULHAM
PALACE
RD

To PUTNEY

GT CHURCH LANE

ERO 88

325

Bound for Hampton Court, LCC Class E/1 car 1780 leaves a colourlight controlled loop in Worple Road, Wimbledon. This weekend service ceased with the introduction of trolleybuses in Wimbledon in 1931. (Courtesy London Borough of Newham Libraries)

Another variant of the "all-red" 1928 livery: Type U2 No.283 heading for Acton on service 89 passes beneath the District Railway bridge in Dalling Road, Hammersmith.
(Hugh Nicol. Courtesy National Tramway Museum)

Fell reported the LUT offer to the Highways Committee on 8 November, pointing out that the scrap value of the cars was £1,800 and the cost of breaking them up would reduce this to £1,300. The company's offer was accepted; the 40 open-top cars remained at Fulwell Depot, where nearly all were broken up in the summer of 1924, while the five open-balcony cars continued in service with the company. At the same time a tower wagon from Chiswick Depot was bought for £450.

Early attempts by the company to establish joint through running over the respective lines had failed, as described elsewhere. The matter was next brought up on 6 November 1923, when Cty. Cllr. J.D.Gilbert asked the LCC Chairman if their cars, terminating at Wimbledon Hill since May 1922, could be extended to Hampton Court. The LCC Tramways Management and General Purposes Sub-Committee (No. 1) reported upon this enquiry on 13 December when A.L.C.Fell said that in view of the existing electrical equipment used on the LUT cars, joint working over the two authorities' lines was quite impracticable. He had considered alternative proposals, (1) that the LCC should offer to lease the lines from Wimbledon to Hampton Court, or (2) that the County Council should operate the through services and the company pay for the mileage worked in their area.

Fell also stated that under existing conditions he could not recommend to the Committee that the company's lines be leased, nor was it reasonable for the London County Council to purchase cars to provide the service. LUT cars were not equipped for conduit operation and were unable to match the speed of those of the LCC. If the company was prepared to obtain new cars or re-equip some from their existing fleet, a scheme of running over the LCC lines might be possible. The Highways Committee instructed Fell to discuss this with the LUT general manager, and to ascertain whether he could agree to suitable terms for LCC cars to run to Hampton Court.

Spencer replied to Fell's enquiry on 27 December 1923, saying that it was thought inadvisable to discuss the matter until current proposals for through running on other routes had borne fruit. Cty. Cllr. Gilbert again raised the matter on 20 March 1924 and Fell recommended that capital expenditure involved in running LCC cars to Kingston and Hampton Court could not be justified in prevailing conditions.

Discussions were resumed later in 1924 but little progress was made until 14 April 1926, when J.K.Bruce, who had succeeded Fell as LCC Tramways Manager on 1 January 1925 wrote to C.J.Spencer referring to a meeting between his traffic manager, T.E.Thomas, and Spencer's deputy, A.V.Mason, at which proposals for weekend through running of LCC cars to Hampton Court were discussed. Earlier, on 12 March 1926, trial journeys had been successfully carried out by the LCC over the route.

Bruce subsequently wrote to Spencer confirming heads of a proposed agreement and asking for an early approval of terms to enable the service to commence in time for the forthcoming Whitsun holiday. Outstanding matters were quickly resolved and the through service commenced between central London and Hampton Court via Wimbledon on Sunday 22 May 1926, and thereafter on Saturday afternoons and evenings, and all day on Sundays and bank holidays in the summer months as well as Saturday afternoons and evenings during the winter months.

Agreed terms for the working by LCC cars as an extension of services 2 and 4 were that their operating expenses be recouped, including premium wages for Sunday and public holiday working, plus capital charges for power supplies in the LCC area. The County Council agreed to pay the company's costs for providing power, superintendence, maintenance of track and electrical equipment. Each party fixed the fares in its own area, while through fares, not to exceed the sum of local fares were agreed between the managers, the LCC retaining receipts from the services initially.

The through service was comparatively short-lived, running for the last time on 30 August 1931, as a result of the imminent conversion to trolleybus operation by the LUT of the Wimbledon to Hampton Court tramway services as from 2 September 1931. This meant that the LUT could no longer work the isolated Haydon's Road tramway with cars from Fulwell Depot. In the meantime, arrangements had been made with the LCC to connect the terminus at the end of Plough Lane, Summerstown with the conduit line in Wimbledon Road, and instal a change-point at the boundary. The LUT track was then extended to close the short gap between the two systems. From 16 April 1931, LCC service 14, working between central London and Wimbledon Road, Summerstown was extended through Plough Lane and Haydon's Road to High Street, Merton, to join the Tooting-Wimbledon line. These arrangements gave the residents of Haydon's Road direct access to and from central London for the first time.

An agreement, supplemental to that of 8 November 1922 varied the terms for the supply of power by the company for LCC cars working over LUT-owned lines. The County Council would continue to pay for the units used by their cars in excess of 1,800,000 per annum, but in the case of the 600-yard section between the change-point at Longley Road, Merton and College Road, Colliers Wood the LCC would pay for all current used in that section. These arrangements necessarily came to an end on 1 July 1933 when all the parties came together under the umbrella of the London Passenger Transport Board.

CHAPTER EIGHTEEN

THE LUT IN THE GREAT WAR

The merger of the three tramway companies in the London & Suburban Traction Company in 1913 enabled the MET, LUT and SMET to pool operational and administrative resources to their mutual benefit. An early result of this was a request by the LST Board to the LUT directors to arrange for LUT car repairs to be carried out at the large MET car works at Hendon. This objective was not immediately realised owing to local objections to the necessary connection between the two systems at Acton, which was not made until 1915 when wartime conditions made it essential, as mentioned in a later paragraph.

During Clifton Robinson's regime the London County Council had resolutely opposed attempts by the company to obtain joint running powers over the LCC lines to central London. The LUT, by virtue of the LST merger, had come under the management of senior staff of the British Electric Traction Company, which also owned the Metropolitan Electric Tramways who already had joint through running agreements with the LCC over lines in north London. This gave rise to consideration that there may be some common ground between the parties.

However, in the summer of 1913, long after the departure of Robinson, senior LCC officers approached the LUT management with a view to the two undertakings initiating joint through services between central London and Hampton Court via Tooting and Wimbledon. A tangible result of this took place on 13 August 1913 when an LCC car was manhandled across the gap between the two systems at Tooting and made trial journeys to and from Hampton Court, although neither undertakings' records mention these trials.

In anticipation of these proposals bearing fruit, James Devonshire, the LUT managing director, undertook to obtain estimates for fitting LUT cars with conduit current collection equipment. The parties were later encouraged to proceed further when, in November 1913 the company submitted a Bill for the 1914 Parliamentary Session, seeking powers to enter into agreements for joint through working over neighbouring systems.

The 1914 Bill also contained clauses seeking postponement of the various local authorities' purchase powers to 42 years from the date of their respective agreements with the company, powers to work trailers and coupled cars and to retain the existing traffic arrangements in Hammersmith after the future sale of the LUT lines there to the LCC. Because there was some doubt as to the right of the company to reserve cars for special purposes, powers were sought to provide vehicles for the use of private parties at other than statutory fares charged on ordinary service cars.

Police regulations insisted that collection of fares was solely the responsibility of conductors, to be done only on the cars. The company wished to allow inspectors to collect fares when necessary, and to arrange for tickets to be sold off the cars at such places as shops or a ticket office on certain routes. The police would not countenance the sale of tickets in the streets and an easing of this restriction was sought, as was a ruling on standing passengers.

The LUT Bill came before a House of Commons Select Committee on 31 March 1914. Its proposals were strenuously opposed over three days by the local councils and other interests. Some claimed that joint through working would double the number of trams passing through their districts and the fiercest opposition was brought to bear upon the proposal to use trailers and coupled cars. A.L.C.Fell, the LCC tramways manager spoke in favour of the LUT proposal for joint through working between adjacent systems. He said that the Council had approached the company with a view to closing the gap between the two systems at Tooting and the establishment of joint LCC/LUT through services between central London and Hampton Court via Wimbledon and Kingston during summer weekends and on bank holidays.

Fell also spoke in favour of the LUT proposal to use trailers and coupled cars, saying that the LCC had started trailer working on the Victoria Embankment-Merton service on 27 July 1913 (the LCC invariably referred to the latter point as "Merton", whereas the LUT called it "Tooting"). He also said that he envisaged the use of trailers through to Hampton Court. The company proposed to use them on all their routes, subject in all cases to Board of Trade and local authority approval.

Opposition to the trailer clause by the local councils, supported by the police, took up most of the Select Committee time, but the evidence given by A.L.C.Fell and Stephen Sellon, the LUT consulting engineer convinced them of the soundness of the company's case. The clause was passed but the use of trailers or coupled cars was expressly disallowed in the urban district of Surbiton, and in the case of the boroughs of Kingston-upon-Thames and Wimbledon existing agreements with the company precluded their use without those bodies' explicit approval. Elsewhere, trailer working was sanctioned subject to Board of Trade approval, after that body had taken into consideration any objections by the Police Commissioner or the local road authority, and to existing service frequencies remaining unchanged.

Police objections to the proposal to reserve cars for hire by private parties or categories of traffic other than timetabled workings at statutory fares were overcome. The company gained the right to reserve cars for the use of women, or for other such special purposes they might consider necessary or desirable, or to prohibit the use of such cars by persons other than those for which they were reserved. The necessary bye-laws were to be made by the Board of Trade.

Standing passengers were always a source of friction with the Metropolitan Police, and conductors were frequently summoned for carrying excess passengers, for which they were fined. The position for the LUT was clarified, allowing cars to carry an additional one-third of the number of passengers they were licensed to carry in the lower saloon in inclement weather; on Sundays or bank or other public holidays throughout the day; on Saturdays after noon or (with the consent of the Police Commissioner) on "special occasions". In the case of the LUT this amounted to ten additional persons on the lower deck.

Restrictions on the method of collecting fares were eased, allowing the company to make bye-laws covering persons, times and places to whom and at which fares may be paid, but no fares were allowed to be taken in the street or any public place without the Police Commissioner's sanction. In practice this meant little to the company and a bye-law made under the 1914 Act on 17 July 1917 merely confirmed the obligation on the part of the passenger to pay the appropriate fare to the conductor. At certain times of heavy traffic additional conductors were employed.

It was not until 21 June 1921 that a bye-law was sealed by the Ministry of Transport confirming the company's right to reserve cars for other then timetabled services, such cars to display notices indicating their special status. These notices took the form of the words SPECIAL CAR, displayed on the roller-blind indicators.

Meanwhile, the 1914 Bill passed through the rest of its stages and received Royal Assent on 31 July 1914. Four days later, on 4 August, the Great War broke out and the main provisions of the new Act fell by the wayside; the authorised joint through running came about many years later, to Hampton Court via Tooting as the LCC originally proposed, but under different conditions. This, and the sole example of trailer working are described elsewhere in this volume.

Consolidation of the three company tramways' interests in the London & Suburban Traction Company enabled the LUT to contemplate a programme of renewing the most badly worn track. Some of this work, in Hounslow, commenced late in 1913 and was partly completed in 1914. Other work, particularly in Brentford, Southall, Ealing, Hanwell and Acton was postponed and the track patched up over the four years' duration of the war. Some badly worn track in Hammersmith was renewed in 1913 by arrangement with the LCC, who advanced money for this purpose.

A provision in the company's act of 1901 and the Kingston Bridge Act of 1911 obliged it to pay the cost of widening Kingston Bridge up to the sum of £10,000, plus one-third of anything in excess of that amount. The £10,000 was paid to the bridge authority during 1913 and work on the bridge was completed in 1914. It was widened on the upstream side and tram services were maintained by replacing the span-wire overhead suspension across the bridge with long bracket arms on the traction poles on the downstream side of it to allow for working in both directions.

At first the war appeared to have little effect upon the company's day-to-day activities, with services being maintained at normal levels for the first few months, until labour and materials shortages began to make themselves felt. There was little munitions traffic on the system as a whole, most being concentrated on the routes north of the Thames, while pleasure traffic on the Surrey lines, especially from Hammersmith and Tooting to Hampton Court did not diminish to any great extent. This was short-lived, however.

A requirement placed upon the company following the outbreak of war was the fitting of small wooden lamp mountings to the offside of each car's dashes to carry an acetylene or carbide lamp of the type then used on bicycles. The lamps were for use in the event of power failure, and when not required were hung on the underside of the staircases. Such lamps were already carried on cars working on the Uxbridge route, which travelled over long stretches of unlit roads and were a requirement of the Board of Trade for that route.

By the time that the war was into its second year, tramway operators had lost many platform staff to the military services, and remaining male conductors were almost all over military age. Shortages were partially made good by retired men returning to service "for the duration". The Metropolitan Police and trades unions initially objected to the engagement of female conductors, but these objections were overcome out of necessity, with the police permitting their employment in October 1915.

One of the best-known conductresses on the LUT system was Mrs.Elizabeth Seal, who described her experiences to Mr.Bryan Woodriff, to whom the author is indebted for material in these paragraphs. Conductresses on the three LST systems were engaged at 4s.6d per day for a six-day week to which was later added a war bonus of 2s.6d. Wages gradually increased to £3 a week. Shifts could run from 4.37a.m. to 9.33a.m. and then from 10.56a.m. until 2.13p.m., and from 2.29p.m.to 7.16p.m., continuing from 8.18p.m. until 12.20a.m. Her duties were mainly on the Ham Boundary and Tolworth routes.

Each conductress wore a uniform consisting of a dark-coloured jacket and

Conductresses were engaged between 1915 and 1919 as a wartime measure. Mrs.Elizabeth Seal worked from Fulwell Depot during this period, mainly on Kingston local services.

(Courtesy Bryan Woodriff)

skirt edged with black leather around the cuffs and hems. Two hats were provided, one of straw for summer use and a second of grey felt, two skirts and a heavy winter coat, again dark grey. These were worn in conjunction with black leather boots reaching half-way to the calf. At first leather gaiters were worn, but later, as skirts became a little shorter, the boots went into use, which were bought at the wearer's expense of some three guineas (£3.3s) a pair. There were no canteen facilities, and car crews took light meals at termini, mainly of sandwiches, with tea from "Thermos" flasks. Following the Armistice in November 1918, men began to return to their old jobs and the last of the conductresses left the service in 1919. No female drivers were employed.

In 1913, as mentioned above, an attempt had been made to connect the LUT Uxbridge Road line with the Metropolitan Electric Tramways system terminating a short distance to the north in Horn Lane, Acton. This failed, mainly owing to objections by Acton UDC and the authorities of St.Mary's Parish Church in King Street. The position was resolved, however, in 1915, when the Ministry of Munitions requisitioned Chiswick Car Works, with the result that the Board of Trade overruled these objections. The necessary 159-yard link in King Street was made with the construction of a single-line track between High Street and Horn Lane. From the end of July 1915, LUT cars made the journey to Hendon, where LUT men worked on their own cars until after the Armistice.

In the autumn of 1915 the German High Command began night bombing raids on London, using "Zeppelin" airships, with crews drawn from the naval and land forces. To combat this offensive the Home Office took steps under the Defence of the Realm Act to restrict lighting. The Lights (London) Order of 26 August 1916 called for tramcar headlamps, already obscured with translucent material to be completely masked, and a low-intensity light to be displayed on each car to the front on either side and a similar red light to be shown on the rear offside.

The necessary fittings, provided at either end of each car, hurriedly made and of makeshift appearance consisted of one nearside front light on a swan-neck fitting extending from the short canopy and a similar offside front light in a wooden box mounted on the staircase landing. This box also displayed the red rear light. The fittings were referred to by staff as "cocoa tins" and "bird boxes" respectively. These modifications were carried out at the cost of £1,000, but a claim for reinbursement as a war expense failed. The fittings, suitably modified for peacetime conditions, remained in place on most of the short-canopy cars for the remainder of their existence.

By the end of 1915 the frequency of Zeppelin attacks had increased and the War Cabinet decided, as a matter of urgency, to establish a ring of searchlights around London, some 10-12 miles outward. The Royal Engineers were ordered to peremptorily requisition any necessary buildings or equipment. The 60cm. lights were hurriedly constructed and mounted upon a variety of platforms, mostly mobile, among them lorries, canal boats and some electric tramcars. Trams taken for this purpose were manned by members of the Royal Engineers.

Each car requisitioned for these duties underwent some modifications. Top deck seats were removed and the light mounted at one end, the other end being covered with a metal shelter for the searchlight crew. The saloon, with the windows boarded over, was occupied by electrical equipment drawing power from the overhead line, with sufficient space being available for crews' messing facilities. The cars were painted dark green, a colour much used during the Great War for vehicles on home duties.

Searchlight trams were located at eleven known points around London, six of them on the MET system. One was stationed on the LUT system at Hounslow Heath terminus. By the end of 1916 purpose-built platforms started to become available and the last trams were stood down in March 1917. A more detailed account of searchlight trams will be found in Volume 1 of the author's *Metropolitan Electric Tramways*.

The intensity of night raids increased as the war continued. Zeppelins, vulnerable to ground and air defences were supplanted by large numbers of faster and more manoeuverable fixed-wing aircraft, which could also operate during daylight. Concern was expressed to the authorities about arcing and flashing from electric tramways and railways. The use of automatic point and frog controllers was one source of this and they were worked manually during hours of darkness. At the same time, interior lighting on the cars was reduced and curtains drawn across windows at dusk. These and other measures put the company to considerable expense, which they were unable to recover.

Power supplies were affected through a variety of causes, chiefly as the result of earlier lack of maintenance aggravated by materials shortages. The 250ft. high stack at Chiswick power station became unsafe and was twice reduced in height. The condition of the coal conveyor had deteriorated to the extent that serious failures were likely to occur at any time, and on 13 October 1915 the directors authorised emergency repairs "to avoid breakdown of services". On 12 October 1916 the Board discussed a proposal to close down the station and take power to work the Middlesex lines from the UERL generating station at Lots Road, Chelsea, but no immediate decision was taken.

Shortages of fuel, and the poor quality of some of the available coal increased the risks of failure of the generating plant. Nevertheless, the question of abandoning Chiswick as a generating station was deferred on several more occasions until, after a number of setbacks and following the end of the war, all power for the system was supplied from Lots Road as from 31 October 1919.

By March 1917 labour and materials shortages coupled with the company's perilous financial position were affecting regular services. On 31 March those to Ham Boundary and Kingston Hill were temporarily suspended owing to a shortage of rolling stock. This brought strong protests from Kingston Corporation, and together with representations made by the Board of Trade, resulted in the restoration of the Kingston Hill service on 1 May. The Hawker Aircraft Company

Type T car 335 heads west from Shepherds Bush c.1914. At the "Askew Arms" junction, seen here, cars turned south for Hammersmith. (Commercial view, Johns series)

334

was building a new factory near the Ham Boundary terminus and this service was reinstated on 29 October. Kingston Corporation insisted that services in the borough as laid down in the LUT 1901 Act should be maintained at all times, and to reinforce this a provision was inserted in the LUT Act of 1918 obliging the company to provide a twenty-minute service from 8a.m. to 8p.m. between King's Road and Ham Boundary and between Kingston Hill and the junction of London Road with Cambridge Road.

Attempts were also being made at this time, as detailed elsewhere, to settle long-standing differences and expensive litigation over the sale of the Hammersmith lines to the LCC. These resulted in an agreement made on 6 December 1917 to conclude the sale within twelve months from the end of the war.

Some services were curtailed from time to time, due mainly to lack of platform and other staff, and also to power breakdowns. The large numbers of people employed at the shell-filling factories at Park Royal made heavy demands on all forms of transport and, as mentioned earlier, LUT cars joined MET cars in providing these. Three MET cars, Nos.1, 20 and 36 were stationed at Acton depot, from where they worked with LUT cars to and from these factories and the aircraft works at Hendon.

Type U car No.280 making headway through floods at Hampton Court in January 1915. It was scrapped in 1923 following accident damage and its top-cover used on another car.

(Courtesy Greater London Record Office)

Bound for Hanwell from Shepherds Bush, No.314 is halted by the traffic policeman at the junction of Uxbridge Road, West Ealing with Northfield Avenue sometime during the Great War. (Courtesy A.D.Packer)

Car No.51 (Type Y) bound for Hammersmith, halts at the Napier works in Acton Vale in summer 1917. A crossover was provided here for short-working cars serving this establishment and the adjacent Eastman dyeworks. (Courtesy National Tramway Museum)

All transport undertakings experienced difficulty in maintaining services at this time and overcrowding came to be largely disregarded. A contemporary photograph taken in Edgware Road, Hendon shows crowded LUT and MET cars passing a large four-wheel cart crowded with workmen and being drawn by a steam wagon, also heavily loaded. Some LUT cars joined MET cars on occasional journeys to Edgware and Canons Park. Despite gaining the necessary powers in 1914, the company made no attempt to operate regular services with trailer cars.

Towards the end of the war the Government called for a 15% reduction in coal consumption, and on 15 May 1918 the directors ordered the suspension of Sunday morning tram services for a period of one month. They were reinstated from 10a.m. on 16 June. On 16 July the board were advised that speed restrictions were to be instituted over the whole system.

The general manager and engineer, A.H.Pott, retired on 31 October 1918. He was granted an honorarium of one year's salary and retained as advisory engineer to the three LST companies at an annual fee of £250. He was succeeded, as manager, on 1 November by Christopher John Spencer, general manager of Bradford City Tramways. Hostilities ceased at 11a.m. on 11 November 1918 with a new manager in place and, with the passing of the LUT 1918 Act on 21 November the company entered upon an era of long-delayed and slow restoration as a working transport undertaking.

CHAPTER NINETEEN

THE POST-WAR YEARS

By the end of the Great War, the new manager, C.J.Spencer, who had built up a fine reputation as general manager of Bradford Corporation Tramways, was faced with the monumental task of restoring the LUT system as a viable undertaking after enforced lack of maintenance during the war years. The problem was compounded by general neglect in earlier years and a continuing critical financial position.

Spencer also held the position of manager of the other two LST tramway companies, the Metropolitan Electric Tramways and the South Metropolitan Electric Tramways & Lighting Company. His predecessor in these posts, A.H.Pott, had held the combined posts of general manager and engineer of the respective companies. On 16 December 1916 Archibald Victor Mason, manager and engineer of the South Metropolitan Electric Tramways Company had been appointed assistant manager and engineer to the three companies and on 21 December 1921 Spencer was designated general manager of the three companies and Mason deputy general manager and engineer.

From 31 October 1919 all electric power for the lines north of the River Thames as well as those in Surrey was being taken from the UERL generating station at Lots Road, Chelsea. The Chiswick station was closed down and a sub-station installed to serve the lines in Hammersmith, Acton, Ealing and Brentford areas. This effectively put an end to the recurring breakdowns at Chiswick generating station which had been causing disruption of services through the war years.

An almost immediate start was made on reconstructing the most badly worn track. The work in Ealing was carried out as from June 1919 by contractors, while at the same time the controversial centre traction poles in the borough were replaced by side poles with span-wire suspension. In Brentford the track was in an equally poor state and reconstruction of this also commenced in the summer of 1919, the company carrying out the work by direct labour. The directors were impressed with the savings achieved by this, and almost all future reconstruction was carried out in this manner, using purpose-built machinery for removing old track and foundations and laying new track.

On 18 July 1919 the LUT directors approved a scheme of partial reconstruction for the track between Hayes Canal Bridge and Uxbridge. This involved renewing the points and crossings at the numerous loops, lifting, packing and relaying the existing rails and renewing the paving. Expenditure of £30,000 was authorised. On 5 December 1919, however, this work was suspended in view of proposals by Middlesex County Council for highways improvements in Uxbridge Road.

Spencer submitted a scheme on 10 October 1920 covering reconstruction and renewals over a three-year period. For the year 1921 he proposed to reconstruct the track between Southall and Hanwell, Richmond Bridge and Twickenham, Coles Bridge and Twickenham, and also the junction at Eden Street, Kingston. For

1922 it was proposed to renew the track between Hounslow "The Bell" and Hounslow Heath and from Twickenham Junction to Stanley Road Junction, while for 1923 the scheme covered the section between Coles Bridge and Busch Corner, Isleworth. The estimated cost of this work amounted to £341,000, while the provision of 30 new cars in each of these years at £2,000 each, brought this projected total up to £521,000.

The sum of £235,000 due to the company upon the sale of the Hammersmith lines was earmarked for reconstruction costs, and formed only a proportion of the projected expenditure. Lack of readily available cash delayed much of the three-year scheme; parts of it were deferred, while the proposed reconstruction of the section between Hounslow "The Bell" and Hounslow Heath and the Richmond Bridge branch did not take place, resulting in these sections being abandoned in 1922 and 1924 respectively. The plan for 90 new cars also did not materialise, while almost ten years were to elapse before partial replacement of the fleet took place in 1931.

A provision of the LUT 1918 Act obliged the company to spend £400,000 on reconstruction and renewals before any dividend on preference or ordinary shares could be declared. This objective was reached in the financial year 1925 by which time £400,810 had been expended.

In addition to the managerial changes already mentioned, others took place among the senior staff of the company. Arthur Lea Barber, Secretary of the MET from 1902 and of the LUT, SMET, LST and the Tramways (MET) Omnibus Company since December 1912, relinquished these posts in January 1921, and was succeeded by Evelyn Boys, who also became the treasurer. Barber was appointed to a new post, that of commercial manager of the Underground Group in succession to Frank Pick, who had become assistant managing director of the UERL.

The long-delayed transfer to the London County Council of the lines in Hammersmith took place on 2 May 1922 but it was several more months before the transaction was finally completed. This included the provision of power supplies to the lines affected. The lease back to the company of the Chiswick workshops was signed on the following day, details of which are described in Chapter 17.

With the exception of the introduction of a service of LCC cars from London Bridge (Hop Exchange) via Putney and Hammersmith to Kew Bridge, together with the replacement of LUT trams between Tooting and Wimbledon, and a direct service by LCC cars at weekends between central London and Hampton Court, there was little other material alteration to daily LUT services.

Having received £235,000 from the LCC the company was in a position to take its rehabilitation scheme forward by improving the existing rolling stock, the 1920 proposal to renew the fleet having been shelved. After trials, 80 car sets of high-powered light-weight motors were ordered from the Metropolitan Vickers Electrical Company in June 1923, which were installed in open and top-covered cars of the 151-300 batch. These cars also received magnetic track brakes and numerous additional improvements, includng new seating and interior decorations, which were made to much of the original fleet, all of which are described in detail elsewhere in this book.

In 1919 the London Traffic Advisory Committee set up to advise the new Ministry of Transport on traffic matters, suggested that the single line link between the LUT and MET at King Street, Acton, provided as a wartime measure in 1915, should be doubled on another alignment and made available for passenger traffic between the two systems.

To facilitate this the Middlesex County Council Bill for 1925 included an application for 316 yards of double line from Horn Lane to High Street, Acton by way of Rectory Road and Steyne Road, both of which would be widened. The Bill was passed in August, empowering the MCC to lay the track and the companies to make the junctions. The time limit for completion of the work was five years. The MCC spent £10,780 on acquiring properties and carried out the road works, but the track was not laid owing to renewed objections by Acton Borough Council. In April 1931 the MCC decided to take no further action, but instead, several years later, powers were granted to the London Passenger Transport Board to make the link for trolleybuses, which was opened on 5 July 1936.

Large numbers of omnibuses came on to the streets of London in the early 1920s, competing not only with the trams but also the UERL-owned London General Omnibus Company. This resulted in legislation giving the tramways some protection against unreasonable competition, as described elsewhere.

Meanwhile, track reconstruction and improvements to the rolling stock continued. These collectively enabled the company to provide speedier and more comfortable journeys. Between 1923 and 1929, a scrapping programme was in progress which dealt with 124 of the original cars, some of which had been out of service for many years. A number of these had been cannibalised to enable parts from them to be used to keep other cars in service. With the later arrival of new trams and trolleybuses in 1931, further cars were scrapped, bringing the once huge fleet down to a total of 150, of which 46 were new.

The Uxbridge Road Problem

The Uxbridge Road scheme was not included in the 1920 programme as consideration had been given in 1918 to abandoning the 5.1 miles of route between the "Hambrough Tavern" at the Southall-Hayes boundary and Uxbridge, the company's 1918 Bill providing for this. The proposal, however, was removed from the Bill and meanwhile Middlesex County Council was considering a scheme of its own for the upgrading of Uxbridge Road west of Hanwell.

During 1922 the MCC again considered making extensive improvements to Uxbridge Road which, beyond Southall was still largely rural in character, with the tramway passing through a succession of single track sections before reaching Uxbridge. The MCC proposed to widen and straighten this road, and that the company seek powers to place the existing tramway upon a reserved sleeper track. Spencer met MCC officers and noted this, but advised the LUT board against seeking powers for reserved track as suggested by the Council, but that the County Council itself should promote any such legislation. Nothing further was done at this time.

In January 1924 the County Council once more agreed in principle to widen sections of the Uxbridge Road to 110ft. and to the reconstruction of the tramway as a reserved sleeper track 35ft. wide, on condition that the LUT contributed to the costs of the improvements. Again, the MCC ruled that the company would be expected to obtain powers for the tramway part of the work and at its own expense.

The MCC submitted a Bill in November 1924 covering the proposed work, and the LUT directors discussed it at length. It was agreed that Spencer should consult the solicitor with a view to ensuring that the company was protected from any obligations arising from the Bill which was passed in 1925, but the LUT was unable to reach any agreement with the County Council on the proposed reserved track. The MCC went ahead with its improvement scheme and Uxbridge Road was widened, and straightened in some places, resulting in the tramway remaining on one stretch of the old alignment.

The General Strike

A serious dispute in the coal mining industry commenced in the spring of 1926, and on 1 May the trades unions representing the employees of many

Bank holiday crowds besiege Type W 235 at Hammersmith bound for Hampton Court in 1919.
In the late 1920s No.235 received a top-cover from a scrapped car.

(Courtesy London Transport Museum)

Car No.89, seen in 1919 near Ealing Common Station carries a poster on the dash panel
announcing the restoration of children's fares in July.

(Courtesy the National Tramway Museum)

A busy scene in High Street, Acton during the town's Charter Day celebrations in October 1921, with No.336 and cars of Types U and Z having passed through the interlaced track section.   (Photo John Goodwin courtesy Mrs.Averil Harper Smith)

Shepherds Bush tram terminus c.1922 with Type Y car No.59 about to be reversed for return to Hounslow while No.81 (Type Z) has just arrived from Hanwell via Acton.
(Commercial view. Courtesy London Borough of Hammersmith & Fulham Libraries)

industries, including transport and manufacturing, called a general strike in support of the miners. A state of emergency was declared in a royal proclamation and, in company with other similar undertakings, regular services on the IUT were suspended from 4 May to 14 May.

The company attempted to provide skeleton services by enlisting the aid of volunteers, among them many students, clerical staff and others. Conductors underwent a hurried course of instruction, while volunteer motormen on the three company systems were trained on the extensive tracks of the Hendon repair works of the MET. The oldest (and slowest) cars were rostered for these duties, but many crews were forced to abandon their cars or retire to the safety of the depots when they came under fire from missiles thrown by strikers. Some cars were derailed by bolts or similar obstructions being inserted into the pointwork. Numerous cars suffered bodywork damage. and for some time after the strike was over, some could be seen on the road with hastily patched-up panels.

The strike was called off on 12 May. Normal services were restored two days later, but as many miners did not return to work until some time after the official end of the dispute, coal shortage was the cause of occasional service reductions. At the shareholders' meeting held on 22 February 1927, the Chairman, discussing the strike of the previous summer, said that the effects of loss of traffic, extraordinary expense arising from the strike, together with subsequent loss of confidence among the public, were still being felt at the time of the meeting.

Partial Rehabilitation of the System

As mentioned elsewhere, an attempt was made subsequent to 1919 to bring the neglected system to an acceptable condition for post-war requirements. Improvements to the existing rolling stock including partial reconstruction of a small number of cars in the mid-1920s, are described in Chapter 21. By 1929 it had become evident that something more comprehensive was needed if the system was to survive and compete with other forms of transport.

In addition to the improvements made to rolling stock, a considerable amount of work was carried out in the depots, where facilities were brought up to date, with car washing machines supplanting hand washing. Where rattan and wooden seating gave way to spring upholstered seats, reverting in some measure to the standards of the fleet when now, vacuum cleaning equipment was installed to deal with upholstery and floors. It is interesting to note that vacuum cleaning was tried at Chiswick Depot in 1903 but not followed up at the time.

Discussions between the LUT and LST management, the UERL and their bankers on a comprehensive scheme covering replacement of rolling stock, and completing the track reconstruction started in 1913, but was halted by the Great War. The new scheme also included completion of improvements to power supplies and depot accommodation which had commenced in 1927, and was submitted by C.J.Spencer to F.Pick on 19 August 1929.

Spencer also proposed the modernisation of the tramways north of Fulwell depot, to reconstruct the route southwards from Stanley Road Junction to Hampton Court and Kingston via Hampton Hill to maintain a through tramway service between Hammersmith and Kingston, and retain tramway access to Fulwell Depot. The scheme included reconstruction of the track in Merton between Wimbledon and Tooting, and as already described, the Uxbridge Road line west of Southall. It was estimated that costs of the Stanley Road to Kingston improvement would be £84,700, and the Merton section £6,500.

The estimate also covered the cost of 126 new trams at £3,000 each. New motors and other electrical equipment purchased between 1923 and 1928 costing £34,610 would be transferred to the new cars, bringing the estimate for these down to £343,390, resulting in the total tramway costs amounting to £534,390. An additional £15,000 covered proposed extensions to Hanwell Depot to

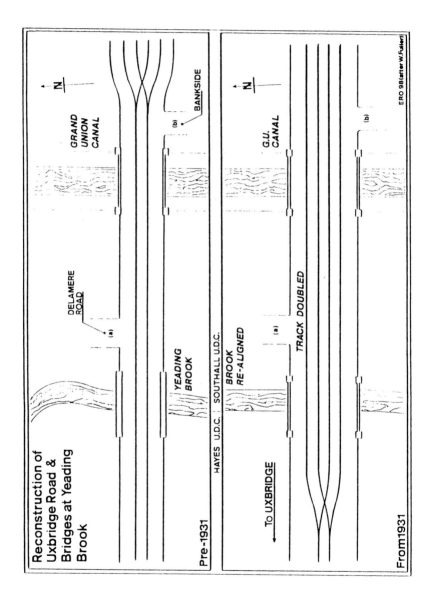

Reconstruction of Uxbridge Road & Bridges at Yeading Brook

Pre-1931

GRAND UNION CANAL

DELAMERE ROAD

(a)

(b)

BANKSIDE

YEADING BROOK

HAYES U.D.C. | SOUTHALL U.D.C.

From 1931

G.U. CANAL

BROOK RE-ALIGNED

(a)

(b)

TRACK DOUBLED

To UXBRIDGE

ERO 98(after W.Fulleri)

Service 55 working between Brentford and Hanwell was extended in the late 1920s to Ealing via West Ealing on weekday rush hours, continuing occasionally to Acton. No.318 (Type T) waits to turn from Boston Road into Uxbridge Road.

(Hugh Nicol. Courtesy National Tramway Museum).

Seen at Beadon Road, Hammersmith c.1931, No.191 of Type W is about to depart for Hampton Court.   (Courtesy London Borough of Hammersmith & Fulham Libraries)

accommodate the new cars and improvements to the power supply and distribution system.

It was also proposed to replace the tramways south of Fulwell via Teddington with trolleybuses, including the route from Stanley Road Junction to Kingston via Teddington, but excluding the Wimbledon-Tooting section and the Haydon's Road branch. Cost of this part of the scheme was estimated at £164,250 including 65 trolleybuses at £94,250. Total estimated cost of the Spencer scheme amounted to £713,840. By this time the tracks in Acton, Brentford, Ealing, Chiswick, Hanwell, Heston & Isleworth (including Hounslow), and Twickenham had been wholly reconstructed and extensive improvements carried out to the lines south of Twickenham.

By January 1930 Spencer had conferred with Lord Ashfield resulting in the scheme being considerably reduced in scale, now comprising provision of 54 new trams (each to seat 100 passengers); replacement of the trams between Hampton Court and Wimbledon by a fleet of 30 trolleybuses; reconstruction of two miles of track between Wimbledon and Tooting; and re-alignment and partial doubling of the Uxbridge Road line beyond Hanwell, at estimated costs of £500,000. The 54 new trams were additional to 46 which had just been ordered on hire purchase terms.

Due to the failure of the proposed application to the Treasury for a grant to meet interest charges upon capital so employed, in part due to the failure of Leeds City Council to gain such a grant, the company revised its scheme on 9 August 1930, dividing its implementation into two phases.

The first phase of the revised scheme included the 46 new cars already ordered; 62 trolleybuses; improvements to Hanwell depot; and the provision of a new sub-station at Southall. This involved expenditure before the end of 1931 of £405,000, which included abandonment costs and the overhead-wire installation for the trolleybuses in the Kingston area. The second phase consisted of a further 74 trams; renewing the track between Stanley Road Junction and Hampton Court via Hampton; and doubling the track between Southall and Uxbridge, involving capital expenditure after 1931 of £426,700.

Considerable delays ensued from this time, owing to uncertainty surrounding the Bills then before Parliament affecting London passenger traffic and, therefore, the position of the company and its associates under the proposed legislation. In the event only the trolleybus conversion between Twickenham and Wimbledon was carried out in 1931; the 46 "Feltham" type tramcars were built; and the alterations to Hanwell Depot and additions to the power supply completed.

On the Uxbridge line, as mentioned previously, only minor work was undertaken, such as the elimination of some of the many single-track sections, renewal of the remaining points and crossings at the loops, and the placing of colour-light signals at the longer single-line sections. The proposed additional 74 new tramcars were not built.

Following the introduction of the "Felthams" and the trolleybuses, little else of note occurred. Established services continued with few alterations, but mostly with improved journey times resulting from the new cars on the Uxbridge Road route, and new motors and improved power supplies over the rest of the system.

CHAPTER TWENTY

ROUTES & SERVICES
DESTINATION & ROUTE INDICATION EQUIPMENT

The Horse Cars

In common with many horse tram operators, especially in London, the LUT allocated cars of a given colour to indicate the route worked. Those used were dark brown for Shepherds Bush-"Askew Arms"; chocolate for Hammersmith-Kew Bridge; yellow for Shepherds Bush-Young's Corner and Kew Bridge-Richmond. This was the situation in 1895, when the track between the "Askew Arms" and Acton was being reconstructed and extended to the new depot being built at Acton Hill. The colours were supplemented by signwritten boards fitted above the saloon windows, and on the upper-deck end panels, while additionally the terminal points of each route were shown on the rocker panels and on the outer stair stringers. There were, however, variations on this scheme, and in some cases the displays on the stairs and the rocker panels were omitted. In other instances boards above the saloon windows displayed terminal and an intermediate point.

Electrification

This chapter is divided into two main periods, 1901-13 and 1914-33. Prior to 1914 the LUT did not use route numbers, relying instead upon various combinations of car colour, inscriptions, route boards and roller blind destination indicators. Route letters or symbols were never used. Service intervals and times of first and last cars were given through company announcements in the local press, upon which much of the following text is based. The information may be incomplete, as services, especially in the early years, were frequently altered as new routes were opened, and again as the traffic pattern settled down. For ease of reference some details are repeated from Chapters 4-9 in Volume One.

In the second period, from mid-1913 to 1933, the LUT was controlled and managed by the London & Suburban Traction Company, in which senior members of the management staff were appointed to posts with the LUT, resulting in the three company-owned systems becoming largely a single entity, but with each undertaking maintaining its outwardly separate identity.

An early result of these changes was the introduction of route numbers and the publication (except in wartime) of a twice-yearly (later annually) Map and Guide covering all three LST systems. These guides form the principal source for the second part of this chapter, although they are not precisely dated. Actual dates on which alterations took place are quoted where known, otherwise the the date shown is that of the first Map and Guide to indicate the altered service.

Uxbridge Road, 1901-1913

Replacing the horse trams, LUT electric cars of series 1-100 commenced operation between Shepherds Bush and Acton Depot on Thursday 4 April 1901, with a service described in the press as "every few minutes until past midnight". The terminus at Shepherds Bush was close to that of the Central London (tube)

Railway, which had opened on 30 July 1900, and provided much traffic for the trams.

The Acton service was extended over the Acton-Ealing boundary at Birch Grove, then via Ealing and Hanwell to Southall Town Hall on Wednesday 10 July 1901. A three-minute service was provided by white cars of series 101-150, with ornate transferred lettering along the upper-deck sides reading:-

SHEPHERDS BUSH   ACTON   EALING   HANWELL   &   SOUTHALL

Extra journeys were provided as far as Ealing, and at the opening banquet it was stated that there was a car to Ealing every minute at peak hours. A photograph exists of a red car of series 1-100 reversing at Ealing Broadway, bearing paper stickers reading:-

SHEPHERDS BUSH   &   EALING

By the time that the extension from Southall to Uxbridge was ready for use, the LUT had become associated financially with the District Railway. As a result, when the line opened on 1 June 1904, the service provided ran to and from Hammersmith using the tracks between there and Acton "Askew Arms" which opened on the same day. Additional cars ran between Hammersmith and Hanwell, both services showing their eastern destination as "Hammersmith District Railway". Some of the Shepherds Bush-Southall cars were sent through to Uxbridge on Sundays, and the Shepherds Bush-Ealing service was extended to Hanwell. So far as is known, the basic headway to Uxbridge on weekdays was a car every twelve minutes.

The Uxbridge service was worked at first by cars lettered:

SHEPHERDS BUSH   ACTON   EALING   HANWELL   SOUTHALL
HAYES   HILLINGDON   &   UXBRIDGE

but this was inflexible and resort soon had to be made to the use of large removable boards which could be clipped into place to amend or obscure some of the original transferred placenames. Examples were a "Hammersmith" board to obscure Shepherds Bush, a "Hanwell Only" board to replace Hanwell & Southall, and a long black board to cover the entire lower line and thus obscure "Hayes - Hillingdon - Uxbridge".

From January to May 1904, Uxbridge Road services were to Southall and Hanwell alternately, with Shepherds Bush and Hammersmith-Uxbridge added in June. In the week ended 10 June, Shepherds Bush-Uxbridge was deleted but restored in the following week.

By the time that the Central London Railway had joined the Underground Group in 1912, the new pattern had become established as daily services between Shepherds Bush and Hanwell, Southall and Uxbridge, and from Hammersmith to Hanwell, extended on Sundays with alternate cars to Southall and Uxbridge.

One of the most unlikely LUT ventures was a through service, tried in 1906-7, between Hammersmith and Uxbridge via Brentford and the Boston Road-Lower Boston Road line. No timetable has been found to show the days and time of operation, but it was evidently unsuccessful, being cut back to Southall in 1907 and then withdrawn entirely, leaving the short line in Lower Boston Road disused.

Permanent lettering on the cars would have been unworkable in the Kingston area, and when services commenced there on 1 March 1906 with cars of the 301-340 series, they carried single-line roller-blind indicators, supplemented by two-line boards fixed above the lower saloon windows. This practice quickly spread to the rest of the fleet and, as the system developed, cars could be re-deployed as traffic demanded.

The Chiswick Routes, 1901-1913

On Thursday 4 April 1901, on the same date as the opening of the Shepherds Bush-Acton line, new electric trams were introduced on the former horse tram routes between Hammersmith Broadway and Kew Bridge and between Shepherds Bush and Kew Bridge, joining at Young's Corner. Red cars of series 1-100 provided a service "every few minutes" on both routes, carrying paper stickers at first and, shortly afterwards, ornate transfer lettering on the upper-deck sides, displaying the terminal points.

The line was extended on 6 July 1901 from Kew Bridge through Brentford to Hounslow "The Bell". Cars now ran every ten minutes on each of four overlapping services:- Hammersmith-Kew Bridge; Hammersmith-Hounslow; Shepherds Bush-Kew Bridge; Shepherds Bush-Hounslow, giving a five-minute service from each terminus. Extra cars ran to and from Kew Bridge and Hammersmith at busy times, especially on bank holidays. The cars were divided into four batches (one for each route) and lettered accordingly. From 13 August 1902 the two Hounslow services were extended from "The Bell" to Hounslow Heath "The Hussar".

On the same day a service began on the branch line between Busch Corner and Twickenham (Cole's Bridge), with through cars to and from both Hammersmith and Shepherds Bush, each every ten minutes, with this addition giving a total of 36 cars an hour through Chiswick. The further extensions of this service to Hampton Court are described later in this chapter. The only other service in this district was a short-lived one on Sunday afternoons from 2 July 1904, between Hounslow and Hampton Court, using the west curve at Busch Corner which, at a later date, was removed.

At Kew Bridge the stub terminus was aligned towards the new (authorised) river bridge, which was to replace the old narrow bridge, which was not suitable for trams. The company hoped to join the Chiswick line with its Kew Bridge (Surrey side)-Richmond horse tramway, with a through electric service via the new bridge, but this did not materialise. When motor buses took much of its traffic, the tram service was reduced to three horse cars (from the nine in stock) and finally to a single "franchise" car. The last horse car ran on 20 April 1912.

The Twickenham Routes, 1902-1913

Having arrived on 13 August 1902 at Cole's Bridge, close by Twickenham Station, the LUT had to await the completion of a large water main and road widenings before proceeding further south. The main line was extended to Twickenham (Cross Deep) on 13 September 1902, together with the branch from Twickenham to Richmond Bridge, while the further extension to Stanley Road Junction near Fulwell Depot opened on 8 November 1902. The services operated from this date were Shepherds Bush-Stanley Road Junction; Richmond Bridge-Stanley Road Junction; and Hammersmith-Twickenham (Cross Deep).

On Thursday 2 April 1903 the Hampton Court Loop (Stanley Road Junction to Stanley Road Junction via Hampton Hill, Hampton Court, Hampton Wick and Teddington) opened just in time for Easter. At that time LUT policy was to allocate cars to specific routes, so the Fulwell Depot fleet was divided into three batches respectively lettered:-

HAMMERSMITH BRENTFORD TWICKENHAM HAMPTON HAMPTON COURT

SHEPHERDS BUSH BRENTFORD TWICKENHAM HAMPTON HAMPTON COURT

RICHMOND BRIDGE TWICKENHAM TEDDINGTON KINGSTON BRIDGE HAMPTON COURT

The cars did not actually venture on to Kingston Bridge, which was not opened to trams until 1906, but used the third side of the triangular junction at the bridge foot.

The basic service was a car every ten minutes from Hammersmith and from Shepherds Bush, giving a combined five-minute service from Youngs Corner. The

Car No.10 (Type Z) stands at "The Hussar" at Hounslow Heath awaiting return to its London terminus. (Commercial view)

Seen c.1907, cars 272 and 274 of Type W at the Wimbledon terminus at the end of Worple Road. No.272, standing on the right, has just arrived, and while the passengers alight the conductor prepares to turn the trolley pole for the return journey to Hammersmith on a special working. No.274 is on a scheduled service to Hampton Court.
(Commercial view courtesy National Tramway Museum)

Richmond Bridge-Teddington-Hampton Court service may have started with a car every five minutes, but was probably cut back later to eight cars an hour. At holiday times a car arrived at Hampton Court every two minutes, but winter traffic proved disappointing and eventually it became necessary to turn alternate cars at Twickenham.

At Hampton Court the layout comprised two stub-ends at right angles linked by a double-track curve. This allowed the operation of circular tours to Hampton Court, out one way and back the other, starting and finishing at the London termini. Circular tour tickets, at one shilling for the 24-mile round trip were issued at Easter 1903, but the practice was short-lived. Most journeys were broken at Hampton Court; but with some at the Garrick's Villa siding.

When the first Kingston lines were opened on 1 March 1906, a 7½- minute service was provided between Kingston Bridge and Dittons (Windows Bridge) alternating with the cars to Hampton Court. Both services were withdrawn in April 1907 and replaced by a five-minute service between Richmond Bridge and Kingston (Eden Street). All services into Kingston carried route boards above the windows, advertisements having taken the place of destination descriptions on the upper-deck side panels.

The Kingston Routes, 1906-1913

The line across Kingston Bridge was opened on 1 March 1906 together with those to Kingston Hill, Tolworth and Windows Bridge (Dittons). The new services, as set out in the *Surrey Comet* were:-

HAMPTON COURT   KINGSTON HILL

RICHMOND BRIDGE   WINDOWS BRIDGE

SURBITON STATION   TOLWORTH

The first of several subsequent changes to Kingston area services took place on 26 May 1906 with the opening of the lines to Richmond Park Gates, Ham Boundary and the Norbiton Park Hotel (later renamed "The Fountain"). The *Surrey Comet* announced the provision of ten-minute services on the routes between Hampton Court & New Malden, Tolworth & Richmond Park Gates, Tolworth & Ham Boundary and Kingston Hill & Surbiton, with the last-named terminating at Windows Bridge at peak hours, the cars carrying boards misspelt as "Winters Bridge". The Richmond Bridge-Windows Bridge service was unaltered. Late evening services were every 20 minutes and start-up times were later than on the other routes.

It quickly became apparent that Kingston services were over-generous. The Ham Boundary service was reduced to a car every 15 minutes, bringing forth a complaint from Kingston Corporation, at whose insistence the line had been built. On 16 April 1907 the LUT board decided on further cuts to save three men and eight cars; Richmond Bridge cars were turned back in Kingston; Kingston Hill cars were to run to Windows Bridge; Richmond Park Gates cars were to run to Tolworth; with a shuttle car working between Ham Boundary and King's Road Junction, passengers changing at that point to cars on other services.

Meanwhile, construction had continued beyond New Malden, the service from Hampton Court being extended to Raynes Park on 27 April 1907, to Wimbledon on 2 May 1907 and finally to Tooting (Longley Road) on 26 June 1907, together with the branch line to Summerstown. The cars providing this last-named service initially ran through from Wimbledon Hill Road, but were later curtailed at High Street, Merton (Haydon's Road Junction) passengers being issued with transfer tickets to enable them to complete their journeys to Wimbledon on the "Tooting" cars.

On 1 January 1905, following advice from American financial consultants the company entered into a contract with an advertising agency, and as a result of this

With a non-uniformed driver, possibly a mechanic, and displaying "Fulwell" on the blind, this car standing in Clarence Street, Kingston is evidently in some difficulty and awaiting assistance. (Commercial postcard)

An early view of car No.180 in Plough Lane on the Haydon's Road branch to Summerstown. (Commercial view)

the upper-deck side and end panels of the cars were given over to advertisements. The destination displays on the sides of the cars then consisted of 13ft.6in. long white boards placed above the saloon windows, in some cases lettered in black with two terminal points e.g:

RICHMOND BRIDGE & HAMPTON COURT

and in others including some intermediate points, e.g.:

TOOTING WIMBLEDON KINGSTON & HAMPTON COURT

The complicated nature of local routes in the Kingston area would have precluded use of the inflexible system first used on the Middlesex lines. When the line across Kingston Bridge opened with new top-covered cars in March 1906, they were fitted with roller-blind destination indicators contained in wooden boxes of a later pattern than those provided on the first cars. Two boards were fitted on each side above the lower saloon windows, each showing one terminal point, which allowed greater flexibility. Almost immediately after the Kingston routes opened the upper-deck side and end panels carried advertisements.

To allow for ease of handling, the boards above the saloon windows were dispensed with from c1910. Five metal brackets were fitted immediately below the lower deck side windows, allowing four separate smaller boards to be displayed, which could be changed from ground level to suit operational requirements. These boards, about four inches deep, were at first blue with white lettering, later white with black lettering, which enabled two terminal and two intermediate points to be shown. After the end of the war lighter brackets were fitted to take a single board, slightly shorter than the combined length of the earlier ones, and narrower, with black lettering on a white ground, and displaying a route number at either end with terminal and a number of intermediate points. All these boards were double sided.

By 1913 the original roller-blind indicator boxes, most of which were of metal construction, had become unserviceable. They were replaced with unglazed wooden boxes, displaying a single-line two-sided slip-board, with a hole in each end to enable the conductor to remove it from the box for reversal, or to change to another route. The open-ended box had space to store a number of the slips. These were illuminated at night by a pair of lamps in swan-neck fittings suspended from the top of the box. In the case of the open balcony cars, the new indicators were placed on the under side of the roof above the top of the stairs on the rear offside, illuminated by a row of lamps fixed to the roof. Most of these remained in use throughout the existence of the tramways.

1914 to 1922

Following the adoption of the use of service numbers on London buses in 1908, the London County Council Tramways did the same in the autumn of 1912, and in their case, used odd numbers for the Northern Division services and even numbers for those on the Southern Division. The London & Suburban Traction Company, which now controlled the LUT and MET decided to follow suit, using numbers chosen to avoid clashing with those of the LCC, or with each other, resulting in even numbers being used by the MET. Odd numbers were allocated to the LUT, with gaps left in the scheme for those LCC north London services which penetrated into the MET area, such as 59 and 79.

Initially, the numbers allocated for the Uxbridge Road services were:-

7	Shepherds Bush-Uxbridge.	9B	Hammersmith-Hanwell.
83	Shepherds Bush-Hanwell.	87	Shepherds Bush-Southall.

These were all daily services and were joined on Sundays by:-

9	Hammersmith-Acton-Uxbridge.	9A	Hammersmith-Acton-Southall.

The branch service from Hanwell to Brentford (Half Acre) was given the number 55.

Those working through Chiswick were:-

57	Shepherds Bush-Hounslow Heath	65	Shepherds Bush-Hampton Court
61	Hammersmith-Hounslow Heath	67	Hammersmith-Hampton Court
63	Shepherds Bush-Kew Bridge	85A	Hammersmith-Kew Bridge

The use of 85A rather than 85 was probably due to a plan (later realised) to use the number 85 for cars working between Hammersmith and Brentford (Ealing Road).

The numbers allocated to the Twickenham route in 1914 (already mentioned) were:- 65 and 67, with the addition of 69 Richmond Bridge-Kingston.

They appear to have overlooked the plan to extend LCC route 9 over MET metals to Barnet, and when this took place on 26 September 1914 it became necessary for LUT 9, 9A and 9B to be renumbered, these becoming 89, 89A and 89B. This gave the following pattern:-

7	Shepherds Bush & Uxbridge	75	Ham Boundary & King's Road
55	Brentford & Hanwell	77	Tolworth & Richmond Park Gates
57	Shepherds Bush & Hounslow	81	Summerstown & Haydon's Road Jcn.
61	Hammersmith & Hounslow Heath	83	Shepherds Bush & Hanwell
63	Shepherds Bush & Kew Bridge	85A	Hammersmith & Kew Bridge
65	Shepherds Bush & Hampton Court	87	Shepherds Bush & Southall
67	Hammersmith & Hampton Court	89	Hammersmith & Uxbridge
69	Kingston & Richmond Bridge	89A	Hammersmith & Southall
71	Tooting & Hampton Court	89B	Hammersmith & Hanwell
73	Kingston Hill & Dittons		

These services operated daily except for 89 and 89A which ran on Sundays only.

The Tramways Map and Guide was not published between 1915 and 1919, and LUT information for those years is therefore incomplete. The worsening financial position in 1917 resulted in service reductions early in the year, with suspension of those to Kingston Hill (73) and to Ham Boundary (75), together with the withdrawal of Sunday service 89 and 89A. The 89B (Hammersmith-Hanwell) was later renumbered 89, becoming a Hammersmith-Acton service on weekdays, extended to Hanwell on Sundays. The Kingston Hill service was reinstated during the summer of 1917, while workmen's cars were run to Ham Boundary at factory shift times as from October, apparently by extending one or two cars of the Kingston-Richmond Bridge service.

The curious arrangement of using the suffix letter "T" after the route number on LUT, MET and SMET services, introduced in 1914 presumably to make a distinction between the numbers carried by the trams from similar ones in use on LGOC buses, continued to be shown in the Maps and Guides until 1922, but the suffixes remained on many cars throughout their existence.

In May 1920, service 75, the Ham Boundary shuttle which had been again reinstated after the war, was withdrawn as a regular service, but a car continued to run at works' times, serving the aircraft factory near the terminus. This was followed by changes in 1921 which included the extension of route 55 (Brentford-Hanwell) to Ealing (for one year), the withdrawal of the Sunday Acton-Hanwell section of 89, and the reduction of service 65 (Shepherds Bush-Hampton Court) to Saturday and Sunday working only.

Service 57 was reduced to Saturdays and Sundays only in 1921, but was reinstated in 1922, and route 61 (Hammersmith-Hounslow) withdrawn in its place, leaving the basic daily services through Brentford as 57 (Shepherds Bush-Hounslow) and 67 (Hammersmith-Hampton Court), a pattern which remained unchanged for the rest of the tramways' existence.

At the Hanwell terminus in Boston Road in the early 1920s, Type Y car No.13 awaits departure for Brentford. The original requirement for trackbraked cars on this route had evidently been waived.

(Photo F.Merton Atkins)

A pair of feeder switch boxes placed on a side-street corner immediately off High Street, Hounslow. The use of these boxes in pairs was a feature of the LUT system as originally constructed.

(S.G.Jackman, courtesy the Science Museum)

Indicators on the cars were modified to enable the new numbers to be displayed. A metal plate was fixed to the right-hand side of each indicator box, either above, below, or on the extreme right-hand end. They were provided with slots into which a black-painted movable plate bearing a route number in white was placed. Later, in a few cases, the fixed plate was painted white and a cut-out stencil was used.

With the limited refurbishment scheme of the 1920s, the 40 Type T cars were fitted with new single-line internally illuminated roller-blind boxes, together with a smaller roller-blind route number indicator above, mounted on the balcony ends above the front advertisement panels. The three type U/2 and five Type WT cars received similar treatment, with the addition of roller-blind route number side indicators placed at the front nearsides and suspended from below the staircase landings. Except for these variations the rest of the fleet retained equipment fitted from 1913-14, except for a small number of Type U cars loaned to the South Metropolitan Electric Tramways, from which route number displays were removed. The equipment used on the 1931 "Feltham" type cars is described elsewhere.

The short line between Haydon's Road Junction at Merton and the LCC boundary at Summerstown was worked as a shuttle service numbered 81. Car No.48 of Type Y is seen on this duty. (Photographer unknown)

Meanwhile, discussions with the LCC regarding their purchase of the Hammersmith lines within the county of London, i.e. those east of Young's Corner and the "Askew Arms", were reaching their conclusion and eventually completed. The LUT continued working to Shepherds Bush and Hammersmith, and the LCC in compensation taking over the working on 2 May 1922 of the line between Tooting (Longley Road) and Wimbledon Hill and extending their services 2 and 4. From the same date, LCC service 26 (Hop Exchange-Hammersmith) was extended to Kew Bridge, but this arrangement this did not appear in the company Map and Guide.

1922-1933

The sections which follow take events forward from June 1922 until all tramways in the London area were taken over by London Transport on 1 July 1933.

Uxbridge Road

Details of the pattern of services:-

7 SHEPHERDS BUSH - Acton - Hanwell - Southall - UXBRIDGE
Daily, every 6 minutes, Journey 81 minutes, Fare 1/-.

55 HANWELL - BRENTFORD (Half Acre)
Daily, every 10 minutes, Journey 13 minutes, Fare 2d.

83 SHEPHERDS BUSH - Acton - HANWELL
Daily, every 2 minutes weekdays, 4 minutes Sundays.
Joint with 7 and 87. Journey 34 minutes, Fare 6d.

87 SHEPHERDS BUSH - Acton - Hanwell - SOUTHALL
Daily, every 6 minutes weekdays, 4 minutes Sundays.
Joint with 7. Journey 44 minutes, Fare 7d.

89 HAMMERSMITH - ACTON DEPOT
Daily, every 4 minutes weekdays, 5 minutes Sundays.
Journey 22 minutes, Fare 3d.

These entries reflect one summer 1922 change, the withdrawal of the 1921 extension of route 55 between Hanwell and Ealing. The 55 ran thereafter as a Hanwell-Brentford shuttle until the reversion from one-man cars to double-deckers in 1928, when it was reinstated at peak hours to work to Ealing Broadway and in 1933 extended to Acton.

The summer of 1924 saw a drastic cut in the running time on Uxbridge Road, following the re-motoring of the cars:

	Journey times (minutes)					
	1922	1924	1925	1928	1930	1932
Shepherds Bush-Uxbridge	81	68	68	68	68	68
Shepherds Bush-Southall	46	40	40	37	--	--
Shepherds Bush-Hanwell	34	--	29	27	--	--
Acton-Hammersmith	22	22	22	19	19	--

At the same time, service 83 (Shepherds Bush-Hanwell) was renumbered 7C and 87 (Shepherds Bush-Southall) became 7A. There was also a 7B between Shepherds Bush and Hayes (Yeading Lane) on Saturdays. The cars made available through speeding up the basic services were used to provide a service every few minutes to Southall, to combat the "Cambrian" independent bus service. The suffix letters A, B and C were discontinued by the time of the issue of the summer 1930 Map and Guide, all cars thereafter showing 7. The 1928 running time remained in force when "Feltham" type cars took over the working of route 7 in January 1931.

Type W 249 departs for Wimbledon from the centre of Kingston in 1922. As from May of that year the LUT service between Wimbledon and Tooting was replaced by LCC cars as an extension of their services 2/4.

(Photo G.Collard courtesy Bryan Woodriff)

In Hanwell Depot yard, car No.268 (Type U) is seen in one of the 1928 experimental "all-red" liveries. The destination indicator box carried two-sided slip-boards, while the service number plate was extended to show the suffix "T", by this time not in general use.

(Photo: LUT. Courtesy G.E.Baddeley)

"Feltham" car 378, heading west to Uxbridge, has passed under the Iron Bridge carrying the Great Western Railway across the road at Southall. Unlike on many other parts of the system, the Uxbridge route was paved mainly with granite setts beyond Southall.

(Photographer Unknown)

The Acton & Hammersmith Service

Route 89, confined to the Acton Depot-Hammersmith section from 1921 to 1927, now underwent a series of interesting changes. From summer 1928, half the service was extended to Hanwell on Saturday afternoons and evenings, and from 28 November the other half of the service was extended to Putney on weekdays, becoming the only LUT service ever to run outside the company's original territory. At first this extension was a joint working of LUT and LCC cars until 30 January 1930, when the LUT ceased to work south of Hammersmith, as terminal arrangements at Putney were considered to be difficult. Nevertheless, they again began to run through to Putney between 16 April and 30 July 1931 and onwards from 28 October 1931. The terminus at Putney was normally at Fawe Park Road, at a crossover in Putney Bridge Road, just west of the Southern Railway low level bridge over the road. Some cars, however, were turned in Fulham High Street at a crossover just north of Putney Bridge.

On 27 May 1933 the Saturday afternoon cars to Hanwell (which had continued to Southall during 1929) were diverted at Hanwell to run to Brentford (Half Acre). No photographs are known to exist of cars showing 89 on Boston Road, and comparison of times in the guide suggest that an end-on merger between services 89 and 55 took place, with a change of number somewhere in Ealing. The link between 89 and 55 continued until the former was replaced by trolleybuses (660) in 1936.

A through service between Acton and Tooting, worked by LCC cars numbered 89, began on 24 June 1933. This was quite likely an arrangement made between the two undertakings to provide such a service, just one week in advance of the LPTB taking over, when all would come under the control of one central management. It was necessary to use LCC cars for this, as none of the LUT cars were equipped with plough carriers.

Services Through Chiswick

57 SHEPHERDS BUSH - Brentford - HOUNSLOW ("The Bell")
Daily, every 5 minutes weekdays, 10 minutes Sundays.
Journey 42 minutes, Fare 7d.

63 SHEPHERDS BUSH - KEW BRIDGE (or BRENTFORD)
Daily, every 4 minutes weekdays, 5 minutes (to Kew) Sundays.
Journey 25 minutes (to Kew 20 minutes), Fare 4d.

67 HAMMERSMITH - Brentford - Twickenham - HAMPTON COURT
Daily, every 6 minutes weekdays, 10 minutes Sundays.
Alternate journeys terminate at Twickenham on weekdays in winter.
Journey to Hampton Court 62 minutes, Fare 10d.

85 HAMMERSMITH - BRENTFORD (Ealing Road)
Daily, every 6 minutes weekdays, 5 minutes Sundays.
Journey 23 minutes, Fare 3d.
Omitted from Winter 1922 guide but later reinstated.

26 (LCC) HOP EXCHANGE - Wandsworth - Putney - KEW BRIDGE
Daily. Not shown in LUT Map and Guide at this date.

The line between Hounslow Heath and Hounslow "The Bell" was abandoned on 11 July 1922, reducing the journey time for route 57 to 42 minutes from its original 51 minutes for the extended journey, (although this was not shown in the then-current guide). In its longer form, this line had briefly served as the first London Airport access in earlier years; in his book "A Social History of Air Transport", Kenneth Hudson relates how, in August 1919, passengers for the first commercial London-Paris service would arrive at the Hounslow Heath airport by tram. Operations were transferred to Croydon Aerodrome in April 1920, with access to it by limousine.

Type U No.224, seen in the mid-1920s, approaching Brentford Bridge on its way to Hammersmith, passes the point where a single-line entry track once led into Brentford Permanent Way Depot. *(S.G.Jackman, courtesy the Science Museum)*

Service 65 (Shepherds Bush-Hampton Court) omitted from the 1922 guide, re-appeared in those for 1923 and 1924 but not those issued subsequently, although continuing to run on Bank Holiday Sundays and Mondays. From 1930, service 63 was extended during weekday rush hours to Isleworth Fire Station, continuing until conversion to trolleybus operation in 1935.

LCC service 26, which had been extended to Kew Bridge, was augmented on Bank Holiday Sundays and Mondays with additional cars from Camberwell to Kew Bridge, displaying EX stencils. Occasionally, LCC cars ventured beyond Kew Bridge, but these were for staff or school outings from the Wandsworth area to Bushey Park and Hampton Court, and were otherwise not available to the public. First and last cars on route 26 were advertised as to and from Youngs Corner, for Chiswick Depot.

Services Through Kingston

69 RICHMOND BRIDGE - Teddington - KINGSTON
    Daily, every 7 minutes, Journey 36 minutes, Fare 5d.

71 HAMPTON COURT - Kingston - Malden - WIMBLEDON
    Daily, every 5 minutes, Journey 44 minutes, Fare 6d.

73 KINGSTON HILL - Surbiton - THE DITTONS
    Daily, every 10 minutes, Journey 28 minutes, Fare 3d.
    Additional cars between Kingston and The Dittons.

77 TOLWORTH - Surbiton - RICHMOND PARK GATES
    Daily, every 7 minutes weekdays. 10 minutes Sundays,
    Journey 28 minutes, Fare 3d.

The Piccadilly tube railway station at Hammersmith was extensively reconstructed between 1930 and 1932. A Type W car on the Hammersmith-Hampton Court service passes over the excavations on temporary track laid above the new works.

(Courtesy London Borough of Hammersmith & Fulham Libraries)

Some of the Type T cars were displaced from Uxbridge Road with the arrival of the "Felthams". No.324 awaits departure from Shepherds Bush for Hounslow in the summer of 1933. (G.N.Southerden courtesy London Borough of Newham Libraries)

Erstwhile blue car 216 just out from the Fulwell paint shop in July, 1924, repainted in "Underground" red and white and with many former decorative features omitted.

(Courtesy London Transport Museum U2755)

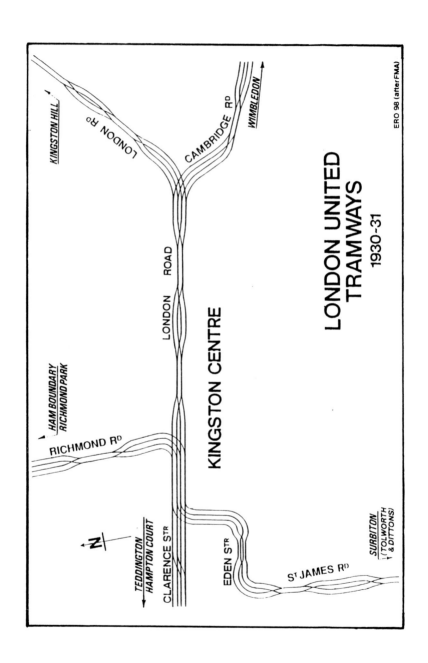

LONDON UNITED
TRAMWAYS
1930-31

KINGSTON CENTRE

ERO 98 (after FMA)

KINGSTON HILL

LONDON RD

CAMBRIDGE RD

WIMBLEDON

LONDON   ROAD

HAM BOUNDARY
RICHMOND PARK

RICHMOND RD

TEDDINGTON
HAMPTON COURT

CLARENCE STR

EDEN STR

ST JAMES RD

SURBITON
(TOLWORTH
& DITTONS)

N

Other Services

81 SUMMERSTOWN - HAYDON'S ROAD JUNCTION
Daily, every 20 minutes, Journey 6 minutes, Fare 1½d.

2/4 (LCC) VICTORIA EMBANKMENT - Tooting - WIMBLEDON HILL
Daily, every 3 minutes, Journey 56 minutes, Fare 5d.

With the Tooting-Wimbledon Hill line covered since 1922 by LCC cars working on services 2 and 4, the only LUT car to run east of Wimbledon was now the single car working service 81 along Haydon's Road. Service 75 to Ham Boundary had ceased in May 1920 except for a workmen's car serving the Hawker aircraft works at factory shift times.

In the winter of 1922-23 an experiment was conducted affecting services 67, 69 and 71. This decision was taken too late to amend the map itself, which carried an overprint. From 4 October 1922, service 67, Hammersmith-Hampton Court, was extended to Kingston, and service 71 from Wimbledon was diverted away from Hampton Court to run to Richmond Bridge, replacing the 69. The running times were 79 minutes for service 67, and 69 minutes for the 71. The reason for this change is unknown; it possibly saved one or two cars, and may have increased shopping traffic from Hampton to Kingston by avoiding the change at Hampton Court. The services concerned reverted to their previous form in the summer of 1923. On 1 October 1924 the LUT withdrew from the Twickenham-Richmond Bridge section, route 69 now becoming Twickenham-Kingston.

From 22 May 1926, alternate journeys on LCC services 2 and 4 were extended on Saturday afternoons and evenings and on summer Sundays to Hampton Court, and a corresponding reduction was made to LUT service 71. In theory, each operator's eight-minute service gave a four-minute combined headway, but in practice, the faster LCC cars would catch up with and follow the LUT cars (and suffer from overheated resistances). The second crossover at Hampton Court was

Type U No.300 about to return from Kingston to Hammersmith on a busy day in winter 1922. This service was extended from Hampton Court to Kingston for this one winter season.

(Photo courtesy Bryan Woodriff)

365

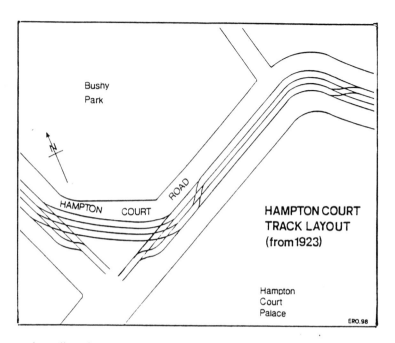

Bushy
Park

HAMPTON COURT ROAD

HAMPTON COURT
TRACK LAYOUT
(from 1923)

Hampton
Court
Palace

ERO.98

used to allow the LCC cars to leave Hampton Court just ahead of the LUT vehicles, but even so, each would catch up with the previous LUT car before reaching Wimbledon.

The replacement of trams with trolleybuses in the Kingston and Wimbledon areas in September 1931, spelt the end for the through Saturday and Sunday service from London, which ran for the last time during the weekend of 29/30 August. Thereafter, cars on services 2 and 4 were confined to their terminus at Wimbledon Hill until the trolleybuses were extended from Ely's Corner to Wimbledon Town Hall on 15th December 1932, when the trams from London were cut back to a new terminating point outside Wimbledon Town Hall. This conversion also left the cars required for service on the 63 and 67 as the only ones to remain at the vast Fulwell Depot, and surrounded by the new trolleybuses.

CHAPTER TWENTY-ONE

ROLLING STOCK 1913-1933

Design and equipment details of the original LUT car fleet are given in Volume One of this book, and except for the addition of top covers to some cars in 1910-11, the creation of a single-deck private hire saloon car in 1911 and the conversion of two passenger cars for departmental use in 1913, few changes took place until after the Great War of 1914-18.

When the London & Suburban Traction Company was formed in 1912 the three London company-owned tramways came under common management headed by Arthur Henry Pott, general manager and engineer of the Metropolitan Electric Tramways, with head offices at the Manor House, Finsbury Park. One of the first objectives of the new management was to bring all repair and engineering facilities together at the large car works of the MET at Hendon. It was hoped to achieve this during 1913, but as described elsewhere, it was not until 1915 that the transfer could take place. Chiswick Works was then requisitioned for the manufacture of munitions.

At the inception of the MET in 1904 a system of type letters was devised for identification of the different batches of cars, and in 1914 this scheme was extended to the LUT and South Metropolitan companies' fleets. The MET cars were lettered from Type A to H with a number of sub-types to denote variations within a defined group, such as Type B, Type B/1 (indicating a seating variation) and Type B/2 (identifying another group later fitted with top covers). As applied to the LUT the arrangement started from the end of the alphabet, commencing with Z and working back to Types S/1 and S/2, while the SMET were allocated those between J and P. The letters I, N, Q, R and V remained unused.

This arrangement went into use on cars of the LUT system in 1914. Those in the 1-100 series with open-top bodies were classified Type Z, and those fitted with top covers in 1910-11 became Type Y (a variation on the MET scheme). The 101-150 batch, all being in original open-top condition became Type X.

A schedule of LUT cars had been compiled in the period between 1914 and c.1924 by observers who listed every car they saw, the type letter it displayed and its existing Metropolitan Stage Carriage number. The only omissions are some cars out of service due to accidents, some in storage and the 101-150 batch, not then in revenue service. A few early scrappings are also noted.

The next group, numbered between 151 and 300, which had been delivered in 1902 and 1903 from two different builders, received quite different treatment from the rest of the fleet. The list shows that this batch was largely intact except for ten sold after the war, four damaged in accidents and three converted for other purposes. Three distinct classifications are shown, Type W/1, 151-200; Type W/2, 201-210 and Type W/3, 211-239. Nos. 240-264 reverted to Type W/1 and the remainder, all top-covered in 1910-11 were Type U, except No. 175, which was converted to a single-deck private hire saloon car in 1911, No. 275 which was cut down to single deck for departmental use, and another, the number of which is not known, which had been converted to a stores van by 1914.

There is no known reason for dividing the cars of this group into three sub-groups. The letters do not agree with the different makers' batches (Nos. 151-211 and 237-300 for the Milnes cars and Nos. 212-236 for those of the British Electric Car Company). A clue might lie in the 201-210 (Type W/2) group as these were white cars (which, by 1909 had become red) among 140 others in the batch which were originally blue.

Referring further to the type letter scheme, some variations and additions appeared in the 1920s, although these were few in number and will be described in the following text covering the history of the fleet up to July 1933. It had been noted by the observers (previously mentioned) that the type letters sometimes changed with repaints in the case of the Type W cars, and were only consistent where they related to Types Z, Y, T, UCC, S/1 and S/2.

The London & Suburban Traction Company produced an undated set of identification sheets covering the fleets of the three associated companies. These show crude outline drawings of each type of car with some main dimensions. Some of the sheets embody random lists of cars of the 151-300 group with sub-classifications up to U/4, in which the car numbers are in odd small batches. The master sheets for these show a marginal note "Incorrect. See Drg. U 90". A copy of rolling stock table U 90 Issue C lists all surviving LUT cars and their type letters as at 1 July 1933. By the mid-1920s, the classifications of Nos. 151-300 had been simplified, open-top cars becoming Type W, the top-covered versions Type U and U/2. Later, a small number of open-top cars were re-classified Type W/2 and some Type U top-covered cars became Type U/2 in company with Nos. 155, 199 and 288 but finally all remaining cars in the batch reverted to Type W (open-top) and Type U (top-covered) except Nos. 155, 199 and 288 which remained Type U/2.

It has not been found practicable to produce a consistent tabular record of scrapping and disposal of cars because surviving records are incomplete. A return to the Board of Trade dated 1917 gives a total of 338 cars owned, but many of these were stored out of service. The first disposal of cars by scrapping occurred prior to 1922, and this was carried out at Hillingdon Depot, but from 1923 this work was transferred to Fulwell Depot. Further details of disposals and scrapping are given at the end of each section.

Nos. 1-100

With the exception of those fitted with top covers in 1910-11, these remained largely unaltered throughout their existence. Their top covers tended to outlast their bodies, and as there was a large surplus of stock, when a top-covered car was damaged in an accident or otherwise became unserviceable, its cover was removed and transferred to an open-top car in store and in better condition.

An early modification to these cars was the fitting of pairs of rectangular hardwood, or possibly cast-iron blocks between the underframe and truck bolsters. The reason for this addition is not recorded but was probably to improve the cars' riding qualities. It did not, however, improve their appearance, imparting a somewhat "home-made" effect.

During the Great War War several of the cars were stored at Acton Depot, and some were operated from there over the MET system to serve the munitions factories at Park Royal, North Acton and the aircraft works at Edgware Road, Hendon. They were accompanied by three MET cars, Nos. 1, 20 and 36 which were stationed at the depot to assist with the early morning and evening traffic to and from these works.

Wartime wear and tear left the already neglected fleet in a poor state. Armature failures, especially in the GE58 motors fitted into these were a recurring problem. By 1922 the English Electric Company was able to offer motors of improved light-weight designs, and the LUT, in a slightly better financial position

Car No.32 of Type Y, on its way to Hanwell from Brentford passes over the fossilised junction of Lower Boston Road with Upper Boston Road. The indicator has already been changed for the return journey. (Hugh Nicol. Courtesy D.W.K.Jones)

as a result of provisions in their 1918 Act, could consider replacement of some outworn equipment.

Reductions in the fleet from the end of the war saw the scrapping of many in this group. Meanwhile, those remaining, some fitted with top covers from cars scrapped earlier, continued in service, mainly on the local Acton-Shepherds Bush service and the Surrey lines. A minor improvement to the remaining 51 Type Y cars took place in 1927, when the centre two top-deck windows on each side were glazed and arranged to open independently, at the cost of £25 per car. However, one, No. 30, had all upper-deck windows glazed shortly after top-covers were fitted in 1910-11.

In their later years, by then all top-covered, the surviving cars in the group worked mainly on route 71 (Wimbledon and Hampton Court). Road traffic increased heavily in the late 1920s, and in February 1929 20 cars working the Surrey lines were experimentally fitted with red "caution" lights on the rear nearside dashes. These were worked by motormen through a pedal switch and were intended to warn other road users of a tram driver's intentions. However, it was found that as motormen used their brakes at least as much to slow down as to stop, the lights caused confusion to other drivers. The trial was not extended to other routes, but such lights were ultimately fitted to experimental cars built later in 1929 and to new cars built in 1930.

A close-up view of the "Caution" light on the near-side rear dash of Type Y No.24. The light was pedal-operated by the motorman.   (Courtesy London Transport Museum U6140)

LUT Car No. 11: Speed Trials

A series of speed and acceleration trials took place in conjunction with the MET on 7-8, 10-11 and 22-23 December 1929 and 11-12 January 1930, in which four cars took part. These were carried out in Twickenham Road, Isleworth between Busch Corner and Twickenham, a distance of 1½ miles. At this time the MET was investing in new motors and other items for their fleet and had also added a number of new, experimental cars to their stock, which were fitted with various types of electrical equipments. The MET provided a standard top-covered car and two experimental "Feltham" cars, Nos. 320 and 330. No. 320 was fitted with four-motor equipment, but No. 330, built for four motors, had been modified at short notice for two-motor operation.

The LUT car used, No. 11, had been withdrawn in 1923 and written off, but was retained as a snowplough. For the purpose of the tests it was equipped with four motors which had been achieved by modifying and using two pairs of Peckham 14D2 maximum traction trucks from scrapped cars of the 1-100 group. These were cut in half, the trailing ends discarded and the four pairs of driving ends welded together, creating two equal-wheel bogies, in each of which were placed two BTH 509KL 50hp. high-speed motors with roller-bearing armatures. The car's underframe was modified and heavily strengthened.

Tables showing results of these trials indicate that LUT No. 11 achieved the best acceleration at lower speeds, reaching 10 mile/h in 3.2 seconds, 15 mile/h in 5.6 seconds, 20 mile/h in 9.7 seconds and 25 mile/h in 21.5 seconds. Only one car reached 30 mile/h (MET No. 330) but No. 11 gave better figures than all the others up to 20 mile/h. Following these tests No. 11 was stored at Fulwell Depot, where it was scrapped in 1931. It is evident that the results of these tests confirmed the tramway engineers' belief that the latest two-motor equipments would satisfy their requirements for new cars, and further work on four-motor equipment was abandoned.

At the same time as these trials took place No. 94 was fitted with a pair of high-speed light-weight motors of an unknown manufacture which were tested on the Surrey lines. Nothing further is known of these tests but No. 94 reverted to its original equipment by the end of 1930.

Disposals

Sometime prior to 1922 cars Nos. 7 and 17 were scrapped at Hillingdon Depot, No. 17 after a collision at Hammersmith shortly after the war. With the transfer of out of service cars to Fulwell, Type Y cars, Nos. 26, 51, 64, 86, 96, 97 and 100, together with cars Nos. 8, 21, 40, 42 and 50 of Type Z were disposed of from there in 1923. The top covers from those of Type Y were salvaged and fitted to other open-top vehicles.

At this time too, there was a market for tramcar bodies and many were sold from Fulwell Depot for use as garden sheds, while a few were sold for use as living accommodation at a time when few restrictions were placed upon such use.

Another 27 cars were scrapped at Fulwell in 1929, this time employing the services of a contractor for the purpose, Thos.H.Proctor of Wimbledon, who had tendered in the sum of £250. In this case, electrical equipments, wheels, axles and bearings from 16 of the cars would be retained by the LUT. Included in the sale were Nos. 4, 19, 41, 50, 62, 66, 72, 84 and 88 of Type Y and Nos. 3, 5, 6, 16, 20, 23, 33, 34, 45, 52, 53, 54, 57, 60, 63, 73, 77 and 81 of Type Z. However, Nos. 34, 62 and 63 were withdrawn from the sale and retained until 1931.

In 1931, with the impending introduction of trolleybuses, space was required to house these, resulting in the disposal, this time under contract to Messrs. George Cohen, Sons & Co. Ltd. of more cars of Types Y and Z. Included were Nos. 3, 9, 10, 11, 13-15, 18, 23, 29-31, 36, 38, 39, 43, 46, 47, 49, 56, 65, 68, 70,

71, 85, 87, 91, 92, 94 and 98, all of Type Y. To these were later added Nos. 25, 35, 62 (Type Y), and 34 and 63 (Type Z).

Later, by an agreement dated 4 May, Nos. 1, 12, 24, 25, 27, 28, 32, 59, 69, 74, 78, 79 and 92 (Type Y) were added to the contract, while a further eight of the same type, Nos. 37, 48, 61, 67, 75, 76, 93 and 99 followed as from 19 August. Lastly, six open-top Type Z cars, Nos. 44, 55, 58, 60, 83 and 89 were scrapped by Cohen under an agreement dated 9 November.

Prices paid by the contractor varied between £4 and £6.10s. per car but, as before, this mostly excluded electrical equipments and non-ferrous metal, which were retained by the LUT.

Nos. 101-150

Most of these cars were out of service between 1910 and 1912, being stored at Hillingdon and Fulwell depots at first, and later all at Fulwell when Hillingdon Depot was closed and leased away. A few, which had been repainted and fitted with new semi-circular dashes in 1909, replacing the original "concave-convex" type, were retained in operational condition for use at holiday periods, but ultimately, as recorded elsewhere in this volume, 40 of them became part of the 1912 arbitration award on the sale of the Hammersmith lines to the LCC.

Two of these, Nos. 141 and 142 had an interesting history. At times of heavy rainfall the Beverley Brook, at Shannon Corner, New Malden, overflowed its banks and the track in Burlington Road became flooded for a distance of about 500 yards. This affected the tramway service, cars being compelled to stop either side of the flood and passengers to make their way on foot to join cars on the other side. The company had gained powers in their 1914 Act to operate trailers and coupled cars, subject to approval by the Board of Trade, the Metropolitan Police and local authorities, and asked the Board to approve the use of a trailer set to work a passenger-carrying shuttle service over the flooded section.

On 19 February 1917, A.H.Pott, the LUT engineer and general manager wrote to the Board of Trade enclosing a drawing of proposed modifications to a car. This included raising the motors and associated wiring on frames fixed to the trucks, incorporating an additional gear between the motor pinion and the axle spur gear, the whole protruding through the car floor. This car would therefore carry no passengers but alternately tow and push a passenger-carrying car, from which the motors were removed, over a single line through the floods.

Pott explained that there would be no continuous brakes or guards between the cars, but he was prepared to run the set under any conditions laid down by the Board of Trade, and suggested a speed limit of 6 mile/h. Passengers would not be carried except through the flooded section. It was not possible to tow the trailer both ways through the affected area, so the motor car would tow in one direction and push in the other. The towing car would, however, tow the trailer both ways to and from the depot. Pott had previously submitted the scheme to the Metropolitan Police Commissioner, who had not objected provided it met with the approval of the Board of Trade.

Lt.Col.Pringle of the BoT commented on the scheme on 24 February 1917, saying that he did not like the proposal to push the passenger car through the floods and asked the company to reconsider the matter. Pott pointed out difficulties involved in the necessary shunting, and finally, the Colonel accepted the company's position and agreed to the original scheme. Wartime conditions delayed fitting up the cars, and it was reported that the set went into use in 1920. Conversion costs amounted to £517, and No. 142 was fitted up as the towing car.

Each car worked with its trolleypole on the wire, that on the passenger car supplying only its lighting, which, on both vehicles was in use at all times when they were operating. Communication between the cars was achieved by a bell rope

Nos.141-2 of Type X at work on the "Flood Service" at New Malden. No.142 was the powered car. (Fox Photos, courtesy London Transport Museum U23095)

extending through both cars. The set was painted in the early red livery, and worked the flood service until 5 December 1929 at the earliest, when a photograph of it appeared in a London evening newspaper. The service would have necessarily ceased to operate by 2 September 1931 when the Wimbledon-Hampton Court tram route was converted to trolleybus operation. Nos. 141-2 were scrapped, with others, at Fulwell Depot later in 1931.

Car No. 148 was written off in 1923, but retained at Hanwell Depot for use as the staff car, where it remained, kept in good repair, until the end of tramway operation from that depot. When vacuum cleaning plant was installed at the depot in 1930, No. 148 was pressed into service as a "stage" for staff using the vacuum hoses to gain access from its top deck into the upper saloons of cars standing alongside. This is more fully described in the chapter dealing with Works Cars.

A longer-lived example was No. 117, the solitary member of the batch fitted with Brill 22E bogies in 1905, seeing little service from then and nominally scrapped in 1923. However, it was retained and underwent an extensive overhaul at Chiswick in 1927, being fitted with a new top-cover of the 1910-11 pattern but to an improved specification. Two Metropolitan-Vickers MV 104 motors, each of 50hp. replaced the original equipment, but the Westinghouse 90M controllers

The saloon of No.142 was stripped of seats and the motors placed on special cradles at a higher level to avoid flood water penetration.

A close-up view of a motor in No.142 mounted on its cradle bolted to the truck, with additional spur gear interposed between the motor pinion and axle, upon which a second pinion was mounted to maintain the correct gear ratio.

were retained and overhauled with the rest of the car. The body and trucks were reconditioned to high standards. New bearers were fitted and the 5ft. 9in. platforms were extended to 6ft. and new semi-circular dashes fitted. A number of minor features remained which readily distinguished the Type X body from those of Types W and Z. Capital expenditure on this work amounted to £691.

The composite vehicle, which was classified Type XU, took the number 247 from a Type W car which had suffered an unknown fate. In 1928 it was temporarily fitted with GEC WT28KL motors and BTH lineswitch gear, which were later removed and replaced with MV 104 motors and normal Westinghouse 90M controllers. No. 247 was one of the longest surviving LUT cars, spending its last months of service on the western system of the former MET, working from Stonebridge Park Depot until it was withdrawn on 27 August 1936, and scrapped at the MET Hendon Car Works.

Car No. 107 was sold to the MET in 1921 for £425 and parts of it were utilised in the construction of that company's second track-breaking car, which was built at Hendon Works. It worked on the pile-driving hammer principle, the hammer driven by a compressor worked from the overhead wire power supply, taking current via one of two trolleypoles. Now numbered as MET 03, it was put to extensive use over the three companies' systems during the 1920s' reconstruction programme.

Six cars, Nos. 108, 118, 125, 137, 149 and 150 were sold to Blackpool Corporation in 1919, less motors and controllers, for £425 each. They were extensively modified by their new owners, remaining in service in Blackpool for many years. No. 138, the drivers' instruction car, was scrapped in 1923, and all those remaining, except Nos. 117 (247), 141, 142 and 148 were broken up at Fulwell Depot in 1924 and the bodies sold. Many ended as bungalows or caravans at a Surrey beauty spot, where their stay is understood to have been curtailed owing to complaints from local residents.

Disposals

Following completion of the sale of the Hammersmith lines to the LCC in 1922, the 40 cars of this batch which had passed to the LCC remained in storage at Fulwell Depot. Eventually, all were re-purchased by the LUT, to be used as a source of spare parts for other cars in the fleet and, after removing useful components, the company broke 38 of them up in 1924. These were Nos. 101-106, 109-116, 119-124, 126-136 and 139-147.

Nos. 151-300

This was the largest group in the LUT fleet, but many cars were taken out of service during and shortly after the Great War. Of 35 fitted with top-covers in 1910-11, three cars Nos. 280, 289 and 298 were damaged in accidents, No. 280 at a date subsequent to 5 January 1915. Their top covers were salvaged and fitted to Nos. 151, 212 and 262, not necessarily in that order, and the bodies were scrapped in 1923. There was always a large number of cars surplus to daily requirements except at holiday times, consequently many were stored out of service, mainly at Fulwell Depot and, up to c.1921, some at Hillingdon Depot. With such a large surplus of stock, cars damaged in accidents or requiring major overhauls were replaced from those in store. Many were also robbed of parts to keep others in service. In 1923, 43 of them, Nos. 153, 156, 159, 160, 162, 170, 172, 176, 179, 184, 186, 188, 190, 193, 195, 197, 201, 202, 207, 208, 209, 213, 214, 215, 217, 218, 219, 220, 222, 225, 231, 234, 241, 245, 248, 249, 257, 260, 263, 264, 280, 289 and 298, were scrapped at Fulwell Depot, the bodies of some being sold in the locality for use as sheds, with many others going further afield.

Some of the surplus cars were disposed of to other undertakings during the Great War. Two were hired to Erith UDC on 13 October 1915 at an annual rental of £68, followed by two more on 8 December on the same terms. These were Nos.

187, 192, 221 and 252 and they ran in Erith unaltered until their sale was agreed on 20 June 1919 at £570 each. After the sale the UDC partially reconstructed them with full-length canopies and spiral staircases.

Walthamstow UDC hired Nos. 226-30 and 232 for three months from June 1919, with a view to subsequent purchase. Negotiations on a sale price were initially unsuccessful and the cars were retained on hire until April 1920, when agreement was reached and the UDC bought them for £2,910. They ran in Walthamstow unaltered for the remainder of their working lives.

In 1923 the company received £235,000 from the LCC for their Hammersmith lines which sum they were obliged to spend on rehabilitation of the undertaking. Accordingly, on 6 June 1923, after trials, previously mentioned, the directors resolved to spend £40,000 on new motors and magnetic track brakes. On 29 June, they approved a capital requisition covering the purchase of 80 sets of type MV

Type W car No.233 at Fulwell Depot with its destinations' display board on the staircase masked with a sheet of black waterproof material. The last few of these cars were mainly confined to Kingston local services. (Photographer unknown)

104 50hp. high-speed light-weight motors and 120 car sets of magnetic track brakes "plus sundry alterations" to the cars. The contract with the Metropolitan Vickers Electrical Co. Ltd. was sealed on the same day.

The new motors and magnetic track brakes were installed in Nos. 163-168, 173, 174, 180, 182, 183, 185, 189, 191, 194, 196, 200, 203, 204, 206, 210, 212, 216, 223, 237-240, 244, 254 and 259 (Type W) and 151, 154, 158, 204, 205, 210, 212, 224, 235, 236, 250, 251, 255, 262, 265, 267-274, 276-279, 281-288, 290-297 and 299-300 (Type U). In addition, No. 247, the solitary Type XU car, received the new motors, but later ran for a time with GEC WT28KL motors, BTH controllers and lineswitch gear, probably on trial. At the same time the cars were being refurbished internally with improved lighting and seating. The stores van No. 005 also received MV 104 motors, and a nominal four sets were allocated to spares stock. Forty sets of the magnetic track brakes were fitted to cars 301-340, which were at the same time fitted with field shunting equipment to improve the performance of their later equipment.

Nos. 152, 171 and 256 (Type U) and 169, 177, 181, 198, 233, 242, 246, 253 and 258 (Type W) were not included in this scheme and carried their original equipment for the remainder of their existence. They may have been fitted with field-shunting apparatus to improve their performance.

New control equipment was not included in the MV contract, and the existing Westinghouse type 90 controllers in Nos. 151-300 did not provide for magnetic track braking. However, Nos. 101-150 had Westinghouse type 90M controllers as original equipment, designed for use with magnetic track brakes. To keep costs down, 40 pairs of these were salvaged when all but three of the remaining cars of this batch were scrapped in 1924, and reconditioned for use with the new motors, together with those retained from the six Type X cars sold to Blackpool Corporation in 1919. The LCC re-equipped a number of their cars at this time and the company bought from them some of the redundant Westinghouse type 90M controllers for £10 each. These were reconditioned for use in the re-motored Type U and W cars to replace the Westinghouse type 90 controllers currently in use.

Between 1923 and 1929 forty-one cars of the 1-100 batch were broken up and some of their top-covers salvaged. Sixteen of these were fitted to Nos. 152, 154, 156, 158, 171, 204, 205, 210, 224, 235, 236, 250, 251, 255, 256 and 261, bringing the total of top-covered cars in the 151-300 batch to 51, not including No. 247, mentioned earlier. All of these, with the exception of Nos. 171 and 256, were fitted with MV104 motors, reconditioned Westinghouse type 90M controllers and magnetic track brakes, the work being carried out at the Chiswick shops where, under the terms of the 1922 agreement with the London County Council the company was granted use of the overhead travelling crane.

As this work proceeded, the interiors of the cars received attention; layers of dark varnish were stripped from doors, panels and ceilings and replaced by light oak, French grey and white enamel finishes. Lighting was improved and reflective fittings enhanced the new, pleasant atmosphere. At the same time the rattan-covered longitudinal bench seats in the re-motored Type W and U cars were spring-upholstered in Johnstons' blue-grey lozenge pattern "Moquettino" fabric.

Journey times were cut once the scheme neared completion. In 1922 the Shepherds Bush-Hounslow service was timed at 51 minutes. In 1924 it had been reduced to 42 minutes for the journey of just over 7¼ miles, and by 1926 was down to 40 minutes. The Acton-Hammersmith service, taking 22 minutes in 1922-24 using cars of the 1-100 batch, was reduced to 18 minutes in 1926, using re-motored cars from Nos. 151-300.

In 1924-5 a few cars, one of which was No. 223, were fitted with large front-facing boards on the outside of the staircases, displaying a route, e.g., Hammersmith-Hampton Court and five intermediate points vertically. The

This upper-saloon view of Type U car No.205, later No.2362 in the LPTB fleet, shows the retained trolley-mast protruding through the roof together with the arrangements made to collect rainwater and discharge it from the side of the car.

(S.G.Jackman. Courtesy the Science Museum)

signwritten lettering was illuminated at night. In the event of a car being transferred to another route the board was covered by a sheet of black rubberised material. The wrought-iron grilles surrounding the upper decks of a few cars had deteriorated by this time and were replaced by sheet metal panels. The upper deck seating of Type U car No. 300 was reduced from 39 to 36 at an unrecorded date prior to takeover by the LPTB.

The nine unremotored open-top Type W cars, Nos. 169, 177, 181, 198, 233, 242, 246, 253 and 258 remained on the stock list at 31 December 1930. There is no record of the disposal of three of these, Nos. 233, 253 and 258, but not recorded as scrapped or passing to the London Passenger Transport Board. No. 258 was photographed standing derelict at Fulwell Depot in 1931. They might have been damaged in accidents and scrapped by the company before agreements were entered into with Geo. Cohen, Sons & Co. Ltd. in February 1931 for large scale disposals after the arrival of new trams and trolleybuses.

In the autumn of 1931 a loan agreement was concluded with the South Metropolitan Electric Tramways and cars Nos. 267, 268, 269, 271, 272, 276, 278, 286, 290, 293, 297 and 299 went to work on the Sutton and Mitcham lines of that undertaking. Nos. 267, 268, 271, 272, 286 and 297 were subsequently returned to the LUT. Following this, Nos. 267, 268, 271, 272, 285, 286, 287, 291, 292, 294, 295, 296 and 297 were transferred to the Metropolitan Electric Tramways' depot at Stonebridge Park.

A few of the 151-300 batch were adapted for other purposes, commencing with No. 175, converted for private hire use in 1911 and described in Volume 1. By 1913 No. 275, the solitary example fitted with Milnes maximum traction trucks was cut down to single-deck and designated in company records as "the pay car". It later returned to the passenger fleet in the guise of one-man car No. 344, accompanied by Nos. 175 and 178 which became one-man cars Nos. 342 and 343. Another 1913 conversion, its passenger fleet number unrecorded became works fleet No. 005, at first described as a "flat car" and later as an "open stores van". It outlived the LUT system, being transferred to North London after the last ex-LUT tramway routes closed.

Nos. 157, 161, 211, 243 and 261 (Type WT)

A total of 53 cars of the 151-300 group was scrapped, sold and converted for other purposes up to 1923 and the 74 cars re-motored from 1923 left 12 cars in original, or near-original condition. The success of increased speeds and improved passenger comfort led the company to embark upon a more ambitious scheme for some of these cars, commencing in early 1928. Nos. 157, 161, 211, 243 and 261 were chosen to receive this treatment.

Of these, No. 261 had earlier been fitted with a top-cover from another car. It was also the first to be taken in hand, probably as the prototype for the others, and underwent a partial reconstruction, which involved fitting new bearers and increasing the length of the platforms from 5ft.9in. to 6ft., extending the short canopies to full length and the roof covers to match. The trolley mast was removed and the roof strengthened to accommodate a trolley plank and dwarf trolleybase, while the top-deck seating was increased from 39 to 44, by the addition of one seat in the space made available by the removal of the trolley mast, and two on each open balcony, the ends of which were surrounded by half-height sheet metal screens. The lower deck seating remained at 30, on longitudinal benches which were refitted with sprung cushions upholstered in blue-grey "Moquettino" fabric.

New roller-blind destination and route number indicators were fitted above the open-balcony ends, with an additional route number roller blind box on the front nearside, below the staircase landings. Apart from lengthening the platforms, no structural alterations were made to the lower deck, the clerestory ceilings being

379

retained, and lighting and interior decoration improved to standards established earlier. The overall effect was to bring the car to a similar condition externally to the 301-340 batch of 1905-6.

Electrical equipment was replaced, the original Westinghouse 25hp. motors giving way to 50hp. high speed light-weight motors supplied by the General Electric Company. These were to the latest design, with ball and roller bearing armatures and were designated WT28KL. They were ordered on 9 February 1928, part of a batch of 52 sets which, with associated equipment was obtained at the cost of £26,500. Forty sets of these were installed in Type T cars as is described later. The Westinghouse controllers were replaced by BTH B49 units, with lineswitch gear developed jointly by BTH and the MET, being fitted to meet the heavier current demands of the new motors.

No. 261 proved to be satisfactory and Nos. 157, 161, 211 and 243 received almost identical treatment, except that, as they did not already have top-covers, entirely new covers were built, it having been found more practical and economical to do this. The work was carried out at the Chiswick shops at the cost of £4,046.

At first the cars wore an experimental livery which was also being tried on the MET. As applied to LUT cars, both rocker and side panels were red, lined out in white, and all above the lower deck windows was mainly white, relieved with narrow red bands above and below the windows. Dashes were red, with two large white triangular patches, the apex of the triangles reaching either side of the central headlamps. A small red triangle appeared on the white ground on the nearside. The statutory lettering on the rocker panels was also in white. This livery which varied slightly on the few cars which received it, was short-lived, and all reverted to the standard red and white scheme by 1931.

Nos. 155, 199 and 288 (Type U2)

These cars were refurbished at the Chiswick shops at about the same time as the five Type WT vehicles. Of the three, No. 288 underwent the most radical transformation. The body was reposted, retaining the six-windows a side configuration, the clerestory roof was removed and replaced with a plain flat ceiling, while the arched side windows gave way to those with flat-tops which were surmounted by opening quarter-lights. Longitudinal seating in the lower saloon was replaced by two-and-one upholstered transverse seats for 15 passengers, with three-seat benches in each corner, totalling 27 in all. This new arrangement, and the fitting of air bells brought the lower saloon to the standard of the forty Type T cars re-seated from 1925, described later. The two-flight staircases were altered to give a right-angle turn, allowing the upper saloon doors to be moved to one side, thus eliminating the gap at the bottom of the doors and preventing draughts, which had always been a source of discomfort on the upper decks of the early top-covered cars.

Seating in the upper saloon was reduced to 38, presumably by eliminating the single seat next to the trolley-mast, otherwise the top decks remained little changed. Except for reposting, reseating the lower deck and the fitting of air bells, Nos. 155 and 199 received the same treatment as No. 288. All three cars' staircases were fitted with metal shields on the outside, while each received the same type of GEC motors, BTH controllers and lineswitch equipment as the five Type WT cars. The work was carried out at the cost of £2,458.

Disposals

With the arrival of trolleybuses in the Kingston area in 1931 the ten remaining unremotored Type U and W cars were sold under the terms of an agreement of 19 August 1931 to George Cohen for scrap. They were Nos. 152, 171 and 256 (Type U) and Nos. 169, 177, 181, 198, 233, 242 and 246 (Type W) together with remotored open-top car No. 238.

Seen c.1930 and although sold for scrap in September 1931, No.185 (Type W) was exchanged for another car in November and continued in service with the LUT and LPTB until October 1935. It was one of a number latterly fitted with BTH line switch equipment.

(Courtesy Bryan Woodriff)

A further agreement dated 28 September 1931 covered the sale of 26 Type W cars Nos. 163, 164, 165, 166, 168, 173, 174, 180, 182, 183, 185, 189, 191, 194, 196, 200, 203, 206, 216, 223, 237, 240, 244, 254 and 259. After the trolleybus conversions were completed it was found that insufficient cars had been retained to work the remaining tramway routes and Nos. 165, 173, 182, 183, 185, 200, 240, 254 and 259 were withdrawn from the sale on 9 November and exchanged for the remaining Type Z cars Nos. 44, 55, 58, 80, 83 and 89, the two flood service cars Nos. 141 and 142, and the rail grinder No. 002. These were sold for £4 each and scrapped by Cohen's staff at Fulwell Depot, although many of the bodies, as earlier, were disposed of for use as summerhouses or garden sheds. One of those which survived (number unknown at the time of writing) was eventually located and secured for the National Tramway Museum, where it is now awaiting restoration.

After delivery of the trolleybuses was completed, eight of the nine retained trams were put to work on the Shepherds Bush and Hammersmith to Hounslow and Hampton Court services, and had earlier been fitted with BTH line-switch equipment as evidenced by their controller handles. They were then joined by No. 255 in replacement of No. 183, which was taken out of service for an unknown reason after 1 July 1933, following the formation of the LPTB. Shortly afterwards, with the renumbering system adopted by the Board, cars 165, 173, 182, 185, 200, 240, 244, 254 and 259 were given LPTB numbers 2522-9 respectively, while No. 255 became 2370. No. 183, not renumbered, was scrapped at Fulwell Depot in May 1934. All nine cars were disposed of by Cohen at Hampstead Depot in October 1935.

Nos. 301-340

The forty cars of this batch remained intact as a class throughout their existence. When type letters were introduced in 1914 they became Types T/1 and T/2 to distinguish between two classes of electrical equipment. They underwent few alterations until the mid-1920s. An exception was No. 340, which was taken out of service in 1914 to be fitted with air-brakes. This work commenced after

Some Type U cars were loaned to the associated South Metropolitan Electric Tramways and Lighting Company from 1931. No.276 stands at West Croydon terminus on the service to Mitcham Fair Green. (Photo J.Higham courtesy G.E.Baddeley)

Still with its original motors, Type W car No.258 is shown at work on the Richmond Park Gates-Tolworth service on a very wet day, sometime in 1929.

(Hugh Nicol. Courtesy National Tramway Museum)

No.258, still at work on the Richmond Park Gates-Tolworth service, but this time photographed in better weather.　　　(Hugh Nicol. Courtesy National Tramway Museum)

Types U and W cars were overhauled internally: dark varnish was replaced by light-oak finish and white-enamelled ceilings. Lighting was increased with opal lamps enclosed in translucent shades.

(Courtesy London Transport Museum U3580)

Seen in 1925, No.307 has been fitted with moquette-upholstered two-and-one transverse seating, rubber-covered floor, new lighting and generally refurbished interior decorations.

(Courtesy London Transport Museum U3581)

Various forms of lighting were tried in the mid-1920s: No.301 received shielded fittings emitting softly-diffused light along the lower saloon. Rattan benches were at first upholstered in moquette until all Type T cars received transverse lower-deck seating.

(Courtesy London Transport Museum U3582)

The existing wooden seats on the top-deck of No.307 were padded with moquette covering and the car remained the only example so fitted.

(Courtesy London Transport Museum U3584)

Type Y car No.9 in mid-1920s condition. Original luxurious upholstery had long-since been replaced by plain wood-slatted seating, while the interior wood panelling was covered in many layers of dark varnish. (Courtesy Tramway Museum Society)

A.H.Pott, the general manager and engineer, found that the cars in use on the Brentford-Hanwell shuttle service through Boston Road were not equipped with track brakes, a Board of Trade requirement for that route. He wrote to the Board in May 1914, saying that he wished to rectify the matter. The brakes had been fitted to the cars when built, but removed before he assumed management of the company in 1913.

Pott sought advice from manufacturers, while Lt.Col.J.W.Pringle, the BoT inspecting officer on 3 May suggested that the recently developed Spencer-Dawson oil-track brake be tried in London conditions. Pott considered that use of the oil-brake on a bogie car would be of an experimental nature, and recommended an air-wheel brake, to which Col.Pringle agreed, subject to seeing it in operation. Later, the Board of Trade agreed to trials with an air-wheel brake, and the equipment was ordered.

On 10 July 1915, W.F.Marwood of the BoT asked Pott what progress had been made with fitting up the car. Pott, replying on 13 July, said that the necessary equipment was to hand but wartime conditions had created a shortage of steel tubing. Continuing shortages caused the scheme to be shelved until 1920, the car meanwhile lying unused.

Car No. 340 is next mentioned in a 1921 report by Major G.L.Hall, to the Ministry of Transport (which had assumed the responsibilities of the BoT for tramways in 1919) in which he said "car No. 340, fitted with air-wheel brakes, is proving satisfactory but the use of an air-track brake would be a greater improvement". The car was again seen in 1922 in Chiswick, with new dashes, straightened balconies, freshly painted, and with Westinghouse air-wheel brakes. The air brake trials continued until 30 June 1924 at the earliest, but later this equipment was removed, the car receiving magnetic track brakes in common with the rest of the batch.

In 1921, C.J.Spencer, now the manager, in co-operation with L.B.Hewitt, a senior member of the LST companies' engineering staff evolved and patented a device known as "field-shunting apparatus". Used in conjunction with existing motors and controllers, it enabled a car to obtain a higher running speed on level track than that afforded by "full parallel". Field-weakening contactors were used which closed automatically by the release of a relay when motor current had decreased to a pre-determined value, introducing shunt resistances across the motor fields. Increased motor currents, due, for example, to a rising gradient or headwind would operate to release the weak-field contactors, restoring straight full-parallel conditions. The automatic response to road conditions would continue as long as the controller remained in the "full parallel" position. A conveniently-placed switch enabled the motorman to cancel the weak-field feature should he, for example, be running ahead of time. Seventy-six MET cars had already been fitted with this equipment.

To combat increasing onmibus competition on the Uxbridge Road route improved journey times were essential. On 23 February 1923, after receiving advice from C.J.Spencer, the LUT directors approved expenditure of £680 to fit the 40 Type T cars with the field-shunting apparatus, together with magnetic track brakes. This had an immediate effect upon the Uxbridge road services. In winter 1922-3 the journey time for the 12.65 mile Shepherds Bush-Uxbridge service was 81 minutes. By winter 1923-4 this was reduced to 79 minutes, and in summer 1924 the service was running at 68 minutes, the cars working in company with those of the 151-300 batch, which had been fitted with new MV104 motors in the summer of 1923.

In June 1923 Nos. 301, 303 and 305 were fitted with English Electric DK84C, BTH GE67 and Metropolitan Vickers MV 104 motors respectively and underwent extensive speed and acceleration trials on the MET system, between Willesden Green and Canons Park and along Finchley Road between Child's Hill and Church End, Finchley. No. 333 also took part in the trials carrying its original

Type T car No.332 at the Hounslow terminus at "The Bell", being made ready for the return journey to Shepherds Bush.   (Courtesy National Tramway Museum)

Westinghouse type 80 motors with field-shunting apparatus, presumably for comparison purposes. At the time, most of the LUT track was unsuitable for speed trials, but the Edgware Road track to Canons Park had been reconstructed in 1921 and the lengthy Finchley Road stretch had only opened in 1909-10 and was maintained in excellent condition. These trials resulted in the purchase of the eighty sets of MV104 50hp. high-speed motors described earlier in this chapter.

Speeding up services proved popular with the public and the LST companies next turned their attention to passenger comfort. On the LUT in 1925, car No. 307 was fitted with new seating, improved lighting and interior decorations and, for the first time in London, improved seating in the upper saloon. The longitudinal benches seating 30 downstairs were replaced with two-and-one reversible transverse seats for 15, spring-upholstered in "Moquettino" fabric, with four similarly upholstered benches for 12 at the saloon entrances, a total of 27. The company considered the reduction of three seats would be more than compensated for by increased passenger loadings throughout the day.

In the upper saloon, the wooden garden-type seats for 36 were upholstered and covered in the same material. The four wooden seats on each of the balconies were reduced to two, resulting in the total for the car being reduced from 74 to 67. The lower saloon floor was covered with quarter-inch thick rubber sheeting, but traditional wooden slats were retained on the top deck floor. Lighting on both decks was also improved, with additional lamps and white reflectors, while dark-stained and varnished ceilings and woodwork were transformed, with light oak interior panelling, and white-enamelled ceilings.

Apart from repainting and minor bodywork alterations, the car exterior was largely unchanged except for improved destination indicators. The boxes suspended from the roof above the top of the stairs, carrying wooden single-line boards fitted in 1913 were replaced by new single-line roller-blind boxes placed on the balcony panels immediately above the motorman's head. These were surmounted by smaller roller-blind indicators displaying the route number. Similar number boxes were fitted at the front near-sides of the car, suspended below the staircase landings. Air bells replaced pull-cords in the lower saloons which earlier had replaced the original electric bells.

Another car, No. 301, was taken in hand later, but on a slightly less ambitious scale. Longitudinal seating was retained at first but spring upholstered in "Moquettino" fabric. The interior finish was carried out in white and French grey. Air bells were fitted, but the floor remained as before, with wooden slats. A feature of this car was the lower saloon lighting, which consisted of rectangular translucent fittings of two sizes, half of which contained a single lamp and half with two, providing an even distribution of illumination along the saloon. The top deck was unchanged except for re-decoration and improved lighting. The steel mesh guards round the balconies were replaced by slightly higher sheet metal panels. Later, the lower saloon longitudinal seating was replaced to conform with the rest of the batch.

The results of these and similar trials on the MET set a standard for refurbishment of the LST fleets. On 1 April 1926 the LUT board voted to spend £8,000 to treat all the Type T cars in a similar fashion to No. 307. The new seating had met with favourable comment from the public and transverse seats were fitted in all the cars, but No. 307 was the only example with upholstered top-deck seats. Rubber floor covering was found to wear at the saloon entrances, and later there was a reversion to the traditional slatted floors.

The elaborate lower saloon lighting in No. 301 gave way to opal lamps in white reflectors, and interior decorations on both decks were in light oak with white ceilings. The seating capacity was fixed at 71, with 27 in the lower saloon and 44 on the top deck, but the top deck seats in No. 307 remained at 36 in the

Increased speeds led the company to improve passenger comfort. In 1925, Type T No.307 received improved lighting, upholstered transverse lower saloon seating, and the first cushioned top-deck seats in a London tramcar.

(Courtesy London Transport Museum U3578)

saloon and two on each balcony. The destination indicators were placed at a higher level, set in the steel mesh balcony surrounds. Prior to this work being carried out the forty cars had been fitted with magnetic track brakes. On 1 December 1927 the LUT directors authorised £1,782 overspent on the scheme.

On 9 February 1928 Spencer reported to his directors on results obtained from the cars fitted with Metropolitan-Vickers MV104 lightweight high-speed motors in 1923-24. He spoke of improved traffic on the Uxbridge Road route and recommended the purchase of further new equipment, to which the directors agreed, and £30,000 capital expenditure was approved. This time it was decided to replace the original Westinghouse motors in Nos. 301-340 with new ones to the latest lightweight high-speed design.

Fifty-two sets of GEC WT28KL 50hp. high speed lightweight motors with roller-bearing armatures were ordered from the General Electric Company of Witton, Birmingham, 40 sets of which were fitted to Nos. 301-340, replacing the original Westinghouse machines of 1905-6. To enable the existing Westinghouse type 90M controllers to handle the heavy current demands of these motors, BTH

389

line-switch equipment was installed. Five sets of the motors were fitted in the Type WT and three in the Type U2 cars, with another set installed in Type U car No. 255, allowing three spare sets. However, those installed in No. 255 had, by 1 July 1933, been removed and MV104 equipment re-fitted.

Under the 1914 type-letter scheme, Nos. 301-309 and 311, with Westinghouse No. 200 motors of 30hp. were classified Type T, and the remainder, Nos. 310 and 312-40 with Westinghouse No. 80 motors of 40hp. were Type T/2. All became Type T when the GEC WT28KL motors were fitted in 1928.

Ten cars, Nos. 307, 310, 318, 319, 333, 334, 335, 336, 337 and 339 were fitted with drivers' windscreens in 1931, at the cost of £532, and a few cars were painted in the short-lived all-over red livery described earlier in this chapter. Originally bought for the Surrey lines, where they had a short life, the Type T cars spent the greater part of their existence on the Shepherds Bush-Uxbridge route, with a few working on the Hammersmith-Hounslow route, and some workings between Hammersmith and Hampton Court.

All 40 cars passed to the London Passenger Transport Board, surviving until the arrival of trolleybuses in 1936, prior to which a few of them worked from Hanwell Depot on the last section of LUT route in Middlesex to be operated by trams, between Hanwell and Brentford via Boston Road. Later, some were transferred to the former MET system, where they worked from Stonebridge Park Depot.

NEW TYPE CARS
JOURNEY TIMES

SHEPHERDS BUSH TO EALING BROADWAY
20 MINS.

EALING BROADWAY TO SOUTHALL
18 MINS.

RIDE IN COMFORT AND SAVE TIME

Liveries 1913-1933

The original red, white and blue liveries were worn by separate groups of cars which were confined to specific routes. The short-lived all-over white livery of the fifty Type X cars (Nos.101-150) gave way to yellow and white when the extension to Uxbridge opened in the summer of 1904. By October 1909 these cars had undergone yet another change, to the early red and white livery borne by Nos.1-100 and 301-340 from new.

With the 1913 merger of the LUT and the London & Suburban Traction Company, the first signs of future standardisation of colours in the LUT fleet was to be seen, which would ultimately bring the cars of the three companies in the combine into the red and white scheme favoured by the other companies in the UERL group. However, owing to the outbreak of the Great War this was delayed until the early 1920s, and even after that there were still Type W cars at Fulwell depot in their original colours of royal blue and broken white, one surviving until 1933.

Wartime shortages of materials began to make themselves felt; a requirement of the Public Carriage Office was annual repainting of public service vehicles prior to annual relicensing. This was eventually modified to biennial repainting, which in practice amounted to a coat of varnish over the old paint. After a couple of years of this treatment the cars took on a dingy appearance, the blue ones especially, becoming almost black with each successive revarnishing.

Attempts were made to preserve the fleet numerals and decorations on the side and end panels by carefully repainting around them, and as some numbers became almost indecipherable they were replaced with new MET-style transfers, by then in common use by the L&ST companies. This resulted in some cars bearing large ornate LUT numerals at one end and the smaller MET-type numbers at the other. One car, No.27, still carried original LUT-style fleet numbers when it was photographed in 1929.

Red paint was made from a pigment produced in Germany and lack of this resulted in the use of substitutes for such repainting as could be done, coming out as a dirty chocolate colour with light and dark streaks owing to the poor coverage of the paint.

The end of the war brought a breathing space during which for a time the priorities of the company lay in restoring some of the long-standing deficiencies in track and electrical equipment, instead of doing much in the way of restoring paintwork on cars. A decision was eventually taken in 1923 to standardise all cars in the red and broken white colours favoured by the MET, which never embraced the flamboyant schemes employed by the LUT.

As cars entered the Fulwell paint shops they were stripped down and re-primed, receiving the "vermilion and broken-white" colours of the MET. This was a lengthy process, and some blue cars underwent at least one more coat of varnish before receiving their new colours. Lining-out was simplified, consisting of plain black and white lines without corner ornaments, retained until about 1926, when the lining-out became gold and white. The "coat of arms" device on the side panels remained. Fenders and trucks were black, previously red oxide. Wrought iron grilles round the top deck of open-top cars, originally silver-painted, were finished in white.

In 1928 a number of Type T cars and some open-top vehicles appeared in experimental liveries, with dark red waist and rocker panels, dashes and cant rails, and with a red band above the lower saloon windows. Some had bi-colour dashes, red and white, the white part taking the form of two large triangles, the points of which met on either side of the headlamp. The rear offside white portion carried a small red triangle with the words EIGHT WHEEL BRAKES on its three sides. On some cars the white and red triangles were absent and lettering on the side panels

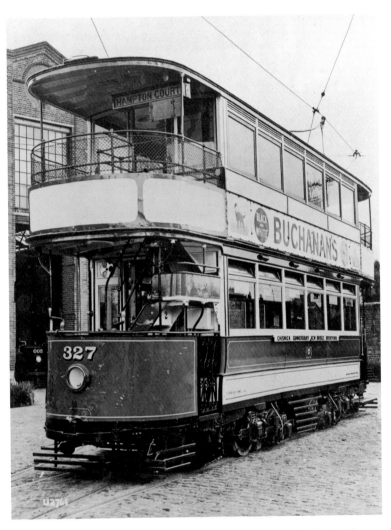

By 1924 No.327 (Type T) had undergone a repaint and displayed the simplified red livery to advantage. Field shunting equipment and magnetic track brakes improved the car's performance on the Uxbridge Road services.

(Courtesy London Transport Museum U2761)

was white, but the central device on the waist panels remained. Conversely, some had no triangles on the dashes, but all were lined out in white.

The "all-red" cars, which at first included the five rebuilt type WT cars of 1928, had all reverted by 1930 to a slightly modified vermilion and white scheme, in which the white triangle bearing the words EIGHT WHEEL BRAKES appeared on the rear nearside dashes and the *faux* coat of arms displayed on the waist panels was replaced by the words LONDON UNITED in "Underground" style gold letters edged in black, which became the final standard for the fleet, except for the remaining type Y and Z cars, most of which had been scrapped by 1930.

Type W2 car No.299 in Glenthorne Road, Hammersmith bound for Acton c.1928. The "all-red" livery is again evident and the small red triangle on the dash indicates "EIGHT WHEEL BRAKES". (Hugh Nicol. Courtesy National Tramway Museum)

With the introduction of the "Feltham" cars, the livery used was, in many ways, similar to that employed on vehicles in other divisions of the Underground Group. Their standard red was applied to the dashes and lower deck side panels, with pale cream on the window surrounds above. The upper deck side panels and window pillars were also of cream, with black lining bands painted to separate each section. Roof colour was initially "silver", but later modified to brown. After the formation of the LPTB, colour arrangements were modified, with the upper saloon side panels being painted L.T. red.

Livery adopted for the trolleybuses was almost identical to that used on the "Feltham" cars, with standard red on the lower part of the body up to the waist rail and light cream above, up to the roof line, each section separated by a series of black bands. The roof colour was also similar to that used on the "Feltham" cars.

CHAPTER TWENTY-TWO

THE ONE-MAN CARS,"POPPY" & THE "FELTHAMS"

Nos. 341-344 (The One-Man Cars)

C.J.Spencer visited North America in 1919 on a study tour, accompanied by other members of the Underground companies' managerial staff. The object of the visit was to observe American methods with a view to their application to the London passenger transport system. He was accompanied by G.J.Shave, maintenance manager of the LGOC, A.R.McCallum, chief assistant (rolling stock) of the UERL and Frank Pick, then commercial manager of the UERL and the LGOC. Transport systems in New York, Philadelphia, Boston, Detroit, Cleveland, Buffalo and a number of other cities were visited. On their return each prepared a paper describing the systems seen, with suggestions for adoption, in London, of some of the American methods, many of which were put into practice, especially in the tramway field.

Spencer's paper drew particular attention to the way in which heavy traffic was quickly dealt with by the use of coupled cars with all axles motored. A lightweight "safety car", seating 35 passengers, running on a four-wheel truck and operated by one man, was proving very economical and was helping tramways to overcome competition by the small "jitney"-type omnibuses, which proliferated in American cities from the end of the war. He also specifically noted American techniques of track construction and maintenance, already highly mechanised there, whereas in the British Isles little, if at all, had changed from the labour-intensive methods used at the beginning of the century.

The value of the single-deck one-man car on lightly trafficked outlying routes, and trailers on other suitable routes was recognised. The use of trailers was always looked upon with disfavour by the Board of Trade and local authorities and, in London, by the Metropolitan Police. Clifton Robinson had favoured the use of trailers from 1899, when he had gained the approval of Heston & Isleworth UDC to use them at busy times, but the police opposed their use and trailer powers were not obtained by the LUT until 1914.

It was originally intended to experiment with one-man working on the Alexandra Palace routes of the Metropolitan Electric Tramways, but an exceptionally steep gradient on one of the two branches precluded this. It was therefore decided to carry out initial trials on the Richmond Park Gates-Tolworth via Kingston route of the LUT. One of the single-deck 36-seat MET cars used on the Palace routes, No. 132, was chosen for conversion to one-man operation. The "six-windows a side" body was reduced to five windows, enabling the short single-deck platforms to be lengthened, reducing the capacity of the car from 36 to 30, but retaining the overall length at 33ft.10in. The bulkheads and their doors were removed and sliding entrance-exit doors placed at the front near-side ends.

The body of the car remained on its Brush 8ft.6in. radial axle truck, which was fitted with Spencer-Dawson hydraulic track brakes, designed by Spencer when he was manager of the Bradford Corporation Tramways. A "dead man" attachment to the oil-brake handle ensured that, in the event of the motorman's hand pressure being removed from the handle, the brake was immediately applied, and power from the controller cut off. The rheostatic brake was retained and hand brakes of the vertical hand-wheel type replaced the normal goose-neck handles. The original roof-mounted headlamps were retained until further alterations were made to the car at a later date.

The motorman was provided with a stool next to a ticket issuing machine, and immediately behind a railing which prevented access from the saloon to the driving position. The sliding doors and folding steps, working in unison, were operated manually by the motorman through a lever interlocked with the control circuit, ensuring that the car could not be moved when the door was open. Fares were collected and tickets issued by the motorman, and a notice at the entrance asked passengers to tender the exact fare for their journey. Another notice read "PLEASE PAY AS YOU ENTER CAR". The fully-vestibuled car, the first such in London, was fitted with a moving indicator intended to inform passengers of their whereabouts on the journey. This was worked through gears from one of the car axles.

Conversion was carried out in 1921 at the MET Car Works at Hendon, and the car was finished in the standard red and white livery and lettering of that company. No. 132 was acquired by the LUT for £703, to which was added £168 for the hydraulic brake equipment, and £300 for alterations to the bodywork. It was renumbered 341 in the LUT fleet.

Major G.L.Hall of the Ministry of Transport saw the car during its conversion at Hendon Works and made no adverse comments. However, Supt. Alfred Bassom of the Metropolitan Police inspected it at Fulwell Depot on 4 May 1922 and reported adversely on the "Road Guide" indicator. At the time the LST companies were considering fitting Road Guides in all their cars.

The object of the guide, marketed as the "Mileometer", was to indicate to passengers their whereabouts on the route, important landmarks such as churches, theatres and road intersections being shown. In addition, at various points advertisements were also displayed on the moving screen, which as the journey progressed, displayed locations at their appropriate positions and the route for half a mile ahead. The apparatus was housed in a rectangular box fixed to the ceiling, close to the quarter lights over the side windows. A photograph appeared in the 7 July 1922 edition of *Advertiser's Weekly.* An earlier, short-lived version of the "Road Guide" consisted of a plain box, mounted at one end of the saloon, containing a vertically-moving screen showing terminal and intermediate points of the route traversed, but with no advertising material.

Bassom objected to the later indicators on the grounds that a passenger quickly rising from a seat might catch his/her head on the indicator frame. Other objections were to "the obstruction of light and ventilation and increase of advertising in and on the car". He reported to the Commissioner that one third only of the display was "route guide", the rest advertisements, an increase in which, he said, was the real objective. He reluctantly conceded that there "might be no objection to the combination of a route guide with advertising, providing objections pointed out could be eliminated".

No. 341 underwent tests on the Richmond Park Gates-Tolworth via Kingston service for a short time, but the Police asked for an extended trial on a quieter route, avoiding the busy Kingston town centre. Numerous minor alterations to the bodywork and fittings of the car were made at Bassom's behest following the earlier trial, and on 14 March 1923 approval was given for the car's operation on the Brentford (Half Acre)-Hanwell shuttle service, a distance of two miles, and to work in conjunction with double-deck two-man operated cars. It was reported that no difficulty was experienced in keeping to schedule when running in company with the standard cars.

Passengers boarding No.341 at the front. There were no rear doors and this format was retained after the car was modified later and fitted with bogies.

(Courtesy London Transport Museum U16113)

Longitudinal seating in No.341 was retained, the bench seats being leather-upholstered with wood-slatted backs. The improved style of lighting was criticised by the Metropolitan Police.

(Courtesy London Transport Museum U3067)

Little time was lost in extending one-man operation, and on 26 January 1923, in advance of approval to operate No. 341 on the Boston Road route, the LUT board sanctioned conversion of four further cars to single-deck one-man working, at a cost of £750 each. The later conversions were to be of a more radical nature than that carried out on No. 341, and were stated to include provision of new trucks and air brakes. As previously, the design work was carried out by the company's engineering department at Manor House offices, under the supervision of L.B.Hewitt, who later succeeded H.J.Troughton as Chief Mechanical Engineer.

Although the LUT directors approved the conversion of a further four cars, three only were taken in hand. They were Nos. 175 (the private hire saloon); 178 (a standard open-top double decker) and 275 (the solitary Type W car fitted with Milnes bogies and later cut down to single-deck for departmental use), becoming Nos. 342-4 in that order.

Passengers boarded and left No. 341 at the front, which resulted in delays. As designed, the new cars were arranged for front entrance and rear exit, doors and steps operating in unison as before. Both doors were held closed when the car was in motion, and were of the two-leaf folding type. A tread-plate, painted red, was placed at each rear exit, acting only when a passenger stood on it, opening the door and lowering the step immediately prior to the car coming to a standstill. The door closed and the step lifted immediately the passenger had left the car, preventing boarding at the rear. The cars were fully vestibuled, windscreen wipers were fitted, and as previously, the motorman was seated next to a "Shanklin" ticket-issuing machine, with the addition of an American-made Brandt "Universo" coin-paying machine for giving change, both pedal operated. Passengers dropped coins into a fare-box on entering the car. Overall dimensions of the cars were unchanged.

Control equipment was similar to that in No. 341, including the "dead-man grip" brake handle. The original Westinghouse controllers in the three cars were replaced by reconditioned BTH B18 controllers taken from scrapped Type Z cars. Unlike No. 341, the later cars were fitted with air-wheel and air-track brakes, as well as the rheostatic brake. These, and the air engines working the doors, were supplied by G.D.Peters & Co. Ltd. The air compressors were housed in boxes on the roofs of the cars.

By removing the inner panels of the bulkheads and their doors, allowing a clear view throughout, the seating capacity of each car was increased from 30 to 32, these consisting of sprung leather upholstered longitudinal benches. The interior was finished in light oak and white enamel, and lighting was improved, with opal-shaded lamps spaced along the clerestory ceiling and above passengers'heads. Pull-cord bells were superseded by air-bells, with brass bell-pushes placed at the top of each window pillar. A modified form of the road guide as fitted to No. 341 was fitted in one of these cars but soon removed, the equipment having proved unreliable in service.

One of the cars, No. 342, underwent air-brake tests on 15 November 1924 and was shown to the technical press on the same day. Meanwhile, the car had been inspected on behalf of the Metropolitan Police on 24 September by Supt. Bassom, who reported that "the opening of the rear exit doors was unsatisfactory", but did not specify in what respect this was so. He also said the "hanging lights" were too low. Subject to these points receiving attention the car was approved for trial on 25 September. On 18 December 1924 Bassom reported to his superiors that "as long as an extension to busy routes is not asked for the experiment may proceed, under close supervision". A further brake test was undertaken on 29 November.

Whilst Nos. 342-4 were being converted, No. 341 was fitted with a pair of Brill 22E bogies, replacing the Brush single truck and displacing the Spencer-Dawson oil-brakes. The body was re-posted to six windows a side, reverting to its

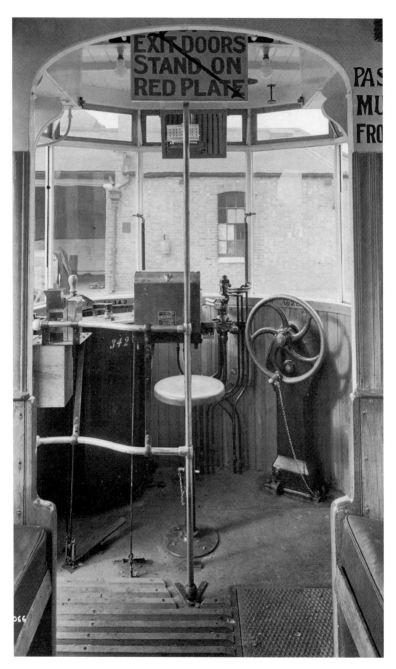

Front entrance and driving platform of one-man car No.342 showing features described in the text. The "Shanklin" ticket issuing machine and "Brandt" change-giving machine were pedal-operated by the motorman. (Courtesy London Transport Museum U3046)

No.342, the second one-man car seen at Hanwell Depot in 1924. The front entrance/rear exit arrangement was later abandoned and passengers used the front entrances for both boarding and alighting. (Courtesy London Transport Museum U3063)

original format, the windows reduced in width, and the length of the saloon remaining unchanged, still seating 30 passengers. No. 341 originally had its destination indicators below the roof, but they were moved outside to the top of the roof in conformity with 342-4. The headlamps were moved from the roof to the dashes. The front exit and entrance door arrangement was retained.

From 2 September 1925 the Brentford-Hanwell service was provided by the four one-man cars, with occasional rush-hour assistance from double-deck cars. To relieve the motorman from the task of swinging the trolley pole, automatic trolley reversers were fitted at each end of the route. Each car carried a bamboo retriever for use in case of dewirement. The four one-man cars provided an eight-minute service on week days, (six minutes on Sundays) at 2d for the full two-mile journey, which took 13 minutes.

The door operating mechanisms on Nos. 342-4 were prone to failure; on one occasion a car and its passengers were taken into Hanwell Depot where fitters took a considerable time to release the trapped passengers. After this the front entrances were used for both boarding and alighting. A notice by the doors reading PLEASE HAVE FARE READY was displayed on the dash, and the left-hand door pillar was then vertically lettered ENTRANCE & EXIT. Early in 1926 the Ministry of Transport issued a regulation requiring each front-exit tramcar to carry notices on the nearside dash at each end, in red on white, reading FRONT EXIT CAR. Nos. 342-4 then bore notices on a white oval patch, FRONT EXIT AND ENTRANCE CAR, No. 341 bearing the legend FRONT EXIT CAR.

At the Tramways & Light Railways Association Congress in 1927, C.J.Spencer conceded that one-man cars were not popular with the travelling public. Meanwhile, Nos. 341-4 continued to work the Hanwell-Brentford shuttle service until 9 November 1928, when they were unexpectedly withdrawn and replaced with double-deck two-man cars of the 1-100 batch. No reason was given for this, and no report on the results of one-man operation has become available. The four one-man cars lay derelict at Fulwell Depot for nearly three years, and were later removed outside to the Stanley Road yard. They were sold to George Cohen, Sons & Co. Ltd, together with 30 double-deck cars, for £221 under the terms of an agreement of 4 February 1931, and broken up where they stood.

Nos. 345-349

These numbers were not used.

No. 350, "Poppy" (Ex-MET 319)

Two experimental cars were built in 1926, one at the Metropolitan Electric Tramways' Hendon Works. The first, No. 318 in the MET fleet, was a light-weight double-deck car seating 71 passengers. It weighed four tons less than the standard cars then in use, and was fitted with high-speed light-weight motors achieving higher rates of acceleration. No. 318, identified officially as "Bluebell" on account of its all-over light blue livery, was fitted with BTH railway-type control equipment, with no rheostatic or magnetic track braking, both wheel and track braking being by air and hand.

At the same time as No. 318 was being built another car was under construction for the MET at the LGOC Chiswick Works. In this case there was no attempt at producing a light-weight vehicle, as the completed car weighed 16 tons, the same as the standard MET cars. The body was of composite construction with metal panels on an ash frame, in traditional LGOC Type NS 'bus fashion. The underframe was of Z-section nickel steel. With no bulkheads or internal partitions the car presented a light and airy interior, with both saloons finished in white enamel and French grey. Lighting throughout consisted of opal lamps set in 'bus-type circular white reflectors, similar to those in the latest LGOC vehicles. The window arrangements and unusually deep side panels will be evident from the illustrations. Like No. 318, the new car, numbered 319 in the MET fleet, was given an official designation, "Type: Chiswick", and was known, and referred to in official notices, as "Poppy". It was painted in LGOC red and white with black lining similar in style to that used on the 'buses.

No. 319 was designed with passenger comfort in mind, and with a total of 64 seats, capacity was comparatively low, but 16 standing passengers could be carried. Seats in both saloons were of the semi-bucket, deep-sprung type upholstered in standard "Moquettino" fabric. The transverse seats were turned round as pairs by the conductor at termini. There were corner seats for 12 and double transverse seats for 16 in the lower saloon, and the seating for 36 in the upper saloon was similar to the transverse seats below. Electric bells replaced the traditional mechanical bells, sounding distinctive tones for the two decks.

Passengers boarded and alighted from the car at the rear end, the platforms protected by double folding doors. At the front nearsides, narrow single doors, some 18in. wide were provided for emergency use, but were closed off after a short time in service. The entrance-exit doors were manually operated by a lever, in conjunction with the platform steps. The motorman's position at either end was open to the elements, but was closed off from the saloon.

A feature of the upper deck was the saloon windows, which were of the horizontally sliding type as fitted to the LGOC 'buses of type "NS", but with additional draught preventers, as the vehicle was bi-directional. A standard single-line roller blind destination indicator was fitted at each end immediately beneath the upper deck window, while the traditional tramcar-style headlamps were replaced at either end by two motor-car type lamps mounted below the projecting canopies above the driving platforms, and angled downward onto the track. These were also arranged to serve as front and rear "police lights". Later, normal dash-mounted headlamps were fitted.

"Poppy", in red livery after transfer from the MET to the LUT in 1928, seen in High Road, Chiswick. It is bound for Shepherds Bush accompanied by a Morris "Doctor's Coupe" motor-car and a solid-tyred NS-type omnibus.

(Courtesy London Transport Museum U8447C)

Maximum traction swing-bolster trucks of 4ft.6in. wheelbase, built by the Brush Electrical Engineering Company, with Hoffman roller-bearing axleboxes, were fitted. The motors were of BTH 509AS 50hp. light-weight type and the use of 28in. diameter driving wheels instead of the normal 32in. allowed the provision of a straight-through floor and a lower step between platform and road. Control equipment was of the Metropolitan-Vickers camshaft type, with lineswitch gear from the same supplier. Air brakes by G.D.Peters & Co. were fitted, acting on the wheels and the track, together with Peacock staffless handbrakes, as were air sanders. Emergency air cocks were provided at either end of the car for use by conductors and passengers.

"Poppy" was removed from Chiswick Works by an intricate night-time operation, involving the breakdown gang from Wood Green MET Depot. The car was at the end of a long setted drive and some 90° turns had to be negotiated to get it in position before the trucks were chained together and it could be moved along the drive by two petrol-driven tractors. Once on High Road, Chiswick the car was manhandled onto the tracks, and after a hitch when it was found that the control circuit was incorrectly wired, it was driven to Hounslow Depot, whence it left next morning for Hendon Works. After trials and an inspection it went into service from Finchley Depot on the Whetstone-Cricklewood route in April 1927.

Later the car failed in service. Faults in the wiring were found and rectified at Wood Green MET Depot, from whence "Poppy" then worked on local routes until 17 June 1927. On this day, No. 318 "Bluebell" ran away out of control down Barnet Hill, its air-brake having failed, and collided with a lorry, which resulted in the death of the motorman. "Poppy" had the same braking system as No. 318, relying upon air and hand brakes only and was immediately taken out of service. Following an inquiry into the causes of the accident, both cars were fitted with BTH B49 controllers with lineswitch gear and direct control, giving rheostatic and magnetic track braking, although air-wheel braking was retained.

401

No.350 ("Poppy") was designed by the London General Omnibus Company at their Chiswick
Works. Construction details of the lower saloon show a close affinity with that company's
omnibus designs of the period.   (Courtesy London Transport Museum U4368)

Upper-saloon seating in "Poppy" was to the same high standard as that used on the lower-
deck, a comparatively new departure in tramcar accommodation.
                    (Courtesy London Transport Museum U4367)

The original trucks upon which "Poppy" was mounted were transferred to another car, and here, at Shepherds Bush, and by now in red and white livery, the re-trucked car stands prior to departure for Kew Bridge. (Courtesy A.D.Packer)

On 4 November 1927 "Poppy" was inspected by Colonel Trench of the Ministry of Transport and passed for service as modified. On 16 November the car was transferred to the LUT for £1,715, the sum spent by the MET on its construction. "Poppy" became No. 350 in the LUT fleet. Later the Brush-built trucks were removed for use under another experimental car, and were replaced by a pair of similar pattern, flame-cut from solid steel plate at Hendon Works. At the same time an EMB quick-release valve was fitted to ensure that the air-wheel brakes were released when the controller handle was moved to the magnetic brake notches. Other minor changes included the removal of the twin lamps from beneath to above the canopies, and the fitting of traditional dash-mounted headlamps. The car then stayed in this condition for the remainder of its existence, working on service 57 between Shepherds Bush and Hounslow.

The "Feltham" Cars

In April 1928 Lord Ashfield instructed W.S.Graff-Baker, assistant engineer to the Underground railway companies, to produce designs for new tramcars to replace the ageing LUT and MET fleets. This work commenced at Graff-Baker's headquarters, the Ealing Common works offices of the London Electric Railway Company in co-operation with the Tramway engineering staff at the Manor House, Finsbury Park. Extensive research into the needs of London passenger traffic resulted in the construction of two experimental tramcars in 1929, followed by a third in 1930. The three cars were unlike anything seen in London up to that time. They were built by the Union Construction & Finance Company Ltd, (formerly the Union Construction Company Ltd.), at their works in Victoria Road, Feltham, Middlesex. This company was formed by Charles Tyson Yerkes in 1902 at the time he founded the UERL Ltd, by which it was owned.

Early in 1929 the parties interested in the LUT (the LST, UERL and their bankers) were in agreement that, despite the difficult state of the company's finances, an attempt should be made to obtain new rolling stock, the experimental cars of 1928 and 1929 (known as "Felthams" in deference to their place of origin), having been originally built with a view to early replacement of the worn-out LUT fleet. On 13 February the LUT directors approved the purchase of 46 cars to the "Feltham" design for £146,500. The contract with the Union Construction & Finance Company for their construction, however, was not signed until 28 August 1930 and was for 45 cars with GEC equipment at £3,250 each, and for one car with English Electric trucks and equipment at £4,444. Spare sets of equipment brought the total value of the contract to £152,654.

A body-bracing system devised for the "Felthams" was patented by UCC on 16 December 1929. The patents were assigned to the English Electric Company on 19 April 1934. The standard "Feltham" body design was registered at the Patent Office for five years from 24 March 1930. The spring fenders and improved drawgear was protected by UCC on 16 December 1929 under patent No. 338037.

The cars were built almost entirely of steel, the use of jigs and fixtures ensuring accurate matching of parts and facilitating quick and easy replacement of body sections damaged in traffic accidents. The underframe of a standard "Feltham" consisted of mild steel rolled sections and gussets, riveted together and covered with sheet steel floor plates, leaving apertures for access to the motors. The body was built up from this, with main pillars of 1½in. x 1½in. x ³⁄₁₆in. angle steel, with lighter steel angle section ⅛in. thick, and flat section ¹⁄₈in. to ¼in. thick for the waist and cant rails and other horizontal members.

The first "Feltham"-type car, No.351, was delivered to Hanwell Depot in December 1930. "STOP" flags and additional destination displays were fitted after the cars had entered service.
(Courtesy London Transport Museum)

Below the lower deck waist rail the bodywork was braced by angle steel and flat steel strip to a patented design. The experimental cars had aluminium side panels but the production batches of "Felthams" had exterior main panelling of mild steel sheet, which was also used for the staircases. A heavier gauge steel sheet was used for the dashes. These changes meant that the production cars, at 18 tons 6 cwt, were over a ton heavier than the second prototype car, MET No. 330.

The roof was built up from tongued and grooved deal boards, on steel framing and covered with heavy grade canvas, with timber mountings for the two trolley bases. The domed roof ends were of steel sheet, formed to shape. Brass rainwater guttering was fitted to the sides of the roof, discharging into downpipes carried through the body pillars to points below the underframe.

As each body shell was completed, it was conveyed on a specially-built trailer hauled by a steam traction engine to the London United Tramways' workshops at Fulwell Depot, some three miles distant from Feltham. Here two bays had been set aside for completing the cars, where all mechanical and electrical work was carried out, together with interior and exterior finishing.

Layout of the body closely followed that of the first experimental car, MET No. 320. Entry for passengers to the rear platform was via a pair of doors, each 2ft.3in. wide, which retracted when open into a pocket between the lobby and body side. To achieve this, the rearmost door was swung and folded against the other one, both then sliding into the pocket. This hand operation was carried out by the conductor when reversing at termini. When the doors were closed, as at the front end, the gap between them and the platform edge was bridged over.

The front exit consisted of a single air-operated door under the control of the motorman. This opened by sliding into a pocket between the staircase and the body side, giving a clear opening of 2ft.4½in. When closed, an automatic gap filler covered the space between door and platform edge. The door was worked by a National air engine, and the mechanism was interlocked by a door-catch and switch in the traction circuit preventing the car from moving until the exit door was closed. All doors were made from one-piece Alpax aluminium alloy castings and suspended from the top on ball-bearing runners, with the bottom edges running in guides, as on the London Underground trains.

Passenger accommodation was finished to the highest standards yet seen on any London tramcar. The lower saloon had side panels of plywood covered with scratch-proof crocodile-finish blue rexine, set in silver-grey chuglam wood framing, in removable units secured to battens screwed into wood inserts in the body frame members. Seating, for 22, was on double transverse seats fully upholstered in "Moquettino" fabric, the reversible seats having chromium plated ball-type grab handles. The end transverse seats were fixed, a single seat backing on to the stairs and a double seat on to a glazed panel. A measure of heating was obtained in the lower saloon from the resistors, which were placed below the stairs. This could be adjusted by opening a vent to the outside and closing an internal one.

Trials with linoleum or cork floor coverings in earlier cars were not successful. The floors in both saloons of the production "Felthams" were finished in grooved boards (varnished light brown) as in Underground railway stock. The ceilings of both saloons were in "Sundeala" board (a form of compressed fibre sheeting) which was painted in white Enamellas.

The upper saloon layout bore no resemblance to earlier practice, closely following design features embodied in the two experimental cars. The body sides were tapered in, from 7ft.1¾in. at the lower deck waist to 6ft.8in. at the roof, giving a symmetrical effect and increasing the clearance between passing cars. There was no upper-deck bulkhead, and passengers could reach the front exit by using the front stairs. At the top of each staircase was a grab-pole of steel tubing

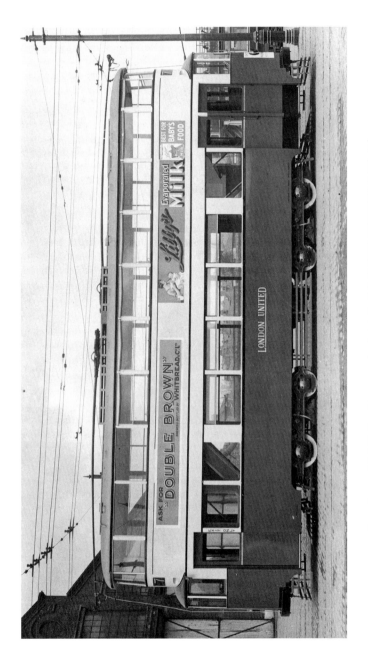

A newly-completed "Feltham" type car stands outside Fulwell Depot resplendent in red and white livery with black relief. The first of these cars entered service on 5 January 1931.
(Courtesy London Transport Museum U8492)

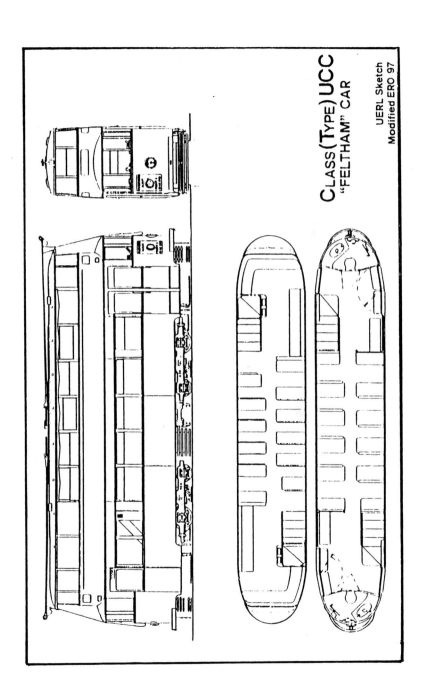

CLASS (TYPE) UCC
"FELTHAM" CAR

UERL Sketch
Modified ERO 97

407

covered with non-inflammable blue Doverite. These poles were structural members which ran through the lower-deck lobbies to the underframe. Blue Doverite was also applied to the other grab-poles.

Upper-deck seating for 42 was a combination of reversible transverse seats (for sixteen), bench-type seats facing the staircases, curved lounge-type seats round the ends of the saloon, and fixed transverse seats for one at the top of each staircase and for two on the opposite side of the gangway. The seats in the upper saloon were staggered, while those below were placed symmetrically.

Reversible seats in both saloons were to a new design. They were semi-bucket shaped, with the metal parts concealed, and the legs and struts placed to avoid contact with passengers' clothing. Each seat squab tilted slightly when the back was reversed, and all components were easily detachable from the frames. The upper saloon seats were upholstered in grained red rexine, with grab-handles similar to those downstairs. The staircases were panelled in blue and the handrails covered in red rexine. Spacious platform lobbies, each capable of accommodating a maximum of ten standing passengers, increased the capacity of the car to 84. The staircases had seven steps and were straight except for the bottom pair, which were angled to face the entrance doors.

Lighting in the lower saloon consisted of sixteen 40-watt traction lamps inset in the ceiling with vitreous enamelled reflectors; there were eighteen similar lamps in the upper saloon. There was one lamp on each platform, and at the front exit door a step lamp which lit automatically when the door was opened. Lower deck ventilation was by four windows on each side with top lights hinged to open inwards, while in the upper saloon it was by seven half-drop windows on either side, a drop window at each end (opening to 11½in. deep) and four "Ashanco" ventilators in the roof. Rain shields were fitted to the tops of all opening windows. Beneath the bench seats opposite the staircases were 6ft. heating tubes, controlled by the conductor.

The driving cabs were glazed all round, with a hinged window surmounting the windscreen. Below this window, on the first few cars, was an eight-inch gap, required by police regulations, which resulted in motormen wearing waterproof aprons in wet weather. The regulations were amended before all the cars were delivered, and a second hinged window was fitted below the first. A mirror fixed outside the car, but adjustable from inside, enabled the motorman to see the rear entrance steps. The controller, air and hand brakes, sanding gear, exit door control and lifeguard re-set controls were all placed suitably for a seated motorman, and the lighting switches, compressor switch, fuses, circuit breakers, gong, bells and destination indication control equipment were all located in the cab.

The motorman's compartment was raised by 11¾in. bringing the level of vision of the seated motorman to about the level of the standing motorman of older cars, and also enabling him to see through the car to the rear entrance door. On the inside of the cab door was a hinged seat, and when the motorman took his seat a bolt engaged in a socket on the floor, preventing the door from opening. As the motorman stood up, the seat lifted and disengaged the bolt. The cab was fully enclosed, and separated from the car body by a glazed partition containing the swing door, opening into the saloon.

Bells for giving signals between conductor and motorman were worked by air; signals between passengers (or conductor) from the body of the car were by electric bells with distinctive tones, one for upper-deck use where there were two pushes, the other for the lower saloon with six bell pushes. A press button to sound a buzzer could be used by a passenger to request that the front door be opened.

Early consideration was given to the use of four motor equipments, but improvements in motor design had shown that maximum traction two-motor

Nos.303 and 351 seen in Hanwell Depot yard shortly after the UCC cars entered service. This
photograph was taken on behalf of a German news agency.   (Courtesy J.H.Price)

"Feltham" No.356 at Uxbridge terminus in April 1933 awaits departure for Shepherds Bush.
(M.J.O'Connor. Courtesy National Tramway Museum)

equipments were capable of attaining the speeds and acceleration required in London conditions at less cost than four motors in equal-wheel trucks. Smaller diameter wheels allowed by advances in motor design permitted a reduction in height from road to step. In view of these advantages the well-tried formula of two-motor equipment in maximum traction bogies was retained for the production batches of the new cars.

The trucks chosen were swing-bolster bogies with a wheelbase of 4ft.6in., similar to those in use on other London tramways. They were built by the English Electric Company of Preston, with SKF roller-bearing axle boxes, into which were fitted 28in. diameter driving wheels and 22in. diameter pony wheels. The distance between the bolster centres of the two trucks was 13ft.8in., and the total wheelbase was 17ft.8in.

Each truck contained one GEC WT 29P1 high-speed lightweight motor of 70hp. manufactured by the General Electric Company Ltd. GEC type KB5 horizontal camshaft controllers with five series and four parallel power and seven braking notches were fitted. The controllers were of standard height and mounted on a sub-floor below the cab floor. Line-switches were also installed, the contactors of which would not close while the front door was open.

Combined rheostatic and magnetic track brakes, Peacock staffless hand brakes and a straight air-wheel brake supplied by the Consolidated Air Brake and Engineering Co. Ltd., a subsidiary of G.D.Peters & Co. Ltd., who featured a "Feltham" car in their advertisements, completed the driving equipment. This was supplemented by emergency air-brake valves on the platforms, for use by conductors or passengers. The magnetic track brakes were interconnected with the wheel brakes, and an electro-pneumatic release valve was provided, to ensure that the air-wheel and magnetic track brakes could not be applied simultaneously, thereby preventing the wheels from locking.

Standard MET-type pedal-operated sanding gear was fitted, linked to an additional air cylinder activated by depressing the motorman's brake valve. Air sanders were also fitted to control wheel slip that could otherwise occur on starting when high-powered light-weight motors were fitted in maximum traction trucks. The compressed air for brakes and doors was supplied by a KLL1 (Oerlikon) two-stage rotary air-compressor directly coupled to a 500-600 volt dc motor, having a minimum output of 6.8 cubic feet of air per minute at 70lb. psi. The air was stored in two main reservoirs, carried with the compressor below the car floor.

External car lighting consisted of a single headlamp on each dash, manually dipped from the cab; the statutory police lights mounted above either side of the cabs, which also illuminated the cab interiors if required, and a red caution light on each dash on the side nearest to the entrances. The caution light was surrounded by a white square lettered CAUTION FRONT EXIT PASSENGERS. Application of the brakes switched on the light at the rear end of the car, while opening the front door at night illuminated the warning notice. After a short period in operation, the white square was extended vertically to form a rectangle with the lettering PASSENGERS ALIGHT FRONT AND REAR ENDS, divided equally above and below the caution light.

Two trolleypoles were fitted, one for each direction of travel. This was necessary as, due to the overall length of the cars the trolley bases were mounted one on either side of the centre of the roof line and at a distance of 2ft.9in. on either side of the transverse centre line of the body.

LUT cars did not work over the LCC conduit tracks, and plough carriers for conduit operation were not fitted. However, provision was made for them to be installed on the undersides of the car bodies and the necessary electrical connections were put in place enabling the cars to be readily adapted for conduit operation if necessary. This ultimately took place after the LUT had ceased to exist, and when the Uxbridge route was converted to trolleybus working on 15 November 1936.

Destination blinds, deeper than normal and controlled from the driving cabs were displayed immediately above each cab, and on each corner of the car at the same level was a route number indicator, in the form of a stencil which was changed from inside the car. Additional route information was given by boards with a four-line display placed at the top of the rear nearside windows.

The total length of a "Feltham" car was 40ft.3¾in. over the spring fenders. Width across the lower deck waist rail was 7ft.1¾in., inside height of lower saloon 6ft.2¾in., inside height of upper saloon 5ft.11in., height from rail to trolley plank 15ft.2½in. Seating was for 64 passengers. The unladen weight was 18 tons 6 cwt.

The first eight cars went into service on the Shepherds Bush-Uxbridge route 7 on Monday 5 January 1931, accompanied by cars of the original fleet dating from 1902-3 and 1906, which had earlier been re-equipped with powerful high speed light-weight motors. Delivery of the remaining cars was completed by 20 June. The first few cars delivered to Hanwell Depot carried the type classification "UC"; shortly afterwards the whole class became Type UCC. These were always restricted to the Uxbridge Road route except on Sundays, when a small number worked the Hanwell-Brentford shuttle service through Boston Road. The journey time between Uxbridge and Shepherds Bush was, by 1926, shown as 69 minutes, but by 1932, with the "Felthams", it had been reduced to 68 minutes.

Before the UCC cars entered service a series of tests was carried out on Christmas Day 1930, including a "race" between an LUT and a MET "Feltham" along Southbury Road between Ponders End and Enfield Town on the MET system. The object of these tests was to compare the performance of the two companies' versions, the MET cars having BTH electrical equipment against the GEC motors and controllers in the LUT vehicles.

No report of these tests has been seen in official records, but it is understood that the Metropolitan Police completely closed Southbury Road after the Christmas Day tram service had ceased as usual at 4pm., with police officers stationed at each intersection. Both tracks were used in the same direction, the crossover point blades being fixed out of use. The cars were loaded with bags of sand on both decks, simulating a full load of passengers, and they also carried recording equipment for checking acceleration, current consumption, braking forces and other functions. Before the tests were carried out the track was checked throughout and the rails thoroughly cleaned and watered.

The tests indicated that the respective batches of cars had been fitted with the correct equipment to suit the characteristics of each system. The GEC equipment on the LUT car proved most suitable for their undertaking with its considerable mileage of quieter traffic with stops at longer intervals. Test runs were also carried out on the Kingston-Hampton Court section, but regular operation on most LUT routes other than Uxbridge was found impracticable owing to tight clearances on curves.

It was found that the front exits on the UCC cars caused confusion to some drivers of other road vehicles, and the Ministry of Transport asked the companies to find a solution to the problem. It was decided that in addition to the rear caution light, some indication that the car was being stopped, was desirable nearer the front of it, which should take the form of a signal arm which would operate on opening the exit door. Considerable research was carried out by the MET, LER and the LGOC, proposing the use of air, electricity and mechanically operated devices. No design came up to the requirements of prompt operation, which called for a signal to be fully extended at a right angle to the car before the door was opened sufficiently for a small child to leave the vehicle.

Deep-cushioned seats and abundant lighting with white-enamelled ceilings combined to make riding in both saloons of the "Felthams" a pleasurable experience. The photograph illustrates the lower saloon of No.355.   (Courtesy London Transport Museum U7873)

Upper-saloons of the "Felthams" were no less luxurious than those below. Seats were upholstered in red Rexine and there was a clear view from one end of the car to the other. The example shown is of a MET car.   (Courtesy London Transport Museum)

A long-serving member of the MET staff undertook to produce such a device. A "STOP" signal was made, to be fully displayed before the door was opened by more than three inches. It was mechanically worked, through linkages, by the opening of the door. A prototype was made up by its designer, and in July 1929 it was fitted to MET car No. 329 and demonstrated at Wood Green Depot before representatives of the Ministry of Transport, senior officers of the Underground Group and the Metropolitan Police.

The prototype flag was made up as a "sandwich" consisting of two pieces of "Balata" rubberised machine belting between which was a piece of flat spring steel. Double linkage with the operating mechanism ensured that if another vehicle fouled the flag when it was extended the spring and mechanical connections returned it to the correct position.

Both companies' "Feltham" fleets were fitted with the signals. In the production run the flags were made from moulded rubber, painted red and displaying the word "STOP" in white lettering. A Ministry of Transport official told the companies that it was not for them to say "stop" to anyone and asked for it to be changed to "STOPPING", but this was not done. The inventor of the device, the late Philip Pugh, received an award and commendation from C.J.Spencer in recognition of his efforts.

One LUT "Feltham", No. 396, the last of the batch, was fitted with a pair of English Electric "Liverpool pattern" equal-wheel monomotor frameless trucks, with 26in. diameter wheels and flexible bevel worm gear quill drives. Each truck was fitted with one 66hp. EE DK120 motor with roller bearing armature, together with magnetic track and air-wheel brakes. A pair of EE DK CDB2 Form 5 controllers completed this order by the MET on behalf of the UCC on 21 March 1930. The motors were replaced by 66hp. DK131 motors prior to 17 February

No.396 was unique. Internal variations are described in the text and the special "Liverpool" pattern frameless trucks were later replaced by the MET-built second set from No.350 ("Poppy"). (Photo: Chas.F.Klapper)

One of the "Liverpool" pattern bogies built for No.396 at the English Electric Company's Preston works. The design was not repeated.

(English Electric Company courtesy Roy Brook)

1932 when No. 396 underwent braking and acceleration tests between Busch Corner and Twickenham, a distance of 1½ miles. Later, on 10 December and 3 August 1933 the car underwent exhaustive air braking tests.

No. 396 also differed from the rest of the "Felthams" in a number of other, minor respects. A noticeable feature was the interior lighting, which consisted of lamps shielded by traditional style circular frosted glass fittings engraved with a decorative "star" pattern, instead of the recessed white reflectors used on the rest of the fleet.

Difficulties with the unorthodox drives and other non-standard features led to the car being frequently out of service and the experiment with the monomotor trucks was abandoned. By 1935 No. 396, renumbered 2165 by the LPTB had been fitted with the Hendon-built maximum traction trucks (with plain axle-box bearings) and their BTH 510AS motors which had been taken from experimental car No. 350 ("Poppy"), together with a pair of BTH B49 controllers removed from a re-equipped MET car. Poppy", renumbered 2317 by the LPTB was shortly afterwards scrapped at the MET Hendon Works.

Disposal Of The "Felthams"

With the conversion of route 7 (Shepherds Bush-Uxbridge) to trolleybus operation, the ex-LUT "Feltham" fleet, now LPTB 2120-2165, together with the "Felthams" from the ex-MET system, were transferred to the South London lines. Those which survived the rigours of the 1939-45 war remained in service there until the evening of 7/8 April 1951, after which 92 were sold to the City of Leeds, where most continued to work until the end of tramway operation in that city in November 1959. An exception was the former 396 (LPTB No. 2165), which had already been scrapped by Geo. Cohen, Sons & Co. at the erstwhile Croydon Corporation Tramways depot at Purley in December 1949.

Disposals: General Notes

Details of the methods used in disposing of the cars scrapped between 1923 and 1929, mainly at Fulwell Depot, are uncertain, but it is known that many car bodies were sold for a variety of purposes. When the scrapping of large numbers of cars commenced in 1931 following the arrival of the new trolleybuses and the "Feltham" cars, contracts were entered into with Messrs. George Cohen for the disposal of these.

In some cases certain parts of redundant cars were retained by the company, and later the LPTB, mainly non-ferrous metal parts such as axle-bearings, motors and controllers, but the treatment of individual batches of cars varied. For LUT cars there four main scrapping vanues, firstly at Fulwell Depot and, in LT days at Hampstead and Aurelia Road Depots; and Hendon Works.

Large scale scrapping operations brought complaints from residents in built-up areas; the burning of car bodies in particular was a source of annoyance. The ten cars scrapped at Hampstead, which was in the centre of a closely-built-up residential area, were broken up manually with sledge hammers and picks, the debris being removed and disposed of elsewhere.

When the Uxbridge Road, Hounslow and Hampton Court routes closed in 1935 and 1936, scrapping was transferred to the large site at Hendon, at that time a mixed industrial and residential district. An extensive operation was mounted there, where 62 ex-LUT cars were dealt with. A temporary double track was laid into a neighbouring field where the bodies were burned. Cohen had agreed to burn one body at a time to comply with the requirements of the fire brigade.

Each car was stripped of useful parts, the body lifted, the trucks run out and the body placed upon a wooden bogie. The vehicle was then pushed by another car into the field where the body was pulled on to its side, the bogie taken back and the body burned. This was found to be taking too long and the numbers of cars awaiting disposal began to build up. To speed up the process the number of cars dealt with at one time was increased until five were burning at once, the fifth being driven from the rear end, complete with its motors into the four already burning. To avoid damaging the overhead wiring, the driver tied down the trolley pole before leaving the stricken vehicle. On one occasion the wind changed, the fire got out of hand and strenuous efforts were made to prevent it spreading to adjacent property.

CHAPTER TWENTY-THREE

WORKS & DEPARTMENTAL ROLLING STOCK

Little is known of LUT works or departmental vehicles in the pre-electric era. However, a photograph exists of a small water car, taken at Chiswick Depot. The vehicle is being drawn by a donkey.

The initial fleet of LUT electric works and departmental vehicles consisted of three four-wheel water cars and a four-wheel box stores and ticket van, all of which were constructed by the British Electric Car Company Ltd. at their works at Trafford Park, Manchester. The first water car was in use at the start of electric operation in 1901, the second later in that year or early in 1902 and the third by 1903. The box van was delivered during 1903.

All three water cars ran on 5ft.6in. "Columbian" trucks built by the McGuire Manufacturing Company and each carried a rectangular tank holding 1,600 gallons of water. These were fitted with wash-plates and were raised on wooden bearers to provide a good head of water, directed through half-inch nozzles towards the rail grooves. When the line was extended to Southall in July 1901, the Southall-Norwood UDC complained about the quantity of water being used, resulting in the nozzles being reduced in size to restrict the flow.

The first car delivered was fitted with two 25hp. BTH GE58 motors and BTH B18 controllers and was numbered 1. The other two, numbered 2 and 3, were fitted with Westinghouse 25hp. type 49B motors and Westinghouse type 90 controllers. Car No.1 formed part of the initial contract with BTH which covered the first 100 passenger tramcars and the equipment of the electrified horse tramways. All three wore royal blue livery and were lettered on the tank-sides "MOTOR WATER CAR" in large sans-serif gold shaded characters. On a white panel beneath the tank the words "LONDON UNITED TRAMWAYS" appeared in smaller but similar characters, together with James Clifton Robinson's name and his designation as Managing Director. When the LUT was combined with the MET and SMET in association with the London & Suburban Traction Company in 1913, their original numbers were prefixed with 00.

One water car was adapted for use as a rail grinder in 1905 to assist with renovating worn track on the Uxbridge Road route, and later the other two were similarly modified, all serving the dual purpose of rail grinding and track watering. At an unknown date in the 1920s, No.003 was re-trucked, or the original truck heavily modified, and all three received 40hp. BTH GE67 motors displaced from re-motored MET cars. They retained their original controllers, and the resistances, originally beneath the cars, were moved to rectangular boxes placed along the roof line. The trolley masts were removed and replaced by dwarf trolley bases mounted on the roof boxes. All three cars had normal handbrakes and rheostatic braking.

No.001 was transferred, on loan, to the MET in the early 1920's, and based at Wood Green Depot, but could occasionally be seen at Finchley Depot. No.002 became surplus to requirements in 1931 following conversion of the Surrey lines for trolleybus operation, and was scrapped by George Cohen Sons & Co. at

Fulwell Depot in November 1931 under the terms of an agreement dated 28 September. Nos.001 and 003 passed to the London Passenger Transport Board on 1 July 1933.

Supplies of tickets and other items were at first conveyed between the stores at Brentford and Chiswick and the various depots and offices by passenger cars. As the system expanded, a purpose-built vehicle became necessary to cope with the increased amount of material being handled. In the summer of 1903 the company ordered a four-wheel ticket and stores van from the British Electric Car Company, which was delivered in the autumn of that year. This vehicle, of neat design and fully canopied, consisted of a 16ft.-long box body of stout timber construction, with generously-sized platforms, making the vehicle 24ft. in length, which was mounted on a 5ft.6in. BEC type BE56 four-wheel truck.

Electrical equipment, by the British Westinghouse Electric & Manufacturing Co. consisted of two 25hp. motors of type 49B and type 90 controllers. Rheostatic and hand braking completed the specification. The box body had wide, double sliding doors on each side, and a small jib crane on rollers suspended from the roof which was capable of being extended outward for up to two feet from either side to enable materials to be lifted from ground level into the car and vice versa, while a ladder gave access to the roof, which was strengthened to carry heavy items and surrounded by a railing.

In common with the three water cars and the 1902-03 passenger cars, the stores van received the same royal blue livery and was lettered "VAN No.4 LONDON UNITED ELECTRIC TRAMWAYS" along the sides, bearing the fleet number 4 on each dash. It was still in blue in late 1909, but from 1913 was numbered 004 and the livery changed to brown, in common with the other works vehicles. It was later scrapped or sold at an unknown date.

A second stores van came into existence in 1913 and was numbered 005. At first it was described as a "flat car" and later as a "stores van (open)". In this condition it consisted of the strengthened underframe of one of the 151-300 batch of cars, mounted on Brill 22E maximum traction bogies and with short platforms. Later, a short box-body of timber construction was fitted, allowing spacious open accommodation at the ends.

A fabricated steel gantry was placed longitudinally along the roof of the box body, upon which was fixed the trolley base, and which also supported at each end a swivelling arm along which a chain-operated block and tackle was free to move to transfer heavy items between ground level and the open sections of the vehicle.

This car was at first fitted with the then-standard Westinghouse type 49B motors and type 90 controllers, with hand and rheostatic braking. At a later date Westinghouse air-wheel brakes were fitted and the original motors were replaced by Metropolitan-Vickers type MV104 motors of 50hp. Track brakes were not installed, and braking was always hand, air-wheel and rheostatic. The car wore a plain brown livery and was lettered "L.U.T. STORES VAN" in gold characters. In later years, No.005 worked between the LUT and MET systems via the Acton link and King Street and passed, with its number unchanged, into the ownership of the LPTB.

A further rail grinder was added to the fleet in 1928. The LUT associated company, the South Metropolitan Electric Tramways & Lighting Company, purchased 12 cars from Croydon Corporation in 1927, one of which was sold to the LUT in the following year for £60. This was Croydon No.13, a 1901 Milnes-built open-top car on a 6ft. Brill 21E truck, with BTH GE52 motors of 27hp. and BTH B18 controllers. Braking was hand and rheostatic. The company removed the staircases, boarded over the windows, placed a water tank in the saloon and fitted rail-grinding equipment to the truck. The upper deck was left unchanged except for removal of the seats, while the original GE52 motors were exchanged for a

One of three water cars built for the LUT between 1901 and 1903 by the British Electric Car Company. They were later converted to operate as rail grinders and worked as required over the LST systems. (Tramway & Railway World. Courtesy National Tramway Museum)

Water car 002 together with two one-man cars awaiting the breakers at Fulwell Depot in 1931.
(Hugh Nicol. Courtesy the National Tramway Museum)

pair of 40hp. BTH GE67 motors, which had been removed from a re-motored MET car. The Croydon livery was exchanged for the standard works fleet brown, and the car became LUT No.006. It survived thus into the LPTB era.

Car No.148 was unique. When vacuum cleaning equipment was installed in LUT depots, stages were provided alongside the tracks to allow the cleaning staff to pass vacuum hoses through the open windows and into the upper decks of the "Feltham" type cars. The exception to this arrangement was at Hanwell Depot, where No.148 was pressed into service to act as a mobile stage. This car, which had been a staff car at Fulwell Depot and was a survivor of the 101-150 batch dating from 1901, was modified by removing the grille-work round the upper deck, thereby allowing vacuum hoses to be passed across to a car on the adjacent track.

In otherwise original 1901 condition and wearing the early red and white livery, No.148 was also fitted at an unknown date with revolving snow-sweeping brushes beneath the platforms. A lever was placed at each nearside front end of the underframe, which was used to lower and raise the brushes, and also probably to engage a chain drive from an axle of the car. It was maintained in smart condition at Hanwell Depot until the end of tramway operation. It was the last surviving example of an original LUT open-top car.

An early conversion of a passenger car for departmental use was that of No.275, and was the only vehicle in the fleet to be fitted with Milnes maximum traction trucks. By 1913 it was described in the stock list as the "pay car" and was cut down to single deck formation. The car was observed in the early 1920s, still painted in a blue livery, making regular visits on Thursdays and Fridays to Acton Depot. It was also one of three cars which had been converted for one-man working in 1924, as is described elsewhere.

No purpose-built snow clearance vehicles were added to the fleet, but Type Z car, No.11 was written off in 1923 but retained as a snowplough. Nos.44, 55, 58, 80 and 83 were also listed in the works fleet as snowploughs. These cars were

Stores van No.4 (later 004) was built by the British Electric Car Co. Ltd. in 1903, and referred to as a "ticket van". It was later converted for track maintenance purposes with electrical equipment worked by power taken from the overhead line.

(Tramway & Railway World: Courtesy National Tramway Museum)

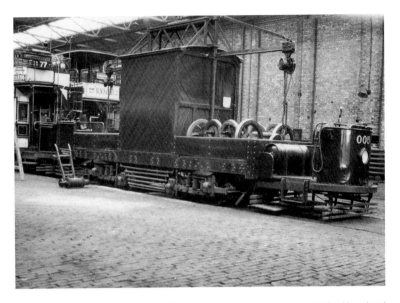

Stores van 005 inside Fulwell Depot with a part-load of wheelsets and in the freshly-painted brown livery of the works fleet. The car was fitted with powerful Westinghouse air-wheel brakes.   (Hugh Nicol. Courtesy National Tramway Museum)

adapted for this purpose by the fitting of ploughs which were hooked on to the front fenders. All, except No.11, whose ultimate fate is not recorded, were scrapped at Fulwell Depot under the terms of correspondence dated 9 November 1931 between the company and George Cohen, Sons & Co.Ltd.

Road Vehicles

Complete records of the original road departmental and works vehicles of the LUT have not survived. It is known that initially a number of horse-drawn tower wagons were obtained from the specialist builder, S.Rawlinson for use in the electrification of the former West Metropolitan lines, and during this period and the subsequent extensions to the system some may have been hired. Many horse-drawn tip-carts and wagons of various types were in use at this time, also hired from haulage contractors. Steam traction engines were available for heavy haulage but their use was not encouraged by various local authorities, who held that they broke up the roads.

At the beginning of the century some horse-drawn private carriages were retained for use by senior LUT staff members, while oher horse-drawn vehicles were widely used for transferring larger numbers of outdoor staff to work sites. Motor vehicles started to become popular from about 1902, and Clifton Robinson and his son were early and enthusiastic users of motor cars from that time.

For everyday purposes, however, the horse remained the main motive power for some years to come, and the earliest proposal for the use of mechanical propulsion for heavier road vehicles came in December 1905, when Clifton Robinson produced quotations for the supply of 20hp. tower wagons. Three companies tendered; James & Browne Ltd., in the sum of £550 each, or £2,200 for four wagons, complete with towers and raising gear; J.I.Thornycroft & Co. Ltd.

with one wagon for £650, or £2,340 for four, and Milnes-Daimler Ltd. quoted £775 for one wagon or £3,000 for four. These quotations were presented to the directors but no contract was authorised. It was to be 4 August 1909 when Robinson next raised the subject of motor tower wagons, when he strongly recommended their adoption. The directors agreed that the proposal was desirable, but could not see their way clear to sanction the expenditure.

When management of the company passed to Albert Stanley in 1910, he was immediately faced with heavy expenditure to make good arrears of track and other maintenance. On 27 July he obtained the directors' agreement to the purchase of a new "Foden" 5-ton steam wagon for use by the permanent way department. This vehicle was fitted with a hand-worked crane, which in later years was replaced by a swivelling hydraulic crane, worked from the wagon's engine. The vehicle carried Foden works number 2246 and registration number M2726. Many years later, on 6 December 1928, acquisition of a second 5-ton Foden of a later pattern, for £450 was sanctioned. It carried Foden works number 9840 and registration number MA3093 and had been built in 1920. It was obtained secondhand from Stevens & Co. of Oxford and the LUT equipped it with a hydraulic crane to the same pattern as the previous one. Both wagons worked over the LST systems as required, and survived to pass to the LTPB.

Stanley next recommended the use of petrol-driven tower wagons in place of the cumbersome horse-drawn vehicles, and the purchase of one on 19 June 1911. The directors sanctioned this and a wagon was obtained from the Leyland Motor Company. At the same time the acquisition of a Leyland motor lorry for use by the breakdown gang was authorised, and on 9 November 1911 the purchase of a smaller, 16hp. lorry from the Albion Motor Car Co. Ltd. was authorised for the use of the stores department.

During and after the Great War there were still several horse-drawn tower wagons and other vehicles in service. By 1922 the company was able to undertake

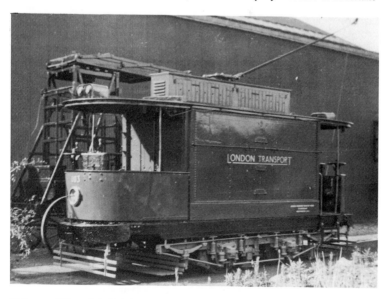

Water car 003 at Fulwell Depot in LPTB livery with modified truck and BTH electrical equipment from a remotored MET car, the resistances having been transferred from beneath the platforms to the box on the roof. (Hugh Nicol. Courtesy D.W.K.Jones)

This "Foden" steam wagon was the second of two in the LUT works fleet. A hydraulic crane, worked off the engine, enabled up to eight 36ft. lengths of rail to be loaded, carried and conveniently placed at work sites. In this view it is in Lordship Lane, Wood Green on the MET system.
(Courtesy London Transport Museum U22901)

a restricted programme of replacement. On 24 April sanction was given for purchase of two lorries for the permanent way department for £600, and £975 for a petrol chassis and construction of a tower and suitable shed. On 16 May 1922, £1,000 was approved for the purchase of two AEC "B" type chassis and lorry bodies, while on 1 June 1923 sanction was given for the purchase of a further "B" type chassis for £300. Another conversion was approved on 6 December 1928, which involved the fitting of a tower from a horse-drawn wagon on to a secondhand "B" type chassis for £350, these being obtained from the London General Omnibus Company, which at that time was scrapping large numbers of "B" type omnibuses.

These second-hand additions were of a stop-gap nature. The conversion of the LUT Surrey lines for trolleybus working provided the impetus for a new approach to the subject of maintenance equipment. The tramway companies, although still preserving the outward appearance of separate entities had, by the mid-1920s become largely integrated; consequently works and other departmental vehicles were increasingly seen on each others' systems.

One result of this came about when a large order was placed through the "combine" purchasing department for ten chassis from the Associated Daimler Company, an offshoot of the Associated Equipment Company. Seven of the chassis were nominally ordered for the LUT, whose directors approved their purchase on 13 February 1930 for £3,325, to include the cost of fitting existing towers to them, which had been removed from life-expired chassis. Of these, only four became part of the company's fleet. Their registration numbers were HX386,

HX581, HX881 and PL1484 and works' fleet numbers 2, 1, 3 and 4 respectively. These passed to the LPTB and survived until 1949. The remaining six became part of the MET fleet. Despite these acquisitions, horse-drawn tower wagons survived until 1936 at the earliest, when one was seen working on the trolleybus conversion work between Acton and Hammersmith.

In 1919, a Siddeley-Deasy saloon car used by LUT officials was sold to the MET for £150, while in 1922, a "Clark" tractor was obtained from Millar's Machinery Co. Ltd. for £500. The MET already had a number of these vehicles which were in extensive use over the three systems to assist with track reconstruction and maintenance. The purchase of two Morris Commercial motor vans for £167.10s was authorised by the directors on 7 February 1929 and 5 June 1930 respectively.

A late addition to the motor fleet was a Raleigh "Carryall", a small three-wheel vehicle based on a motor-cycle frame suitably modified, with two rear wheels and fitted with a small open body, with ordinary motor-cycle steering. Its registration number was MV1516, and it was possibly utilised for conveyance of lighter items over short distances. It was seen in Teddington in new condition on 28 September 1932, but no record of its subsequent history has been seen.

Most vehicles in the "combine" group of tramways wore a dark brown livery; tower wagons were an exception to this rule, being painted dark green, but in red later.

CHAPTER TWENTY-FOUR

THE LUT TROLLEYBUSES

An early trolleybus trial, mentioned elsewhere, took place on part of the LUT Haydon's Road tramway in Wimbledon early in 1922. A single-deck four-wheel vehicle, built by the Associated Equipment Company, then based at Walthamstow, underwent trials from 2 January, a negative wire having been added to the tramway overhead wiring. The AEC was a member of the UERL group of companies and specialised in road vehicle construction, a large part of their output being specifically for the London General Omnibus Company.

Poor traffic returns, coupled with the need for reconstruction of the tram track between Twickenham town centre and Richmond Bridge caused C.J.Spencer, the LUT general manager to consider conversion of the 1.1 miles section for trolleybus operation. The AEC had just produced their new "railless trolley omnibus" for which they were seeking markets. This was the first of this type to be designed by that company, and consisted of a 36-seat wooden body built by Strachan & Brown of Acton, mounted upon an AEC four-wheel chassis which was built up of ash with nickel-steel flitch plates.

Earlier trolleybus designers had followed the tramway principle of series-parallel control with two-motor equipments and separate drives to the rear axle, with consequent heavy maintenance costs. The AEC vehicle was fitted with a single 33.5hp. BTH motor of tramway type with purely rheostatic control. The motor was mounted "amidships" horizontally in the chassis and the drive to the rear axle differential was through worm gearing. Mechanical foot and hand brakes worked on drums attached to the rear wheels.

Steering was by worm and nut, and the steering column was forward of the front wheels. Twin trolleypoles were mounted on a common ball-bearing base. Photographs of the vehicle indicate that shortly after initial trials a steel channel section collision fender, of full width and perforated throughout its length was added to the front chassis members. The unladen weight of the vehicle was 4 tons 18 cwt.

Trials with the vehicle, classified as AEC Type 602, were initially in chassis form, and fitted with a gantry upon which the trolleypoles were mounted. On 10 February, while still in this condition, it was undergoing service trials, making 15-second stops when a cyclist who emerged from a side turning was in collision with it, striking the side of the vehicle. The cyclist was killed, and an inquest was held on 14 February at which a verdict of "Accidental Death" was recorded. At the inquest it was stated that the chassis was fitted with a number of seats, and in addition to the driver two other members of the AEC staff were present. A senior member of the LUT engineering staff, L.B.Hewitt was also present and seated next to the driver, indicating that the LUT was at this time interested in trolleybus developments.

Six examples of the AEC type 602 trolleybus involved in the Haydon's Road trials were built. With another, the Haydon's Road example was sold to the Mexborough & Swinton Tramways Company later in 1922, the two becoming

Nos.25 and 26 in that company's fleet, joined by a further one, No.31, in 1924. Two were sold to the city of Leeds and the sixth to the city of Wellington in New Zealand.

Whilst these trials were taking place the LUT advised Twickenham UDC that they did not propose to reconstruct the worn-out track between Twickenham Junction and Richmond Bridge and were considering its conversion for trolleybus operation, for which Parliamentary powers would be sought.

At the Tramways & Light Railways Association Congress in Bournemouth on 22-23 June 1922 a double-deck 4-wheel trolleybus designed by Trackless Cars Ltd. of Leeds was demonstrated. This was a 64-seat vehicle, accommodating 30 passengers on the lower deck and 34 in the upper saloon. It had entrance and exit doors set back from the front end of the saloon and a staircase close to the centre. The body was built by the Blackburn Aeroplane and Motor Company of Leeds. All the seating, mainly of the transverse type, had sprung cushions and padded backrests.

An unusual feature was the stepped-frame chassis, which allowed the whole of the traction equipment to be placed at the front. It also enabled the body to be set at a lower level, reducing the height of the step. The motors were placed upon a fore-carriage, each front wheel being driven by one of the two traction motors through a pinion on the motor spindle and an internal gear ring fixed to the wheel. At the conclusion of the TLRA Congress the vehicle was taken to Fulwell Depot and inspected there by senior LST tramways staff. It is not known if it was tested on the Haydon's Road tramway, but it is understood that another trolleybus was tried out there in June 1922, of which no firm description has come to light.

As previously mentioned in Chapter 14 (Volume 1) the LUT had considered submitting proposals to convert the Twickenham Junction-Richmond Bridge line for trolleybus operation. A Bill to authorise this, presented in 1924, failed on account of objections by Twickenham UDC to the use of side streets to provide turning circles. The Bill was withdrawn, the tramway service ceased to operate on 1 October 1924, was replaced by LGOC omnibuses, and the track lifted without delay.

Trolleybuses: The First Moves

C.J.Spencer, a firm believer in the use of trams for heavily trafficked trunk routes, was fully aware of the advantages of trolleybuses for suburban routes and smaller towns, and by 1929 had drawn up plans to carry out a long-delayed rehabilitation scheme for the LUT system. This entailed replacing the tramways south of Twickenham with trolleybuses as far as Wimbledon Town Hall, and the provision of new trams for the remainder of the system, together with the necessary additions to the power supply and depot accommodation.

A Bill deposited in November 1929 for the 1930 Parliamentary Session sought powers to convert for trolleybus operation all or part of the existing tramways in Middlesex and Surrey. The powers were gained with little difficulty, agreement having been reached with Twickenham UDC on the question of turning circles. However, conversion of the tramways in Middlesex from a point north of Twickenham station in London Road and those in Surrey eastward of the junction of Victoria Crescent with The Broadway, Merton Road were specifically disallowed in the resulting London United Tramways Act 1930, which received Royal Assent on 1 August. The line east from Wimbledon was being operated by the London County Council and that in London Road, Twickenham northwards had only recently been reconstructed.

On 3 July 1930 the LUT directors approved the acquisition, by hire purchase, of 35 trolleybuses from the associated company, the Union Construction & Finance Co. Ltd. (formerly known as the Union Construction Company), who would manufacture the bodies and assemble the vehicles. Expenditure of

A 60-seater full-fronted AEC-English Electric trolleybus bearing fleet number 11 was demonstrated from Fulwell Depot on 1 October 1930. The tramway overhead wiring had been modified as far as Teddington to allow test runs to be made with the new vehicle.

(Courtesy London Transport Museum U7337)

Trolleybus No.8 on the tilt-test rig at the UCC Works on 13 May 1931. It passed the tests satisfactorily and the MOT inspector recommended approval of the results of these.

(Courtesy London Transport Museum U8740)

£133,435 sanctioned included conversion of the first 11 miles of route from Twickenham to Kingston and the local lines radiating from the latter. At a later date a further 25 vehicles were ordered, again from UCF, and similar in most respects to the first batch but with BTH electrical equipment. Conversion of the remaining seven miles of overhead between Kingston and Wimbledon and to Hampton Court was also authorised. The hire purchase arrangements for these acquisitions were made through the UCF, who in turn were financed by the LST, and ultimately the UERL and their bankers.

A Practical Demonstration

In September 1930 a negative wire was strung from Fulwell Depot through Stanley Road and along Broad Street, Teddington to a turning circle at Church Road, a distance of ¾-mile, along which a six-wheeled trolleybus was demonstrated on 1 October. This vehicle consisted of a chassis built by the Associated Equipment Company, an associate of the UERL group, with half-cab bodywork by the English Electric Company. The electrical equipment was also supplied by EEC, including an 80hp. motor with rheostatic braking assisted by vacuum-servo operation on all six wheels. A powerful handbrake was also fitted and the motor was mounted under the bonnet at the front of the vehicle.

The AEC, whose works had earlier been moved from Walthamstow to Southall were using their type 663 chassis for new LGOC omnibuses of the LT type which were marketed as the "Renown". It was a development of this which was used for the trolleybus and designated 663T. The motor drove both rear axles via a cardan shaft with a differential on each. The body had an enclosed full fronted cab, while the lower saloon was fitted with five windows a side, together with matching windows on the upper deck and a further shaped window at the rear. It seated 60 passengers, 27 downstairs on eight forward-facing double seats and two inward-facing benches at the rear, and 33 on the upper deck on 14 forward-facing pairs of seats and one for five at the back of the vehicle.

The trial run was undertaken at short notice and was of brief duration, the vehicle also being demonstrated elsewhere in London on the same day. When photographed at Fulwell Depot it bore the fleet number 11 on the rear panel, but no other lettering was visible and no trade plate appears in the photograph.

The LUT Trolleybuses: Design

Meanwhile, an outline drawing of the vehicles that the LUT proposed to use had been sent to the Ministry of Transport on 23 August. A few days later A.V.Mason, the LUT deputy general manager and engineer sent a detailed drawing to the Ministry, saying that if the design was approved 35 vehicles would be put in hand "at once". They would be fitted with air and rheostatic braking and the half-cab bodies would be mounted upon the "Renown" type chassis. The electrical equipment of each vehicle, similar in many respects to that used on the demonstration vehicle, would consist of an English Electric DK 130A 80hp. motor, housed in the bonnet, and a six-notch power controller, the last notch providing weak field. A two-notch rheostatic braking controller was designed to operate on the first stroke of the brake pedal and further depression of the pedal would bring in the vacuum-servo brake, to be supplied by the Clayton Dewandre Co. Ltd.

On 5 September Mason, accompanied by Superintendent H.Claro and Inspector Woods of the Metropolitan Police together with representatives of the Union Construction & Finance Company visited the MoT, where a large model of the new vehicle was on view. Claro criticised the cab design, right-hand signalling facilities, windscreen wipers and other details. He asked for safety glass in the windscreen and, with a protection rail in the front window of the upper deck. There was one seat too many in the upper saloon, but if the tilting angle was satisfactory, this "may be permitted". Numerous minor points were raised by

Claro, such as knee room between seats, and he looked askance at the proposed use of vacuum-servo braking, saying the Westinghouse air-brake was "more powerful". The company wished to adopt the servo braking system to standardise equipment with the new LGOC omnibuses. The MoT representative present at this meeting was Col.A.C.Trench.

Despite these criticisms the design and equipment in general was approved at this meeting, subject to attention being given to the points raised and to approval of the cab layout on a full-size sample yet to be constructed. Provisional approval was given by the Minister on 15 September. Col.Trench and Supt.Claro visited the UCF works on 22 September, when the cab design was agreed subject to a minor alteration to the support structure, and on 2 October this was formally approved. On 14 January 1931 Mason advised the MoT that a sample vehicle was ready for inspection.

Reconstruction of Overhead Wiring

In the meantime, conversion of the tramway overhead wiring between Twickenham and Teddington was under way, the work being carried out by Clough, Smith & Co. Ltd. An uncommon form of suspension using double span wires was adopted. Most of the original tramway poles were retained, having been strengthened during the mid 1920s by the insertion of steel reinforcing rods and filling the poles with concrete. Many of the poles were also lengthened by having an additional short section placed over the top of each one. The spans carrying the traction wires were strung from the poles in the usual fashion, except that they were divided in the centre and joined there through small metal rings. Secondary spans, fixed near the tops of the poles, also divided, were joined through the same rings, relieving the main span wires of some of the additional weight of the double trolley wires and fittings. Street lamps in Teddington were suspended from the central rings.

The first section of overhead wiring for trolleybuses was strung between Fulwell Depot and Teddington in 1930, for the purpose of testing the new vehicles. Existing towers were mounted on new Associated Daimler chassis to facilitate the work.   (Bus and Tram Journal)

The First Trolleybus

Lt.Col.E.Woodhouse R.E. inspected the new trolleybus on 26 January, accompanied by Supt.Claro and Insp.Edwards. Col.Woodhouse's report, dated 9 February, described it in detail, noting that the overall length was 27ft.7½in., width 7ft.5½in. and height over trolley base 15ft.2½in. The mean wheelbase was 16ft.6in., front track width, 6ft.5¾in., rear track width 6ft.2¾in. The total unladen weight was 8 tons 2 cwt 2 qtrs, and the addition for 56 passengers and two-man crew amounted to 3 tons 12 cwt 2 qtrs, equal to a total laden weight of 11 tons 15 cwt.

The vehicle was originally designed to seat 33 on the upper deck on 14 double seats and one seat at the rear for five. The stated capacity of this seat was reduced to four prior to the inspection and the inspector asked for arm-rests to be fitted on it to prevent it being occupied by more than four persons. The inspector also asked for a number of minor alterations to the interior of the vehicle, including the addition of grab rails, some adjustments to the staircase and, again, the replacement of ordinary glass in the cab by safety glass. He noted that there was no emergency lighting for use in the event of dewirement. The vehicle ran smoothly and quietly under test and, subject to attention to the points raised and adjustment of the suspension to increase the tilt angle to 28°, Col.Woodhouse recommended that its form, dimensions and construction be approved. Shortly afterwards the company placed an order with the UCF for a further 25 vehicles, similar in all material respects to the previous batch but with electrical equipment by the British Thomson-Houston Company Ltd.

Modifications

On 23 March 1931 Mason wrote to the MoT and commented upon matters raised by Col.Woodhouse. He said that a notice would be fitted above the row of seats at the back of the upper deck restricting it to four persons. The sample trolleybus was fitted with a trailing skate to allow it to work over tramway track using the rail as a negative return, and this would be fitted with a safety device to protect the conductor from shock when handling the skate. The tilting angle would be discussed at a meeting with MoT officers.

The police were still concerned about the seating capacity of the top deck and this was re-arranged by removing the last double transverse seat on the rear nearside and extending the seat for four round to the near side to seat six, thus taking the place of the last double transverse seat and making the upper deck seating a total of 32. As a result of these modifications the MoT told the company on 18 April that they were now prepared to accept a tilt angle of 25° in lieu of the 28° originally called for.

A tilt test was undertaken at the UCF works on 13 May 1931. The top deck of the vehicle was loaded with sandbags placed on the seats to simulate 32 passengers at 10 stones each and two crew members. The results of the test were within the prescribed limits. Representatives of the police were present, together with Col.Trench, who told them that the Ministry saw no objection to licensing the vehicles for public service.

The New Vehicles In Service

The various modifications to the sample trolleybus were applied to the rest of the 35 vehicles. By 6 May eight vehicles were completed to MoT requirements and the overhead wiring inspected and approved by Ministry officers. These eight vehicles were sufficient to allow the company to commence a service on the first 2mls.704yds. of route between King Street, in the centre of Twickenham and the turning circle at Church Road, Teddington. The first two trolleybuses, which had been delivered on 24 January and 21 February 1931 were used to teach tramway motormen to drive the new vehicles. On the morning of 16 May, the official inauguration of the first regular trolleybus service in the London area took place.

LUT trolleybus services were inaugurated on 16 May 1931. Nos.4 and 5 are seen leaving King Street, Twickenham for Teddington, No.4 being started on the opening run by the Mayor of Teddington, Alderman J.O.Owen. The motorman of No.254 looks on with interest.

(Courtesy National Tramway Museum)

By this time the eight vehicles had been licensed and No.4 'led the opening procession, followed by No.3, both decorated for the occasion. The ceremony was performed by the Mayor of Twickenham, Alderman J.Owen who, using a special controller mounted on the rear platform of No.4, started the inaugural journey from the "King's Head" Hotel, Twickenham to Fulwell Depot. Here, a celebratory lunch was held, attended by the Mayor, aldermen and councillors, together with senior LUT and UERL officers, and presided over by Frank Pick. Immediately following the opening ceremony public service between Twickenham and Teddington commenced.

Further Extensions

By 5 June the overhead wiring terminating at Teddington had been extended to Kingston Hill, where a loop was formed through Park Road, linking London Road and King's Road. This provided a service through the centre of Kingston, while the loop eliminated the dead-end termini at the top of Kingston Hill and in King's Road at Richmond Park Gates. A result of this was the abandonment of 180 yards of route in King's Road and half a mile at the end of the Kingston Hill route, together with the track to the terminus at Ham Boundary. On this day the first trolleybus to cross Kingston Bridge carried an official party, among whom were the Mayor of Kingston, local councillors, C.J.Spencer and other senior members of the LUT and UERL staff.

Trial runs were carried out over the new sections, and adjustments made to the complicated overhead layout in the centre of Kingston, until the work was finally approved by the MoT. To assist in dealing with the new overhead wiring layout in the centre of Kingston a tower wagon was stationed in the town, with a suitable building provided to accommodate it.

On 15 June the service terminating at Teddington was extended to the Park Road loop at Norbiton, the vehicles using the loop in both directions. At this time the trams from Tolworth and the Dittons terminated in Kingston at Eden Street. On 29 July a service between Eden Street and Tolworth commenced, while from

15 to 29 July a shuttle service was worked by trams between Surbiton and the Dittons until the Dittons and Kingston Hill route was inaugurated a few days later.

The company had entered into a hire-purchase agreement with the Union Construction & Finance Company, covering the acquisition of the 60 trolleybuses and the 46 "Feltham" type trams. Full details of this are not in the public domain, but the agreement was for a term of 15 years bearing interest at 6% per annum. The agreement was formally sealed on 2 July 1931, followed by a later supplemental agreement on 5 November.

Delivery of the 25 BTH-equipped trolleybuses had now started and one was inspected on 12 August by Col.Woodhouse. His report of 14 August was favourable, saying that the bodywork and chassis of the new vehicles were identical with the first batch. The BTH equipment was lighter, which helped to give an improved tilting angle. No.60 differed from the rest in that the bottom of the staircase was turned at a right angle, to face the step, and the seating arrangement was revised to allow 29 in the upper saloon and 27 below, totalling 56. No.60 also differed in having Westinghouse air brakes instead of the vacuum-servo brakes fitted to the other vehicles.

The BTH 82hp. motor and rheostatic braking were controlled by contactor gear energised from the overhead, which was considered an improvement upon the drum-type controllers in the English Electric equipment of Nos.1-35. Servo braking equipment was also provided, and it was noted that on Nos.36-60 the exhauster motor for this feature did not continue to run when the vehicle was stationary. It is possible that this continuous noise from the exhauster gave rise to these vehicles being nicknamed "Diddlers". Col.Woodhouse said that the BTH equipment was "thoroughly satisfactory", and on 14 August signed his formal approval for the vehicles' use in public service.

Trolleybuses In Wimbledon

Little time was lost by the contractors dealing with the overhead conversion in completing the lengthy section between Norbiton and Wimbledon and from Kingston Bridge to Hampton Court via Hampton Wick. Insufficient vehicles had been delivered for a full service between Wimbledon and Hampton Court, and on 2 September 1931 a partial trolleybus service commenced, the shortage being made up by the retention of nine trams already sold to the scrap merchants, until another delivery of trolleybuses permitted a full service over the route. At first the trolleybuses reversed at the St.George's Road-Francis Grove loop in Wimbledon at the end of Worple Road, in an anti-clockwise direction instead of the clockwise movement followed by the trams. Meanwhile, the LCC summer week-end through tram services 2 and 4 from Victoria Embankment to Hampton Court ceased to run on 30 August.

LCC trams had taken over operation of the line from the county boundary at Longley Road, Tooting through Merton to Wimbledon Hill terminus in 1922. These arrangements were reviewed in 1931, which resulted in the LUT and LCC agreeing to cut back the line from its terminus at Wimbledon Hill to a new one in the Broadway at its junction with Queens Road and almost outside Wimbledon Town Hall. On 11 February 1932 the LUT directors approved expenditure of £1,000 to extend the trolleybus overhead wiring by 275 yards from the end of Worple Road to a turning loop at the Town Hall. Expenditure of £800 was also authorised to provide turning circles at Teddington, Heath Road (Twickenham), Malden and Surbiton.

The extension of the Wimbledon route to the Town Hall was carried out during the autumn of 1932. The work involved widening the road and the construction of a large, irregularly-shaped traffic island in the Broadway facing the Town Hall and Queen's Road, on to which the LCC trams ran for unloading and loading passengers, providing a convenient interchange with the trolleybuses.

A busy scene at Ely's Corner, Wimbledon with "Diddler" trolleybuses, motor buses and general road traffic moving smoothly with the assistance of the traffic policeman.

(Courtesy London Transport Museum)

432

A scissors crossover immediately east of the island facilitated rapid reversals for the trams. The trolleybus wiring was extended into the Broadway to end in a circle surrounding the island. With the removal of the tram track between these two points, it was necessary to provide a negative power feed return cable, and this was laid to connect with the cable in Worple Road. Total expenditure on this work amounted to £5,343, with Wimbledon Corporation contributing £1,000 towards the cost of the roadworks. The new traffic arrangements went into use on 15 December 1932 and marked the completion of the conversions authorised in the LUT Act of 1930.

The Final Extension

By 5 November 1931 all 60 trolleybuses were in full operation and on 5 January 1932 the LUT shareholders approved an application to the MoT for a Provisional Order to extend the route by 1496 yards from the "Red Lion" at Tolworth via Ewell Road and Warren Drive to terminate at a triangle near the "Toby Jug" public house in a service road adjacent to the Kingston By-pass Road. The Order was confirmed in an Act which received Royal Assent on 12 July 1932. Meanwhile the company had negotiated with the London & Home Counties Joint Electricity Authority for the provision of a new sub-station at Tolworth and £517 was authorised for the supply of mains, panels and switches. The sub-station went into use on 4 April 1932.

Expenditure on cables and overhead wiring for the extension amounted to £2,483 and a contribution of £933 was made to Surrey County Council towards the cost of making the service road. Construction of the extension was completed by the LUT's successors, the London Passenger Transport Board, who opened it for service on 20 September 1933. An uncommon feature of this short length of route was the use of reinforced concrete traction poles.

Generalities

An unforeseen effect of trolleybus operation was interference with radio broadcasts, and following complaints from residents near the routes and subsequent tests the directors agreed on 1 October 1931 to fit the 60 vehicles with choke coils, which were fitted forward of the trolleypoles, at the cost of £270. Expenditure of £105 to fit the vehicles with lightning arresters was also sanctioned.

On 4 January 1932 Spencer submitted a report to the directors on the new trolleybuses. Their capacity of 56 set them at some disadvantage against the trams and consideration was being given to the construction of a larger and higher-capacity vehicle. There was also some concern about the current consumption of the new trolleybuses, and on 25 February 1932 a BTH 110HA motor was obtained and fitted to No.54. This was of the "super-saturated" type and Spencer reported to the directors on 1 December on trials with this motor, but details have not become available. No further motors of the type were ordered but No.54 retained the motor until at least 1941.

Trolleybuses were subject to rules and regulations drawn up by the Ministry of Transport, and on 26 May 1932 Regulations and Byelaws were published, covering construction of the vehicles; lighting; brakes and other matters. The maximum speed allowed was 25 mile/h.; the company had asked for a maximum speed of 30 mile/h., but this was disallowed. Speed was restricted to 15 mile/h. in Broad Street and High Street, Teddington; in Upper Teddington Road; High Street, Hampton Wick; over Kingston Bridge and in Clarence Street and Richmond Road, Kingston; between Hampton Wick Station bridge and Kingston Station bridge; in London Road, Kingston between Richmond Road and Queen Elizabeth Road; in Park Road, Kingston except when passing Borough Road and Brunswick Road, where speed was restricted to 10 mile/h.; in London Road, Kingston when passing Coombe Road on the descending journey; in Surbiton

The tram track has gone from Clarence Street, Kingston and "Diddlers" reign supreme. The complexity of trolleybus overhead wiring is clearly brought out in this view along the street.
(Commercial card: Valentine's series)

Road and Surbiton Crescent; in Eden Street, St. James's Road and Penrhyn Road, Kingston between Clarence Street and the Council Offices; in Victoria Road, Surbiton and in Hill Road, Wimbledon.

When passing under bridges 10 mile/h. was stipulated, except beneath the Southern Railway bridge over Kingston Road, Malden, where speed was restricted to 5 mile/h. This limit was also imposed when passing through overhead wire junctions and crossings; when rounding right-angle bends at street intersections; when rounding the curve between Park Road and King's Road, Kingston; crossing Malden Road, Kingston and crossing the road junction at Surbiton Station.

Compulsory stops were called for before entering turning circles and triangles, and in Stanley Road, Teddington before crossing the Southern Railway bridge; in Stanley Road at Hampton Road on the northbound journey; in Hampton Road at Staines Road on the northbound journey; in High Street and Kingston Road, Teddington at St. Alban's Corner; in Park Road, Kingston at London Road; at the foot of St. Mark's Hill on the descending journey; before passing beneath the Southern Railway bridge in Kingston Road, Malden; in Burlington Road, New Malden at Shannon Corner and at the junction of Worple Road and Francis Grove, Wimbledon.

Estimated cost of the trolleybuses amounted to £2,100 each, but the final actual cost of the 60 vehicles was £139,260 or £2,321 each. Conversion of the overhead wiring, using most of the existing tramway installation, cost £24,000 and abandonment of track with associated road works accounted for a further £71,000.

With completion of the works authorised by the 1930 and 1932 Acts the LUT directors learned on 6 October 1932 that £9,896 excess expenditure had been incurred, and agreed to approve this, together with a further £4,056 for purchase of 200 ticket issuing machines ("TIM") for use on the new vehicles. The total costs of the conversion amounted to £162,346.

From January 1932 Spencer and his staff co-operated with the AEC engineers to produce a design for a trolleybus to match the carrying capacity of the standard London tramcar. By February 1933 their efforts had borne fruit in the form of an experimental six-wheel 74-seat vehicle, of all-metal construction, with English Electric electrical equipment, the chassis built at the AEC works at Southall and the body at the London General Omnibus Company's Chiswick Works.

A specially-designed chassis allowed for the fitting of a stepless central entrance and exit, with the staircase opposite the doors. The motor, placed horizontally in the chassis was close to the rear wheels, permitting the use of one short driving shaft with differentials to the rear wheels. With the electrical equipment the chassis weighed no more than 4 tons 5 cwt 3 qtrs.

Records indicate that an English Electric DK403 80hp. light-weight motor was ordered for the vehicle, but a later version, DK404 also of 80hp. was actually used. This was of the field control series type. An EEC DK23 Form 6 controller of the latest type was fitted. Braking was on all six wheels, foot-operated and of the internal expandng type, assisted by Lockheed hydraulic mechanism, together with a powerful hand-operated mechanical brake.

Bodywork, of all-metal construction consisted of a steel frame with light alloy panelling and again every effort was made to keep weight to the minimum consistent with safety and smooth running. Unlike Nos.1-60 with the motor-bus style half-cabs, the new vehicle was full-fronted and overall of less angular appearance. Double sliding doors, which allowed a clear opening of 4ft.3in., were worked by Peters pneumatic door engines, controlled by the driver from his cab. A conductor's valve for emergency use was placed on the staircase panelling. The door engines were interlocked with the traction control circuit, making it impossible to start the vehicle until both doors were closed.

Seating, for 40 in the upper saloon and 34 below was mainly of double transverse style, fully upholstered and with Dunlop rubber-filled squabs and backs. A row of four longitudinal seats was accommodated in the front nearside end and a similar row of three in the upper saloon above the entrance and facing the stairs. The driver's compartment was screened from the saloon to the nearside and behind his seat.

Following an inspection by the technical press at the AEC works at Southall on 23 February 1933, the new vehicle underwent extensive trials but little information has become available on the results of these. It was designed to reach a speed of 30 mile/h. with a full load of 74 passengers on a level road. When trials commenced it was given the fleet number 61, but was never owned by the LUT. as, during this period the company and its undertaking passed into the ownership of the London Passenger Transport Board on 1 July. The new authority became responsible for financial arrangements with the AEC. After trials No.61 went into service on the Kingston area routes, and in outline appearance at least, it was the forerunner of the huge trolleybus fleet built up later by the LPTB.

London United trolleybus services at the end of 1932 were:

    Route 1: Twickenham Junction-Tolworth.

    Route 2: Tolworth-Kingston Hill Loop.

    Route 3: The Dittons-Kingston Hill Loop.

    Route 4: Hampton Court-Wimbledon Station.

The author gratefully acknowledges the assistance given by Messrs. G.E.Baddeley and K.C.Blacker in the compilation of this chapter.

CHAPTER TWENTY-FIVE

DEPOTS & WORKS

The electric cars of the London United Tramways were housed at six depots, at Chiswick, Acton, Hanwell, Hounslow, Fulwell and Hillingdon. Their combined capacities were quoted as 414 cars (not including workshop bays), which was substantially in excess of the maximum number of cars in stock at any one time (340 passenger and 4 works cars c1906-1913). Furthermore, the rolling stock purchased was considerably in excess of service requirements, many cars having been bought in anticipation of extensions which were never built, either through North Kensington or further afield in Middlesex and Surrey. The stored cars occupied part of the excess depot space, and when in the early 1920s they had been eliminated from the fleet the daily duties could be covered from four of the depots (Acton, Hanwell, Hounslow and Fulwell), Chiswick being sold to the LCC, while Hillingdon (later re-named Hayes) was leased away for industrial use.

The depots were open-fronted and were entered through track fans allowing direct access to each road. The plans accompanying this chapter show each depot at its maximum extent, except for Hanwell, which was enlarged in 1930 to accommodate new and larger cars, and in this case, both versions are shown. Miscellaneous properties are described at the end of this chapter except for Clifton Robinson's erstwhile residence, Garrick's Villa, which is described in Appendix 3, Volume One.

Chiswick Depot

From the formation of the LUT in 1894, operations were conducted from 88 High Road, Chiswick (later renumbered 74), which contained on one site the head office, traffic office, overhaul works and power station and, until the advent of electric traction in 1901, extensive stabling and a large granary (the latter building still standing at the time of writing). The site occupied an area of 14,128 square yards, or a little under three acres and was leased by the West Metropolitan Tramways Company at the commencement of their operations on 24 June 1883 at an annual rent of £220 and for a term of sixty years. The lease was assigned to the LUT in 1894.

The land was originally an orchard and the entrance to it was quite narrow, situated between two existing properties, and to allow access to the greater part of it to the rear, a house which lay at the western boundary of the property some 30 yards from the main road was demolished. Lying on the north side of the High Road, the ground was bounded at the back by the tracks of the London & South Western and the Metropolitan District railways between Stamford Brook and Turnham Green stations. It was also a little more than a quarter of a mile west from Young's Corner, where the boundary between the Hammersmith and Chiswick parishes lay. This boundary was also that of the area then covered by the Metropolitan Board of Works which, in 1889 became vested in, and administered by, the London County Council.

When the site came into the hands of the LUT it contained a three-track car shed accommodating 20 trams, stabling for up to 170 horses, some small workshop buildings, and at the front, a small building stood at the western boundary by the entrance from the main road, serving as office accommodation. There was also a row of cottages, then named Tramway Avenue, which provided accommodation for members of the WMT staff, and immediately behind these was a large paddock, necessary for the wellbeing of the horses. Another paddock lay along the north-west boundary of the site.

These meagre facilities deteriorated during the tenure of the WMT who had neglected maintenance of the property. August Krauss, in accordance with his contracts with the LUT built an additional four-track car shed immediately east of the existing building (described in Volume 1). In addition, to cope with arrears of maintenance of the rolling stock and other facilities, Krauss installed machinery which was used to refurbish existing trams, such equipment having been virtually non-existent hitherto. The new machinery was driven by a Tangye gas engine and the work, carried out between 1895 and 1896, as part of a general rehabilitation of the erstwhile WMT undertaking, placed the system on a sound footing as a horse tramway pending the later adoption of electric traction.

The first stages of the electrification scheme were embarked upon in 1898 and, early in 1899 additional car sheds were built to either side of the shed built in 1896, resulting in a total of eleven tracks. One of these two sheds was 400ft. long and the other extended to 270ft. Additional space was made by bringing all the tracks slightly closer together, and there was ample provision by way of pits for inspection and repairs to trucks and motors. The arched elevation of the whole range of buildings presented an uncluttered and clean appearance, at variance with the architecture of the day, and indeed, the sheds provided an interesting comparison with the classical style of the adjacent power station.

In addition to Chiswick's main function, it was also, at first, the head and administrative offices of the company, the range of buildings for this purpose

This view of Chiswick Depot was taken in the afternoon of 27 December 1900 with cars of the 1-100 series standing ready to commence electric services.

(Courtesy Bristol Record Office)

437

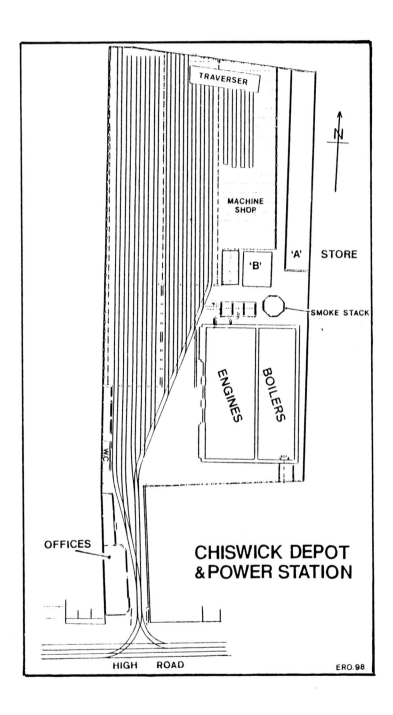

TRAVERSER

MACHINE SHOP

'A' STORE

'B'

SMOKE STACK

ENGINES

BOILERS

W.C.

OFFICES

CHISWICK DEPOT & POWER STATION

HIGH ROAD

ERO.98

N

438

being placed along the west boundary of the narrow entrance from the High Road. The site, which was never extended throughout its existence had, by the time the car sheds were extended in 1899 become fairly cramped. Some additional storage space became available in the north-east corner, when the introduction of electric traction allowed the stables there to be utilised for other purposes. The other building to be erected at Chiswick was the generating station, space for which was made by the demolition of the row of cottages along the south boundary, and by using the paddock immediately north of the cottages.

Company policy was, wherever possible, to become the owners of any premises it occupied, and following negotiations with the freeholders the property was conveyed to the LUT on 13 May 1902 for the price of £14,000. Despite the Chiswick site containing such a large proportion of the company's facilities it was not the largest in area. On the 14,128 square yards of ground that it occupied, 4,878 were covered with car sheds, 1,680 with workshops, 2,027 with the power station, 700 with office accommodation, with 700 for storage space. The maximum capacity of the running sheds was 75 cars.

Chiswick Works

The works complex attached to Chiswick Depot lay on the north-east corner of the site immediately adjacent to the second car shed. It consisted of an extensive machine shop, with a wheel lathe, heavy boring machines and a large range of light and heavy machine tools capable of being used to carry out any necessary work on car bodies, trucks and electrical equipment, as well as maintenance of some of the equipment in the power station. A smithy took care of repairs to and replacement of such items as brake rigging, lifeguards and other ironwork. Fitting shop staff carried out stripping and re-assembly of trucks and other mechanical parts and maintained axle bearings, while an extensive range of woodworking machinery, which included a 30in. circular saw, panel planer, combination saw and other equipment was used to deal with body repairs. Electrical repairs to motors, controllers and switches were carried out in a separate workshop. Machinery in the shops was driven by d.c. motors via underfloor shafting. Pits beneath the tracks were equipped with hydraulic jacks for removal and replacement of motors, and a three-ton overhead travelling crane spanned the area, able to move motors, trucks and other heavy items from place to place with minimum effort.

Two tracks were occupied by the paintshop, which allowed for four cars to be dealt with at once. A traverser at the extreme north end of the workshop reaching the two most westerly tracks in the second car shed, gave access from the sheds to the shops. The Chiswick shops were not large when seen against the number of cars in the fleet, particularly as wear and tear tended to bring them in for attention more frequently when mileage and traffic increased. Consequently, by 1907 some car maintenance work had been transferred to Fulwell Depot, where space was available owing to planned extensions failing to materialise. Some work on car bodies was also done here and later the paintshop was moved from Chiswick to Fulwell, where three tracks, each 150ft. in length on the south-east side of the building were used.

Prior to the resignation of Clifton Robinson and the appointments of Albert Stanley and Z.E.Knapp early in 1910, the company had entered a period of extreme financial difficulty. Large arrears of maintenance of track and rolling stock had accumulated, and the new management found that the car fleet required extensive overhaul to bring it back to serviceable condition and allay complaints from the public and the licensing authorities. Stanley and Knapp re-organised the Chiswick shops and introduced improved working methods, putting each of the 250 cars in the operational fleet through the shops for overhaul and renovation. On 17 February 1911, Stanley was able to tell the LUT Board that the work had been completed. No new electric trams were ever built at Chiswick but in 1910-11, 100 cars were fitted with top-covers there as part of measures to improve the fleet. These were constructed to a light-weight specification at minimum expense. From the mid-1920s a small number of cars were partially reconstructed at Chiswick shops, which by that time had passed to the ownership of the London County Council, but with part leased back to the LUT.

However, during the Great War the Chiswick shops were requisitioned by the Ministry of Munitions and used as a factory for the production of shells and bombs. This took place from July 1915, with arrangements having been made with the MET by an agreement dated 30 June 1915 for the maintenance of LUT cars to be carried out at their Hendon Car Works. To reach Hendon it was necessary to provide a link between the LUT system in High Street, Acton and the MET southern terminus at the south end of Horn Lane, details of which, and of the problems involved in providing it, are given elsewhere. Following resolution of these difficulties, the LUT cars were able to be taken to Hendon, where the Chiswick men worked on them, being conveyed to and from there by special cars which ran mornings and evenings and at mid-day on Saturdays.

Chiswick Works was vacated by the Ministry of Munitions on 25 June 1918 but the LUT staff continued to work on their own cars at Hendon until 30 May 1919 pending rehabilitation of equipment at Chiswick. The Ministry relinquished their tenancy of the works on 30 September 1919 after having paid the LUT a rent of £1,200 annually for the space occupied.

Shortly before the LUT men returned to Chiswick Works the directors voted £1,075 to purchase a Tangye wheel lathe as a matter of urgency, as much of the original plant was coming to the end of its useful life. The future of the Chiswick complex hung in the balance at this time, as a settlement of the long-delayed sale of the Hammersmith lines to the London County Council was imminent. Both the LUT and LCC wished to conclude the transaction without further delay, and it was agreed to effect the sale on 2 May 1922, on which day the whole Chiswick complex together with the LUT lines in the Metropolitan Borough of Hammersmith and 40 trams became the property of the LCC.

An early view of the Chiswick workshops showing heavy engineering machine tools and cars in course of assembly.   (LUT publicity brochure. Courtesy National Tramway Museum)

By arrangement with the LCC, the LUT retained part of the power station as a sub-station, which was fed from the UERL generating station at Lots Road, Chelsea, and served the local lines in Acton and Chiswick and the lines in the Hammersmith area. The LUT rented car shed No.2 with six tracks, the machine shops, armature shop, smithy and general stores from the County Council as workshop space at an annual rent of £1,000. Car shed No.1 with five tracks, the remainder of the power station and the rest of the complex remained in the hands of the LCC who used it for their own purposes. The company did not pay a rent for the part of the power station they retained as a sub-station, but supplied 1,800,000 d.c. units of power annually at no charge to the LCC for their cars to work over LUT metals.

In the mid-1920s the LUT undertook improvements to a number of cars of the original fleet, amounting in some cases to partial reconstruction. To facilitate this work the directors agreed on 1 July 1926 to £800 expenditure to screen the part of the depot they rented from the rest of the building. Earlier, on 1 June 1923 £1,600 was sanctioned to reconstruct the track at the entrance to the depot, from which LCC trams now operated. The LUT gave up their tenancy of car shed No.2, the workshops and other areas rented from the LCC on 24 March 1932 and all LUT repair work was transferred to the MET Car Works at Hendon.

Ownership of the Chiswick complex changed hands yet again when the LUT and LCC tramways passed to the newly-formed London Passenger Transport Board. With the closure of the tramways in the Chiswick and Hammersmith area on 27 October 1935 the depot and shops continued to be used for various transport purposes, but did not become a trolleybus depot. The power station is at the present day used by commercial undertakings but the depot remains in use for bus operation as Stamford Brook Garage.

Acton Depot

A depot on the Uxbridge Road route became necessary when the line from Shepherds Bush was extended through Acton to the top of Acton Hill in 1895. Under the terms of August Krauss' agreement with the LUT on 21 August 1894, he negotiated on the company's behalf with the Hon. Charles Hedley Strutt and the trustees of C.R.Round for the purchase of a plot of land on the south side of High Street, Acton, west of Gunnersbury Lane. The purchase price of the freehold was £1,094 and the deed of conveyance was sealed on 5 November 1895. The irregularly-shaped site measured 255ft.6in. at its maximum depth with a frontage to High Street of 67ft.7in. and to Gunnersbury Lane of 200ft. The back of the site was bounded by a large paddock, which was later built over with houses fronting Gunnersbury Lane together with a new road named Denehurst Gardens. The paddock was used by the company for exercising their horses until they were superseded by electric traction on 4 April 1901.

Designed by a well-known Acton architect, Edward Monson, who had played a prominent part in overcoming local objections to the LUT plans for electrifying the lines, the depot stands almost unchanged to the present day. The brick building consists of four bays, the easternmost of which is set back slightly to compensate for the irregular shape of the site. The two central bays are surmounted by an arched pediment in which was formerly a large clock set in a stone panel, and two end bays by smaller pediments, the westernmost of which carries the 1895 datestone. The brick frontage is relieved by some ornamental stonework and the interior walls are recessed with arched panels, the whole structure being of exceptionally robust construction.

The depot's narrow frontage to High Street was bounded by an 8ft. brick wall with stone capping topped by ornamental wrought-ironwork. Four 9ft. brick gate piers with a main pair of wrought-iron gates centrally placed and flanked either side by smaller gates for pedestrian use, each pier surmounted by an exceptionally

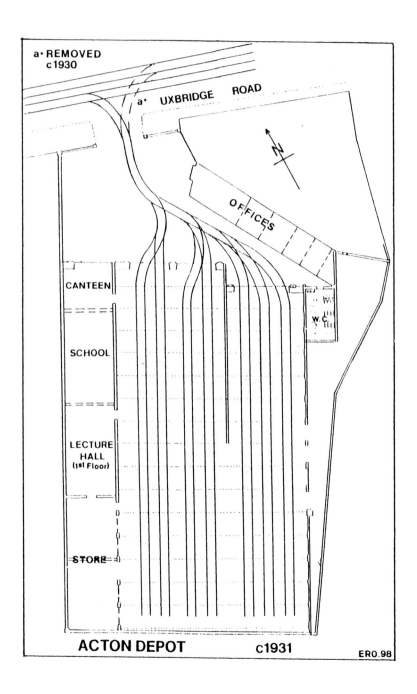

a• REMOVED c1930

a• UXBRIDGE ROAD

N

OFFICES

CANTEEN

W.C.

SCHOOL

LECTURE HALL
(1st Floor)

STORE

ACTON DEPOT   c1931

ERO.98

heavy stone ornamental cap with wrought-iron light fittings, completed the imposing entrance to the premises. At the extreme ends of the wall were further piers identical to the gate piers. Four large stone panels placed on either side of the gates formerly carried the legend LONDON UNITED TRAMWAYS LIMITED in incised lettering. This was obliterated during the 1939-45 war and most of the features described in this paragraph, and much of the wall and ornamental ironwork no longer exist.

A six-room house, since demolished, was built for the depot superintendent. It was placed at an angle to the east end of the main building, with a range of smaller buildings to the rear, used as offices, stables and stores. The depot was built close to the west side of a large property and its garden named "Courtfield House". Its occupier, J.E.Sharpe, assigned his lease of the house to the LUT and the company bought the freehold from the owner, Mrs.Charlotte Meyers, for £1,200 on 9 October 1903. The house was demolished but the company made use of only a small part of the site, the rest of which was later sold.

The depot contained seven tracks, each having space for five electric cars fully under cover. On 20 March 1896 the *Acton Gazette* described the new complex. It stated that there was space for 150 horses and 16 trams, with fodder stores, a smithy and other facilities for horse tramway operation. During the horse tram period most of the space would have been taken up by the stabling and loose-boxes.

An area of 2,929 square yards was occupied by the buildings, and with the superintendent's house and other small buildings the total site area was 4,236 square yards, a little under three quarters of an acre. When the land to the rear and to the west was built over and the "Red Lion" public house east of the depot was extended in 1907, the depot was closely surrounded by other buildings except on the side flanking Gunnersbury Lane, where an already narrow yard was reduced in width still further when Gunnersbury Lane was widened, the company having made a strip of land available to Acton UDC for this purpose.

Acton Depot c.1931 with redundant MET cars and LUT combined water car and rail grinder 003. The east to south track into the depot had by this time been removed.
(Hugh Nicol. Courtesy National Tramway Museum)

Type Y car No.75 on route 89B, standing inside Acton Depot gates having just come "off service". The motorman takes the opportunity to partake of refreshment.

Courtesy National Tramway Museum)

The superintendent's house at Acton Depot. It was latterly used as offices and has been demolished in recent years. (Photo courtesy Mrs.Averil Harper Smith)

Considerable alterations became necessary when electric tram services began on 4 April 1901, at first only as far as the depot, and pending these works it is possible that initial services were worked from Chiswick Depot. Later, on 10 July 1901, the larger depot at Hanwell went into use when the line was extended to Ealing and Southall. After these services had been operating for a short time the LUT directors discussed the completion of works necessary at Acton Depot in conjunction with the conversion from horse to electric working, which was carried out by early 1903.

The bulk of the Uxbridge Road traffic was always worked from Hanwell Depot, which was placed centrally along the route to Uxbridge, but from c1908, following a re-allocation of rolling stock, a large group of the first electric cars (Nos.1-100) worked from Acton Depot, mainly on the Shepherds Bush-Birch Grove (Acton-Ealing boundary) service. These cars became the mainstay of operations from the depot during the Great War when, in 1915, the LUT system was linked to the Metropolitan Electric Tramways' terminus at the south end of Horn Lane, Acton. They were then joined by a number of MET cars to work services from Acton over the MET system to the shell-filling factories at Park Royal, and the aircraft works along Edgware Road, Colindale. Some of the LUT cars also worked regular services from Acton to Willesden Green station and Hendon at this time.

A rifle range was installed at the depot in 1910 and regular competitions between staff of the various LUT departments took place there. From the end of the war, as a result of the merger in 1913 of the three London tramway companies, some departments hitherto at the MET Hendon Works were transferred to Acton Depot. On 25 April 1919 the LUT directors authorised £1,000 expenditure to transfer the MET conductors' and motormens' school to the depot, where facilities for both companies were established at the west end of the building. The staff uniform store, fitting and machine rooms, again for all companies, were brought together at this end of the building. At the same time, and adjacent to the driving school, a lecture hall with projection and other facilities was built, where efficiency meetings were held on a regular basis for the staff of the whole Underground group of companies.

The Uxbridge Road trams were fitted with higher powered motors between 1923 and 1928 and their demands, together with increased service frequencies resulted in the installation of a mercury-arc rectifier sub-station in the south-west corner of the depot, approval for which was given by the directors on 4 October 1928 as described in Vol.1. Later, on 7th March 1929 approval was given for the purchase and installation of a car washing machine, one of three obtained at the time for £1,000.

Powers were granted in the London United Tramways Confirmation Act of 1896 to establish a generating station at the depot, but these were not used. It is possible that the most easterly portion of the main building could have been used for this, as the Act mentions the area adjacent to Gunnersbury Lane. No reason is given in the company's records for allowing the powers to lapse, but it is possible that strong local objections would have been made to such a development in a residential area. The depot and adjacent auxiliary buildings were in place by 1897 and it was found possible to accommodate the company's power station requirements at Chiswick Depot.

Situated at 283 High Street, Acton Depot survived the tram and trolleybus eras: the Hammersmith-Acton section was converted to trolleybus operation (by the LPTB) on 5 April 1936 and these worked from the depot until 12 September 1937, after which it passed into the hands of the LPTB high tension mains department. For many years it has been a terminal point for buses which show destination blinds reading ACTON TRAM DEPOT. In its last tramway days some MET cars, displaced from their routes by new trams in 1931, were stored at the depot and pending disposal were put into use on the LUT system for special services to and from Brentford Football Ground, most of the oldest LUT cars having by then been scrapped and replaced by new trams and trolleybuses.

Acton Depot was the first to be built in the Greater London area for electric tramway operation, notwithstanding that for the first five years of its life it was used for horse trams. At the time of writing (1998) the depot continues to be used for transport purposes as a garage and workshops for services operated by First CentreWest Buses Ltd.

Hanwell Depot

This was the second depot to be built by the LUT and was the main operating centre for electric tramway services on the lengthy Uxbridge Road route. It was situated on the south side of Hanwell Broadway in Uxbridge Road east of Boston Road and was acquired from its owners George Ralph Fitzroy Cole, Edgar Robert George Hopwood, Arthur Frederick Churchill Tollemache and Henry Euan Cole by the LUT on 31 January 1901, but the price paid for the property does not appear in records seen. The acquisition of the site and subsequent construction of the buildings marked a departure from previous practice of using contractors and intermediaries such as August Krauss. The LUT had by this time established its own civil engineering and construction departments and all building work, ·installation of equipment and trackwork construction was carried out by labour engaged and supervised from the company's head office at Chiswick.

Hanwell Depot, as originally built on an odd-shaped site, consisted of the main car shed containing ten tracks accommodating fifty cars. The shed building was parallel to Uxbridge Road and cars entered through a narrow single track entrance from the main road, turning sharply left onto a roughly triangular fan leading directly into the shed, which was placed immediately to the rear of buildings fronting Uxbridge Road. The sub-station occupied a position in the acute angle formed by the extreme west and south-west corner of the yard. Along the west boundary were various store buildings and a sand drier, with offices and a smithy nearer to the entrance. Of the total site area of 8,502 square yards, 2,407 square yards were occupied by the car shed and 300 square yards by the sub-station bulding.

The main building was not quite as Victorian in style as Acton Depot, but construction was still in brick with the front elevation appearing as two gabled bays with five tracks in each, making accommodation available for a total of 50 cars. Unlike Acton Depot, where the cramped site precluded the provision of windows to the sides and the rear, Hanwell Depot was built not only with extensive roof lights but with tall arched windows on the south side of the shed. It went into use for services on the Shepherds Bush-Southall route which was extended from Acton on 10 July 1901, the date of the formal inauguration of the company's electric tramways. Later, from 1906, it also accommodated the cars for the Brentford-Hanwell shuttle service along Boston Road.

In the early years of electric traction considerable attention was paid to the maintenence of the company's assets, but later, the effects of prolonged heavy usage combined with reduced maintenance began to make themselves felt. With the 1910 change of management, a rehabilitation programme was arranged. At Hanwell Depot it was found that considerable work was required to make up these arrears of maintenance and at the same time as this was undertaken staff facilities were improved.

Hanwell Depot's share of post-war improvements came on 3 November 1927 when the LUT directors approved the provision of two car washing machines. The cost of these amounted to £230 and the necessary electrical equipment, wiring, piping and installation in the pits came to a further £270. A third machine was installed following authorisation by the directors on 7 March 1929.

Hanwell Depot c.1926 with Types T, Y and W cars in evidence. This depot was extended in 1930 to accommodate the new "Feltham" cars.

(Courtesy London Transport Museum P5328)

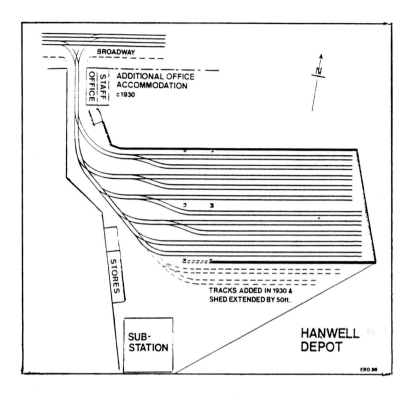

The provision of new rolling stock for the LUT system was finally agreed to, and an order for 46 new cars was authorised on 13 February 1929. These, the celebrated "Felthams", were five feet longer than the existing cars, and as they were required for the Uxbridge Road services, extensive alterations were necessary at Hanwell Depot. Chief among them were the extension of the main shed and reconstruction and realignment of the track fan. Other lesser works were the provision of improved staff facilities, additional inspection pits and ticket stores.

The smithy near the front entrance was moved to a better position at the north-east corner of the site. Some additional land to the east of the depot entrance was bought and on 1 May 1930, £15,000 was voted to carry out the various works, with £4,600 authorised on 3 July to purchase the necessary land. Two houses at the east of the depot entrance, Nos.92 & 94 The Broadway, were bought on 28 October for use as offices, and shortly afterwards, another building next to the two cottages, the Coronation Hall, was bought, but no details of the relevant transactions have become available. The car sheds were lengthened by fifty feet by erecting walls and roofing on metal framing covered with asbestos sheeting, the extension being brought forward, which necessitated the re-design of the fan.

Along the south side of the shed two outdoor tracks were laid, each 220ft. long, with shallow pits and a car washing machine. At about the same time, the Divisional Inspector's office was accommodated at Hanwell. The acquisition of the Coronation Hall, the two houses in the Broadway and the transfer of the smithy from its old position next to these buildings allowed space for improved accommodation for various administration departments, some of which had been transferred from the Chiswick offices when they were sold to the LCC in 1922.

An interesting feature at Hanwell Depot was car No.148, the last survivor of the 101-150 group. It had been the staff car at the depot for many years and, with the advent of upholstered seating and vacuum cleaning equipment, it was retained to gain access to the upper decks for the cleaning staff, and described as the "Vacuum Cleaner Car" in the company's records. In effect it was no more than a moving gantry, but it was also fitted with revolving brushes for snow clearance.

The improvements carried out at the depot to cater for the "Feltham" cars were the most that could be afforded owing to the company's serious financial position at the time. The depot continued to be used, accommodating the new cars and some of the best of the older ones until the trams were superseded by trolleybuses in 1936, for which it underwent extensive reconstruction during the last months of tramway operation.

Types X 148 and U 250 at Hanwell Depot. No.148, still in opentop condition, was retained for works duties and in later years fitted with revolving brushes beneath the platforms for snow clearance.   (D.W.K.Jones courtesy National Tramway Museum)

Hounslow Depot

This was situated on a plot known locally as "Three Rood Piece", and measuring a little over three quarters of an acre in extent. Unusually for LUT depots the site was symmetrical in shape and rectangular in form. It was on the north side of London Road to the west of Spring Grove Road and in the district of Heston and Isleworth but known as and referred to as Hounslow. The freehold site was acquired by the LUT from Alfred Platt and Walter Bricknell by an indenture dated 1 February 1901, but details of the price paid are not known. Construction of the building and the adjacent sub-station was carried out by the LUT outdoor workforce and the depot went into use when the new electric line between Kew Bridge and "The Bell", Hounslow opened on 6 July 1901. Immediately prior to this some horse trams displaced by electric cars on 4 April 1901 were stored there pending disposal.

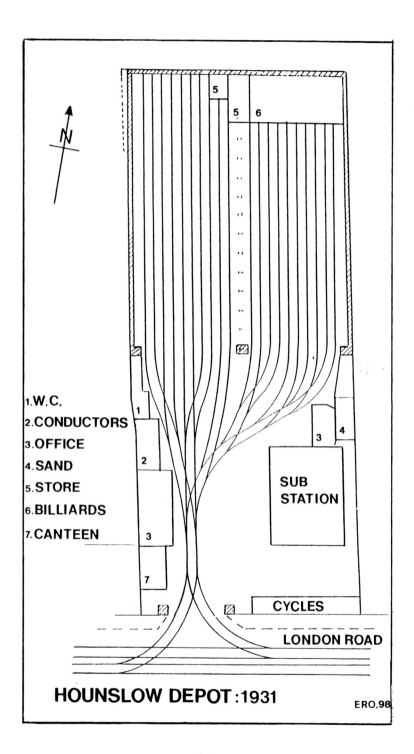

1. W.C.
2. CONDUCTORS
3. OFFICE
4. SAND
5. STORE
6. BILLIARDS
7. CANTEEN

SUB STATION

CYCLES

LONDON ROAD

HOUNSLOW DEPOT:1931

ERO.98

450

Measuring 110ft. by 156ft. the car shed contained ten tracks accommodating forty cars. Entry to the depot was direct from London Road with curves from both directions. The sub-station occupied a position in the yard near the south-east corner and measured 50ft. by 40ft., the architectural style of the buildings being similar to those at Hanwell Depot. Around the perimeter wall of the yard a messroom, cycle sheds and a sand drier were located and the 116ft. frontage to London Road was guarded by a 7ft.6in. brick wall with stone copings. The entrance to the premises was through a pair of ornamental wrought-iron gates supported by 12ft. brick piers with heavy stone caps and wrought-iron light fittings of ornate design.

The track from the main road led directly onto the track fan, passing offices left of the entrance and branching into the ten tracks in the shed, which was built of brick in two spans. Owing to the position of the sub-station in the yard the track fan was assymetrical in form, resulting in the curves into the five most easterly tracks being quite sharp. Few alterations were made to the depot in its earlier years and the site allowed no space for creating additional capacity in the shed.

It was found necessary to provide additional maintenance facilities at the depot in 1914 and £388 was sanctioned to construct more inspection pits. Some re-arrangement of the offices also took place at this time. In 1915 the need arose for training facilities for Army motor transport drivers and James Devonshire, the LUT managing director told his colleagues on 14 April that the depot had been loaned to the London General Omnibus Company, who had undertaken to carry out the necessary training on behalf of the Army authorities. The terms agreed were an annual rent of £1,000 which included £500 per annum to cover the LUT's costs of re-arranging tram services and housing the Hounslow trams in other depots. The tenancy was terminated on 8 May 1917 but it was agreed that the LGOC should retain part of the depot to store bus bodies at a rent of £275 per

Hounslow Depot with Type U, W and Z cars in a photograph taken c.1926.
(Courtesy London Transport Museum P5169)

451

annum. The date this arrangement ceased is not known, but the LUT was able to resume tramway operation from the depot from this time.

The closure of the section of tramway on 5 July 1922 between Hounslow "The Bell" and the terminus at Hounslow Heath "The Hussar", together with the earlier abandonment of powers to reach Baber Bridge and Staines meant that the depot's capacity of forty cars was no longer needed. As members of the Underground group of companies were increasing recreational facilities for their staff, it was decided to provide a billiards room at the depot, which took the form of a space 50ft. by 22ft. in the far north-east corner of the shed, which was suitably partitioned from the rest of the building and covered over with an arched roof. This reduced the capacity of the shed by five cars. On 23 February 1923 the LUT directors approved £200 expenditure for additional equipment for the staff canteen. On 7 March 1929, £367 was authorised to instal a car washing machine in the shed, to the same pattern as those already fitted at most of the other depots.

Hounslow Depot provided accommodation for cars working between Hammersmith and Shepherds Bush termini and Kew Bridge and Hounslow, and during its lifetime it was home to cars of the 1-100, 151-300 and 301-340 groups. Following the transfer of the LUT undertaking to the London Passenger Transport Board, trams working on routes 57 and 63 continued to be housed there, until they were converted to trolleybus operation on 27 October 1935. Renamed as Isleworth in its final years it was sold to the Post Office on 25 January 1968.

Fulwell Depot

Fulwell Depot was planned to accommodate rolling stock for the lines to Hampton Court, Kingston and Wimbledon, together with authorised and proposed lines striking across Hampton Court Bridge to form a second loop taking in the Dittons and reaching Kingston by way of Surbiton. Other lines, proposed in 1901, were from the authorised line at Hampton Court to Sunbury and Staines. These schemes did not materialise and other, more ambitious plans to reach places as far distant as Maidenhead and Reading failed as described elsewhere in this book, with the result that when built had considerable excess capacity.

A site off London Road, Twickenham was initially considered for the new depot, but negotiations with the freeholders did not succeed and another plot, situated immediately south of South Road, Fulwell was secured after lengthy and difficult negotiations with the owners, the Freake Estate Trustees. The freehold could not be obtained at the time, but a 99-years building lease, at an annual rent of £200 was agreed in April 1902, and bulding operations started without delay. The site was awkwardly shaped and is best described as a "cranked rectangle", flanked on its south side by the approach to the Fulwell station of the London and South Western Railway. It occupied an area of 26,954 square yards, or slightly in excess of 5½ acres.

As in previous cases, construction of the buildings and their equipment were carried out by the company's staff, exceptions in this case being the large amount of structural steelwork and a central heating system. The depot was one of the largest in the Greater London area and was the largest owned by any of the three London company-owned tramways. The car shed measured 400ft. by 258ft. and, as it lay close to Stanley Road Junction it had frontages to and access from both Stanley Road from the east and Wellington Road from the west.

Of the 18 tracks provided, the three on the south side of the building could be approached only from the Wellington Road end, the sharp "bend" of the site at the east end of the shed preventing access from Stanley Road. The remaining fifteen tracks were approached by way of fans in the yards at either end of the building. As originally laid out the site contained, in addition to the shed the sub-station, a nearly square building 70ft. by 65ft. which was situated in the extreme south-west corner of the Wellington Road yard, facing an office building in the opposite,

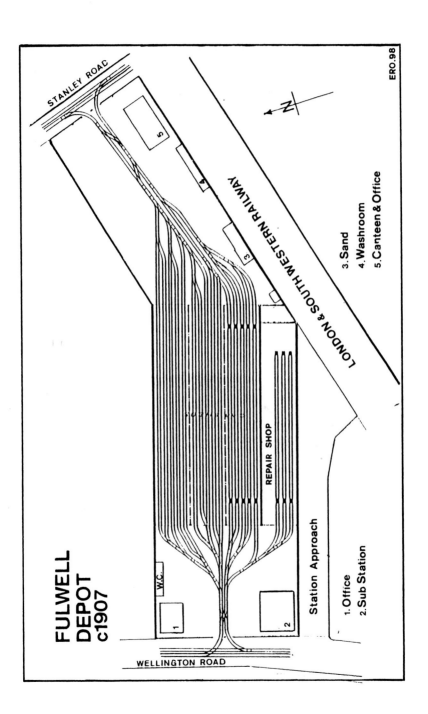

FULWELL DEPOT c1907

STANLEY ROAD

LONDON & SOUTH WESTERN RAILWAY

SOUTHERN

REPAIR SHOP

W.C.

WELLINGTON ROAD

Station Approach

1. Office
2. Sub Station

3. Sand
4. Washroom
5. Canteen & Office

ERO.98

N

south-west corner. On the south-east of the Stanley Road yard there was placed a mess-room, some offices and a sand drier.

While both Hanwell and Hounslow depots had been constructed to a fairly plain architectural pattern, Fulwell was a reversion to a more decorative style, not unlike Edward Monson's design for Acton. The Wellington Road elevation presented four gabled and pedimented spans, each with space beneath for five tracks, the Stanley Road side being cut off at an angle by the LSWR tracks passing close to the corner. The extreme east end of this corner was occupied by a store.

In the southernmost bay, although constructed to accommodate five tracks, were the three which were not accessible from Stanley Road and were shorter than the other fifteen. This portion of the shed was utilised as a repair shop and was divided from the main building. The tracks in this section of the shed accommodated 24 cars, while those in the remainder of the building held 165.

Fulwell Depot was built on a grand scale; each of the four large bays had a span roof with clerestories which were exceptionally lofty. Above the centre of each bay were three large windows, the centre ones being proportionally larger than the other two. The top of each gable had a brick and stone pediment with circular glazed openings, and in one of these a large clock was placed. The elevations and clocks were similar for both ends. The boundary walls fronting Stanley and Wellington Roads were 10ft. tall with stone capped piers spaced at 18ft. intervals, the brickwork relieved by ornamental panels between the piers. Each entrance was guarded by heavy wrought-iron gates, their brick piers supporting ornamental lamp fittings in wrought-iron.

The new establishment went into use on 2 April 1903 providing cars for the Hampton Court services and subsequently, in 1906 and 1907 the extensions to Kingston, Wimbledon, Summerstown and Tooting. Because of its immense capacity it was easily able to supply the requirements of these routes, but the

This panoramic view of Fulwell Depot (Stanley Road end) taken in July 1924 includes cars of Types W, U, Y and Z, together with a water car. Stores van No.005 is just visible, standing at the entrance to the right-hand section of the building.

(Courtesy London Transport Museum U2757)

A July 1924 view of the interior of Fulwell Depot, with a line-up of various types of car. No.63, dressed for service on route 67 stands at the head of the group on the left of the picture.
(Courtesy London Transport Museum U2763)

Type W car, No.198, still with its original motors and without magnetic brakes, awaiting departure from Fulwell Depot for service on the route between Richmond Park Gates and Tolworth via Kingston. (Chas.F.Klapper. Courtesy The Omnibus Society)

distance from the depot to the Tooting and Summerstown termini meant, particularly in later years, that the cars operating on these routes worked considerable and expensive dead mileage.

Excess capacity at Fulwell Depot gave the LUT some much-needed additional workshop space which it started to use at an early date, relieving the main repair shops at Chiswick. Later, after the depot and works at Chiswick were sold to the London County Council in 1922 most maintenance work was carried out at Fulwell, to which some of the machinery at Chiswick was transferred. The Fulwell sub-station was built with future extensions in mind and, with the abandonment of these schemes, part of this building was converted to a canteen after the Great War. On 27 October 1922 a 300-gallon petrol tank and pump were installed in the Stanley Road yard and a new tower wagon shed was built on the opposite side of the yard.

Forty of the cars from the 101-150 batch were sold with the Hammersmith lines to the LCC in 1922. A year later they were bought back by the LUT, having never left the company's possession. Some of these cars had been stored at Hillingdon Depot which was leased away in 1923, with the rest at Fulwell. They subsequently all came together on tracks 1 to 5 at the Stanley Road end until the summer of 1924 when nearly all were broken up, the bodies sold and useful spare parts retained for further use. The space released allowed a redistribution of the stock between the various depots, while the main shed accommodated cars for the services between Shepherds Bush and Hammersmith termini and Hampton Court, these operating from the Wellington Road entrance and those for the Kingston and Wimbledon routes from the Stanley Road side.

In common with the other depots Fulwell received a car washing machine following approval of £367 expenditure on 7 March 1929. As there was ample space in the depot environs a number of smaller departments of the company were accommodated there, mainly in small buildings in the Stanley Road yard, among them being the building and bill-posting departments.

Fulwell Depot made an impression upon the UERL management. Shortly after it opened their General Manager, J.R.Chapman, wrote to Clifton Robinson on 28 May 1903 asking to view the new premises, saying that the UERL wished to provide new depots "and I am anxious to learn how you do it". The ample space at the depot was used to good effect in 1930-31 when newly-built "Feltham" type trams were fitted out and painted there, each one being delivered in shell form from the Union Construction & Finance Company's works at Feltham on a road trailer hauled by a steam traction engine hired from Pickford & Co. At the same time, surplus open-top trams were broken up in the east yard, including some from the South Metropolitan Electric Tramways & Lighting Company.

The depot assumed a new identity from 16 May 1931 when it became the operating base for the first trolleybus services in the London area. This involved the conversion of the five most northerly tracks in the shed to a repair shop and the adjacent five tracks became tne running shed for the new vehicles, trams continuing to work from the next five tracks until 27 October 1935 when the last tram routes working from the depot were converted to trolleybus operation. Fulwell Depot continues in use at the time of writing as a garage for the local bus operator, London United Busways Ltd. It was an exception to the general LUT practice of outright ownership of operational premises wherever possible. The freehold was eventually bought from the owners on 16 February 1937 by the successors to the company, the London Passenger Transport Board.

Hillingdon (later Hayes) Depot

Hillingdon was the last LUT depot to be built. It was intended to serve the outer end of the Uxbridge Road route beyond Southall and additional demands were expected when the line was extended to Uxbridge in 1904. This part of the route was then of a mostly rural character, Hillingdon Village being a favoured beauty spot. The first site chosen for the depot and sub-station was on land owned by Lord Hillingdon, east of the Hillingdon East parish boundary. Negotiations commenced in 1903 but did not succeed and a fresh location was found, half a mile to the west in the parish of Hillingdon East on the north side of Uxbridge Road opposite New Road. The area of the plot amounted to 2,305 square yards. a little under half an acre, irregularly shaped with a frontage to Uxbridge Road of

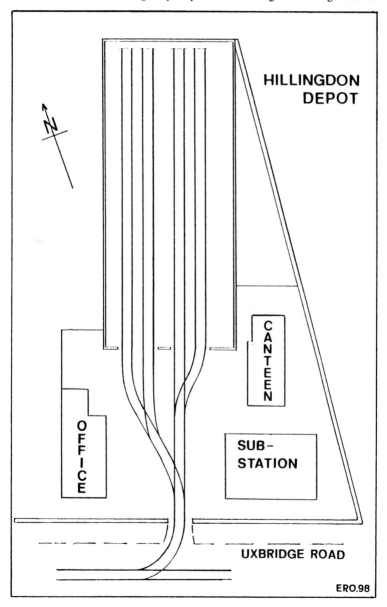

approximately 130ft. A leasehold interest in the site was assigned to the LUT early in 1904 and the freehold was conveyed to the company by the owner, W.Hicks by an indenture dated 3 November 1905, the purchase price being £700.

The car shed had four tracks and accommodated 20 trams. It was of utilitarian design and materials and was flanked by an office building on the west side and on the opposite side by the sub-station. A mess-room and store completed the facilities at this small establishment, which had a short operational life. Plans were drawn up in 1904 for an ambitious programme of extensions, which included the continuation of the line at Uxbridge to High Wycombe. These plans did not materialise, and the depot became of little importance. From 1908-9 it became a store for surplus rolling stock, some of the displaced cars of the 101-150 batch being stored there. Some of the oldest cars of the 1-100 series were scrapped there shortly after the Great War, when the fleet was being drastically reduced.

Later scrappings were carried out at Fulwell Depot which meant that the company had no further use for Hillingdon car shed, and on 7 June 1923 it was leased to the Chemical and Engineering Company, but the sub-station was retained. The premises again became vacant in 1931 and on 5 November were leased to Lang Wheels Ltd., who manufactured there the electrically driven "Dodgem" fairground cars which were introduced from America in the 1920s. The depot is at the time of writing (1998) occupied by a company producing milk products. It remained the property of the successors to the LUT until it was sold by them on 24 March 1950. The sub-station was sold on 6 March 1964.

Brentford Permanent Way Depot & General Stores.

This establishment occupied a site between the Grand Junction Canal at Brentford Bridge and the Great Western Railway branch line to Brentford Dock. It was roughly rectangular in shape, measuring some 600ft. by 150ft. and adjoined the railway and Brentford Dock station on the south-west side. The largely open site contained a range of buildings, mainly on its north-east side and was

A single-line entrance from London Road into Brentford Permanent Way Yard and Stores led to an extensive area with double track and numerous buildings flanking its east side, none of which now remain. (Courtesy London Transport Museum U59381)

458

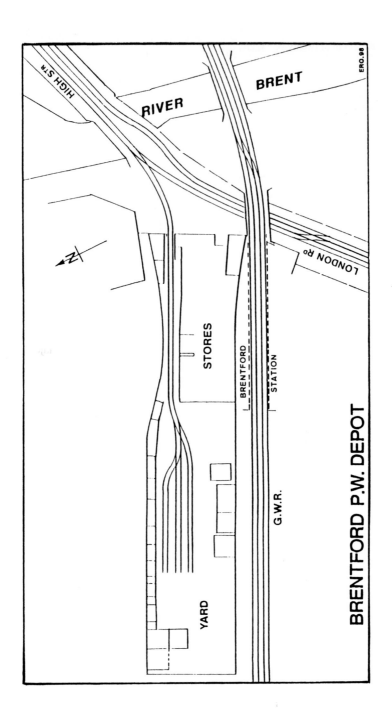

BRENTFORD P.W. DEPOT

459

Part of the electrical store at Brentford Permanent Way Depot c.1925.
(Courtesy London Transport Museum U5549)

approached by a single line from the north side of High Street, Brentford immediately west of Brentford Bridge, which carried the road across the canal. The depot, held on a renewable lease, had come into use by 1898-99, but the precise date is not known. Some of the horse trams displaced by the new electric trams in April 1901 were stored there pending disposal.

Water-borne consignments of rails and other heavy materials had unloading facilities provided at the nearby Goat Wharf, but there was no access from the railway into the yard. The LUT did not, in its earliest years have any railed vehicles for the conveyance of goods apart from a four-wheel box van which was obtained in 1903. The track connection from the street into the yard was through a narrow entry between buildings set well back from the main road. At an engineering meeting on 4 December 1904 presided over by Clifton Robinson, instructions were given to remove the points and crossings at the entrance and thereafter there was no tramway access to the yard for another ten years. Some damage to the premises was done by a fire on 2 October 1908.

The LUT and Heston & Isleworth UDC came to an agreement in 1913 for reconstruction of the track between Hounslow "The Bell" and Brentford Bridge (the bridge being the easternmost boundary of the district). The council noted that the depot approach track and overhead had not been used for many years and asked for them to be removed. On 16 July 1915 the company wrote to the UDC saying that Chiswick Depot had been given over to munitions manufacture and they wished to restore the connection into the yard to keep their water cars and other works vehicles there. The UDC Works Committee assented to this request on 27 August, whereupon the connections were reinstated and remained until after the Great War ended in 1918, but were removed for a second time a few years later, by which time steam and motor wagons had come into use. On 5 December

460

1919 the directors sealed the counterpart of the renewed lease, and from this it appears that the original lease dated from 1898 for a term of twenty-one years.

In addition to outdoor storage of heavy track and paving materials the yard had a range of buildings containing comprehensive stocks of spare parts for rolling stock, overhead equipment and materials for the paintshop, as well as large quantities of miscellaneous consumable items. These required transport to the various depots, and in addition to the electric box van acquired in 1903, a Foden steam wagon and a Leyland motor lorry were bought in 1910 and 1911 for this purpose. Later, in 1913, a larger bogie-fitted stores van was brought into service. Two motor lorries were bought in 1922 and on 27 October 1922 the provision of a 500-gallon petrol storage tank and pump for the depot was authorised. On 12 February 1923 authorisation was given to expend £240 on improvements to be made to the depot offices, and £648 for a motor tower wagon shed and a mess room.

The company's lease of the premises was transferred to the London Passenger Transport Board on 1 July 1933. At dates subsequent to the cessation of tramway operation by the LPTB on 13 December 1936 the area surrounding the depot was extensively redeveloped, and the Great Western Railway Brentford Dock branch line removed.

Proposed Depot Sites for the Surrey Lines

The LUT made two attempts, in 1907 and 1909, to obtain running powers over the London County Council lines through Tooting and Wandsworth to central London. Neither was successful but Clifton Robinson told the directors that he was confident the applications would bear fruit. A depot was required closer to the Wimbledon and Tooting areas to avoid extensive dead mileage already being worked to and from Fulwell.

The company's Act of 1906 authorised the purchase of a large plot of land on the south-east side of High Street, Colliers Wood about 80 yards north of Christchurch Road. The 1907 LUT Bill was accompanied by a map covering the whole LUT system on which was marked the various depots and works of the company, and at the point in High Street, Colliers Wood mentioned in the 1906 Act the map is marked "TOOTING DEPOT". This site was at the time a large open space approached by a narrow gap between some properties to the south of Cavendish Road. There was clearly an intention to establish a depot on this site and the printed map attached to the 1907 Bill is evidence of this. The reference to Tooting Depot is not repeated on the map attached to the 1908 Bill and the company did not exercise their powers to buy the site. The LUT did not secure the powers for joint running with the LCC sought in the 1907 Bill and the 1909 Bill also failed.

A further attempt was made to obtain a suitable site in the Wimbledon area. On 7 May 1907 Clifton Robinson submitted plans to the directors for a depot on a site in Plough Lane on the Summerstown branch, to hold 25 cars. The price asked for the one-acre site was £950 and further adjoining land could, if required, be obtained at the same price, to accommodate a total of 100 cars. The directors authorised Robinson to conclude the purchase of a suitable site "within the price named". On 26 June he had to tell his colleagues that negotiations had failed "owing to exorbitant demands having been made". He said that he had found another site in West Barnes Lane, Raynes Park owned by the Metropolitan Water Board. The MWB had offered him a 99 year lease at an annual ground rent of £110. Negotiations on these terms commenced but difficulties over drainage arose. Discussions were deferred and there is no record of the outcome of any further negotiations.

The subject of a depot in Surrey next arose in October 1909, when tentative

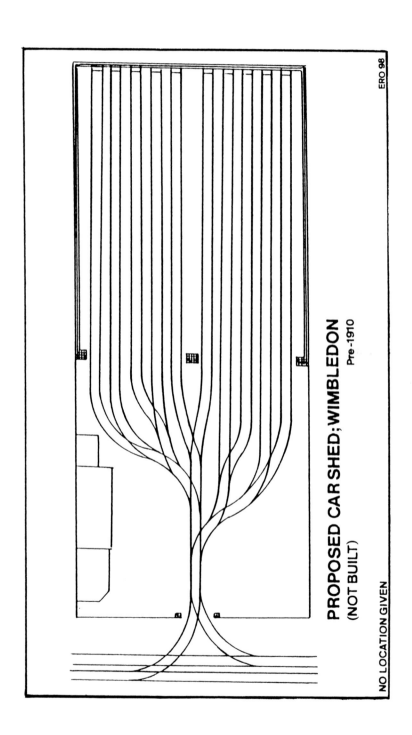

PROPOSED CAR SHED; WIMBLEDON

Pre-1910

(NOT BUILT)

NO LOCATION GIVEN

ERO 98

462

estimates were submitted for provision of a depot on an unidentified site in Wimbledon which may have been the earlier Plough Lane site or another in the same thoroughfare, where there was then much vacant land. Robinson estimated that provision of the depot would save 105,485 "dead" miles in a year at 4.68d per car mile, equal to £2,061 per annum. The annual cost of operating the depot, £535, covered the cost of wages, lighting, telephones and other items. The cost of the land was estimated at £1,000 and construction work at £7,500. Rates, taxes and insurance were estimated at £717 per annum and total costs at £1,252, offering a net annual saving of £809.

On 4 December 1909 Robinson presented a more detailed estimate of the costs of the proposed depot. The shed was expected to cost £16,476 and the mess-room, offices, tower wagon shed, sand drier and lavatories complete with water, drainage and lighting at £5,341 plus 5% for contingencies at £1,091, and the land at £1,500. A plan accompanying these papers shows a ten-track car shed to accommodate forty cars but gives no indication of the whereabouts of the proposed site. The directors gave these figures close consideration, but such was the financial position of the company that, despite the valuable savings offered by the scheme they had to decline, with regret, to implement it. This was Clifton Robinson's last major proposal as managing director and engineer of the LUT.

Richmond Depot

Among the assets acquired by the LUT with the West Metropolitan Tramways undertaking in 1894 was the lease of a small depot for six cars and 20 horses at the southern end of Kew Road, Richmond (No.125) to operate the isolated Kew Bridge-Richmond horse tramway. The freehold of this cramped site was bought c i behalf of the LUT by August Krauss on 12 December 1895 and an adjacent property was acquired by a deed dated 1 April 1898. The extended premises had a capacity of at least ten cars and 30-35 horses. Refurbishment of the old WMT premises was carried out by Krauss under the terms of his 1894 and 1895 agreements with the company. Premises in Kew Foot Road, Richmond were also occupied by the company during the horse tram era, possibly as stabling.

The Kew Road tramway, never electrified, was always isolated from the rest of the LUT system, and its horse cars were taken across Kew Bridge on their flanges to meet the tracks on the north side of the river and thence to Chiswick Works for overhaul. Following the abandonment of the Kew Road line in 1912 the depot was sold to J.R.Wright on 21 July 1915, for an undisclosed sum. The property was used subsequently as a fire station and survives to the present day in a much altered form.

The Shepherds Bush Depots

The first tramway depot on Uxbridge Road was a small establishment on the south side of the road between the Hammersmith & City branch of the Metropolitan Railway and The Lawn at Shepherds Bush Green. The site was then occupied by a number of cottages, stabling and a contractor's yard belonging to W.H.Wallington, who owned the depot of the Harrow Road & Paddington Tramways Company at Trenmar Gardens, Kensal Green. Immediately east of the approach road to Shepherds Bush station was the site of the small depot which housed the two original cars of the Southall, Ealing & Shepherds Bush Tram Railway Company from 1874. At that time the railway station was half-way along the approach road which has since become Shepherds Bush Market. Nothing is known about the depot building, which may have been no more than stabling and a small office, with the two SESB cars standing outside.

After the collapse of the SESB company, the premises were taken over by their successors, the West Metropolitan Tramways Company and the depot was numbered 9 Uxbridge Road (No.9 is now on the west side of the railway). The freeholders of the land were the Ecclesiastical Commissioners and the Homage

Jury of the Manor of Fulham, who presented part of the property to the Library Commissioners, on which the present Shepherds Bush Library at No.7 Uxbridge Road was built at the expense of J.Passmore Edwards and opened by Lord Rosebery on 25 June 1896.

The second Shepherds Bush depot, at No.43A Goldhawk Road, was at the rear of buildings in that road and had capacity for 61 horses and 7 trams, the latter being stored in the yard. It was leased to the WMT by W.J.Apperley on a monthly tenancy at a rental of £41.0.4d, from Autumn 1892. The lease originally granted to the WMT was assigned to the LUT in 1894. The limited space available did not permit extension and the depot did not figure in the improvement scheme agreed between August Krauss and the LUT on 21 August 1894. The LUT retained the Goldhawk Road premises for storage and other purposes until the tenancy was given up in September 1902. The property later served for many years as a wholesale dairy.

Head and Registered Offices

Company head office was initially at 88 (later renumbered 74) High Road, Chiswick, but at the beginning of 1913 was transferred to the chief offices of the Metropolitan Electric Tramways at Manor House, Seven Sisters Road, Finsbury Park as a result of the merger of the tramway companies in the London & Suburban Traction Company.

When the company was founded in 1894, the registered office was at 19 Clare Street, Bristol. By 19 January 1895 it had been transferred to Clare Street House, 28 Clare Street, the headquarters of the Bristol Tramways & Carriage Company. It was again transferred to the head office of the LUT at Chiswick Depot, 88 High Road on 18 November 1897 and from there to 16 Great George Street, Westminster on 30 October 1903. On 9 March 1910, following the management changes described in another chapter, the registered office was moved to Electric Railway House, Broadway, Westminster, S.W.1, the headquarters of the Underground Electric Railways Company of London Ltd. Following the grouping of the company-owned tramways in the London & Suburban Traction Company at the end of 1912 the registered office was transferred to the British Electrical Federation offices at 1 Kingsway, W.C., returning to Electric Railway House in May 1915 following further management changes. The office remained at this address, later defined as 55 Broadway, throughout the rest of the company's existence.

Managing Director's Office & Legal Department

The managing director's office was transferred from 88 High Road, Chiswick to 16 Great George Street, Westminster with the registered office on 30 October 1903, together with the company's legal department which was headed by a partner of the Bristol firm of solicitors, Stanley, Wasbrough, Doggett & Baker. These departments were transferred, at an uncertain date, to the Hamburg-Amerika Building at 15 Cockspur Street, Charing Cross. They were brought together at Electric Railway House, Broadway, Westminster as a result of management changes following the resignation of Clifton Robinson in January 1910.

Ealing Office

A 1902 LUT press advertisement quoted the company's addresses as 88 High Road, Chiswick, 125 Kew Road, Richmond and The Mall, Uxbridge Road, Ealing. The Ealing address does not appear after 1902 and was possibly an enquiry office temporarily established in rented shop premises.

Traffic Offices

The traffic office for the whole of the LUT system was originally at Chiswick Depot. On 15 October 1913 the directors took a number of decisions in anticipation of the sale of the Hammersmith lines to the London County Council. Among them was one to transfer the traffic office from Chiswick to Acton Depot. The Hammersmith sale was deferred for several years but the decision to move the office to Acton held good, and by the time the Hammersmith lines were about to be transferred to the LCC, it was decided on 31 March 1922, to establish a local traffic office for the Surrey lines. Premises at 3 London Road, Kingston were taken on a seven years' lease at £127.10s. per annum. The traffic manager's office of the LUT and MET was established at the MET Manor House offices on the formation of the London & Suburban Traction Company in 1912.

Kingston Tower Wagon Shed

The complicated overhead layout in the centre of Kingston necessitated repair facilities closer to the town than Fulwell Depot. The company obtained a site in London Road close to the traffic office at No.3, and on 7 January 1932 the LUT directors approved expenditure of £495 for preparation of the site, erection of the building and a mess-room and paving of the roadway to the shed. By this time the lines in Kingston had been converted to trolleybus operation and doubtless the greater liability of a trolleybus to dewirement had made this necessary.

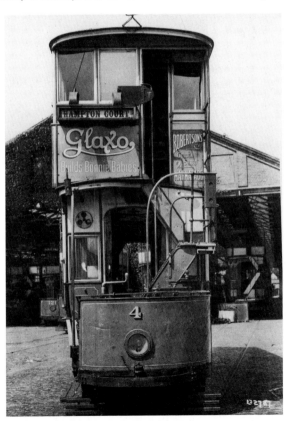

No.4 of Type Y seen at Fulwell Depot in July 1924. Cars in the background include Type X 121, 122 and 142, sold to the LCC in 1922, re-purchased by the LUT and ultimately scrapped at the depot.

(Courtesy London Transport Museum U2787)

CHAPTER TWENTY-SIX

FARES & TICKETS

Of the three electric tramway companies operating in London, the LUT had the lowest fares, averaging ½d per mile (minimum payable 1d) until 1918. These were, in part, inherited from the West Metropolitan horse tramways and competing horse bus companies, but largely came about as a result of demands by the various local authorities who, in return for their assent to the company's extension and electrification proposals, insisted upon exceptionally low fares for the lines in their areas.

In 1895, a minimum fare of 1d was charged on the horse trams of the company, which applied to the journeys between Shepherds Bush-Acton, Shepherds Bush-Young's Corner and Kew-Richmond. The longer Hammersmith-Kew Bridge route had a through fare of 3d for the three mile journey, with three overlapping 1d stages, Hammersmith-Chiswick "Pack Horse & Talbot", Young's Corner-Gunnersbury Station, and Turnham Green-Kew Bridge. In anticipation of electrification, the first and third penny stages were lengthened, becoming Hammersmith-Turnham Green and Chiswick-Kew Bridge.

During the period of horse car operation, fares on the Hammersmith-Kew Bridge route fluctuated, at one point reducing to 2d for the through fare. One 2d ticket has the first stage for the through fare and two further bookings: Young's Corner-Kew Bridge and "Pack Horse & Talbot"-Kew Bridge. The latter were probably used on Sundays when higher fares (3d through fare) prevailed. These the company had promised (in August 1895) would be withdrawn when permission for electrification was obtained. As this was not forthcoming until 1899 the higher Sunday fares remained.

The LUT used the "bell punch" system of accounting, the punches and tickets being obtained initially from T.J.Whiting & Sons, then Foster of Northampton, and finally, from c.1897 and for the rest of the company's existence, from the Bell Punch Company whose tickets, from the beginning of their contract with the LUT were colour-coded according to route and value. However, with the extensions in Twickenham and beyond the ticket colours were standardised, presumably as it was realised separate colour ranges for each route would be too complex to handle.

Ticket layout, during the horse car period and during electrification of the horse lines and the extensions to Hounslow and Uxbridge, was of a fully geographical format, with the stages laid out vertically, except on the longer routes, where the 1d's and in some cases the 2d's had the stages set horizontally, but still in fully geographical format. When more intermediate bookings were added the 1d's came out in "menu" style, with each stage point listed singly, down the centre of the ticket, to avoid the use of longer tickets.

Overlapping stages were applied to the Hounslow route when it opened, the new stages being Brentford (Half Acre), Busch Corner, Isleworth (Pears' Fountain) and Hounslow. The fares from Hammersmith or Shepherds Bush were 2d to Brentford, 3d to Pears' Fountain and 4d to "anywhere in Hounslow", including Hounslow Heath (shown on the tickets also as "Hounslow Terminus" or "Hounslow Barracks"), when this extension opened in 1902.

The non-overlapping stages south of Isleworth could penalise short distance riders crossing a stage boundary, and this applied with even greater force to the Uxbridge route, on which the original stages from Shepherds Bush or Hammersmith were Acton (Birch Grove), Ealing (Eccleston Road), Hanwell Broadway, Southall Town Hall, Hayes Post Office and Uxbridge, with no overlaps. There was a bargain fare of 5d for the full journey of 12 miles, but the short distance rider would pay 2d if he crossed a stage boundary. This was not rectified until 1910.

In Surrey, the local authorities had insisted that the same generous scale as on the company's 1901 lines be applied in their areas. Local fares in Kingston were 1d to or from Teddington, Hampton Court, Surbiton, Malden, Kingston Hill, Richmond Park Gates and Ham Boundary and 2d to Dittons or Tolworth. On the nine-mile route from the LCC boundary at Tooting (Longley Road) the fares were 1d to Wimbledon Station, 2d to Malden (Norbiton Park Hotel, later re-named "The Fountain"), 3d to Kingston and 4d to Hampton Court. There was a local fare of 1d on the Summerstown line. Route codes were applied to the tickets some time between September 1902 and April 1903 ('ST': Shepherds Bush-Twickenham, King St., operated only between between these dates until the route was extended to Hampton Court). These codes were discontinued when the fares structure was altered in 1910, although similar codes re-appeared when the ticket layout changed again in 1915.

The 1902/3 codes used were as follows:-

HHC	Hammersmith - Hampton Court
HH	Hammersmith - Hounslow
HK	Hammersmith - Kew Bridge
RHC	Richmond Bridge - Hampton Court
RK	Richmond - Kew
RT	Richmond Bridge - Twickenham
SHC	Shepherds Bush - Hampton Court
SH	Shepherds Bush - Hounslow
SK	Shepherds Bush - Kew Bridge
ST	Shepherds Bush - Twickenham
SS	Shepherds Bush - Southall

Ticket colours during this period were:-

1d white, 2d blue, 3d pink 4d green, 5d orange and 6d brown.

When the Kingston local routes opened the RHC sets were discontinued, and new sets were produced for Richmond Bridge-Hampton Court-Windows Bridge with a large 'K' overprint.

Also, as the extension to Tooting progressed, tickets overprinted "NM" (referring to New Malden) and carrying stages between Raynes Park and Hampton Court were produced; to be followed by ones for Wimbledon Station-Hampton Court without the 'NM' overprint. Finally 'THC' tickets were produced for the completed route. A range of menu-style tickets was also produced for Richmond Bridge-Tooting, but these were probably very short-lived, if used at all. Values seen only have punch holes for the section Richmond Bridge-Kingston.

The first 6d tickets to appear were for the through fares on the Hampton Court routes from Hammersmith or Shepherds Bush. The Richmond Bridge route to Hampton Court had a 4d fare. There was an "introductory offer" at Easter 1903 of one shilling round trip tickets from Shepherds Bush or Hammersmith to Hampton Court, and it appears that the cars went only one way round via Hampton Hill at first, but one of these has yet to be seen. However, a 5d from the Shepherds Bush/Hammersmith-Hampton Court routes has been seen, and besides having the two normal stages displayed, it has an additional stage at its foot for the through fare from Shepherds Bush/Hammersmith-Hampton Court. It is surmised that this stage was used when cars were loaded only with passengers travelling the whole distance.

No provision was made in the early years for reduced fares for children. The early tariffs advertised in the local press stated that all children occupying seats would be charged the adult fare, but by 1906 this was re-defined as full fare for children of five years or over. Small dogs were admitted to the upper decks for payment of the adult fare, while luggage was charged at 2d per package of up to 28lb. From an unknown date, parcels of newspapers were conveyed to outlying areas at a charge of one penny a parcel, payment being recorded by the use of perforated adhesive stamps. These were engraved with the company title and displayed the legend "PREPAID. NEWSPAPER PARCEL 1d." together with a serial number. No other details of this service are available.

Concession fares for workmen were introduced on the horse tramways in May 1900. On the electric lines these took the form of very cheap single fares in the early mornings only, the rate being one penny for any journey on the sections: Shepherds Bush-Hounslow, Hammersmith-Hounslow, Shepherds Bush-Hanwell, Southall-Uxbridge, Hammersmith-Twickenham, Twickenham-Hampton Court, Twickenham-Kingston and Kingston-Tooting. On the first routes to open they were issued only before about 6.30a.m., but this was later extended to 7a.m. Standard 1d tickets with a diagonal red or green "Workman's Ticket" overprint were issued. The passenger paid the ordinary fare for the return journey.

At the annual general meeting of the company held early in 1903, the chairman announced that they intended to introduce through tickets between the LUT trams and the District Railway at Hammersmith. This had to wait until the District line was electrified, and, in the event, were not introduced until 15 December 1905, the opening date of the Piccadilly tube railway. These were issued in conjunction with both the Piccadilly and District railways, and will be described in a later section of this chapter.

The 1910 to 1917 Period

The new management of 1910 adopted a more equitable fare stage arrangement to encourage short distance riding, while leaving the long-distance fares unchanged. From May 1910 the original 1d stages were divided into three approximately equal sections with a scale giving three of these for 1d, four for 1½d, six for 2d,, seven for 2½d, nine for 3d, ten for 3½d, twelve for 4d, thirteen for 4½d, fifteen for 5d, sixteen for 5½d and eighteen for 6d. The company issued a folding Map and Guide, produced by Johnson, Riddle & Co., publicising the changes and listing all the fare stages, which was the forerunner of similar guides issued by the LST companies from 1914.

With the introduction of odd ½d fares, the tickets for the Hampton Court (via Hampton Hill) routes and the Hounslow routes were initially printed in "menu style" for all values. The conditions on the 1d to 3½d values read: "This ticket must be punched in the Section to which the passenger is entitled to travel". The 4d to 6d values did not have this condition, but instead, at the foot of the tickets was printed: "Passengers must not break their journey", wording that had been incorporated in conditions on earlier examples. The 1910 tickets of the other routes were produced in "fareboard" format, with stages from one terminus printed in route order down the left-hand column and stages to the other terminus down the right-hand column, the "stagger" between the two columns varying according to the number of stages the passenger was permitted to travel for the fare paid. Thus the passenger's journey was fully shown, reading either from left to right or right to left, depending upon the direction of travel.

The conditions of issue were printed vertically in the centre column. Initially, these read: "To be punched opposite the Section...". Subsequently all routes had this style of fareboard ticket, at first with conditions reading: "...punched in the section to which the passenger is entitled to travel..." and finally reading: "...punched in the section indicating the point to which...".

The Kew-Richmond horse tramway was divided into three sections, the intermediate ones being at Victoria Gate and Lion Gate, although these did not appear on the tickets. In any event, as the through fare was 1d, there was no need to publicise these.

To ensure that passengers were not penalised when having to change cars, one-penny transfer tickets were introduced to and from Ham Boundary, together with a series of values up to 4d to and from the Summerstown route and the Tooting-Hampton Court line. There were also 1d and 1½d transfers to cover journeys between Hampton Hill and points in Teddington, changing cars at Stanley Road Junction. There may have been others. Geographical style exchange tickets were issued on the second car, the original ticket being retained by the conductor.

Ticket colours at this time were 1d white, 1½d white/purple stripes (edges), 2d stone, 2½d stone/brown stripes, 3d pink, 3½d red/yellow stripes, 4d green/pink stripes, 5d orange, 5½d orange/blue stripes and 6d blue.

Following the example of the MET (itself influenced by the LCC), reduced fares for children of between five and fifteen years of age at half the adult fare were introduced on the LUT in November 1914 at off-peak times. The minimum child fare of ½d, for which a salmon-coloured ticket was issued, covered the same distance as for the 1d adult (direct or transfer). The special fares were withdrawn as from 1 January 1919, being reinstated later that year, on 1 July, but with a minimum fare of 1d and an even pence structure above that. There were no "odd halfpenny" fares.

After the LGOC had joined the Underground Group late in 1912, tram-to-bus transfers were issued to Windsor from Hounslow, and between Richmnond (The Quadrant), Fulwell, Teddington and Kingston, changing to or from tram 69 at Richmond Bridge terminus. All these transfers became war casualties, but those from Richmond were reinstated (by tram from Twickenham) on the closure of the Richmond Bridge tramway in 1924.

With the formation of the "combine" (T-O-T: Train-Omnibus-Tram), LUT fares and tickets soon came under the control of the group's Traffic and Advertising Departments. Centralised purchasing from the 55 Broadway Office meant that from 1915, LUT tickets took on a resemblance to those of the LGOC, and referred to as "the fareboard system". The fare stages were arranged in pairs down the ticket, separated by a vertical black line and LGOC-style value overprint in red or green, with the route name (e.g. "Uxbridge", "Hounslow", etc.) displayed at the top. Each ticket would be punched at the fare stage boarded, which was opposite the one to which the passenger could travel for the fare paid. When the war affected paper supplies certain of these "route-tickets" had to be combined in a single issue and some non-standard colours had to be used.

Between 1917 and 1922

The company's fares being fixed at very low levels by statute from the start of electric operation in 1901, could not be altered without the sanction of Parliament. By 1917, wartime conditions had brought heavily increased costs and on 12 June the directors were told that fare increases were urgently required. The managing director, James Devonshire, had met Sir William Marwood of the Board of Trade, together with representatives of the Ministry of Munitions, in an attempt to obtain some relaxation of the statutory fares restrictions. Marwood suggested that if the Ministry of Munitions made representations to the BoT, that body might consider providing relief from existing restrictions through the wartime Defence of the Realm Act. These negotiations came to nothing and the Board of Trade advised the company to ask Parliament to authorise fare increases.

A Bill for the 1918 Session was being prepared at this time and a clause was inserted seeking fare increases. The resulting 1918 Act, when passed provided for the division of the routes into half-mile stages and allowed for ordinary fares to be charged at the rate of 1d per mile (two stages) or part thereof, and for workmen up to 3 miles for 1d (six stages), 6-8 stages for 1½d, 9-12 stages for 2d, 13-14 stages for 2½d, and all in excess of 14 stages for 3d. The workmen's tickets were to be singles, issued up to 8a.m. and after 5p.m., and from mid-day to 2p.m. on Saturdays. There were to be no halfpenny fares. The Act also empowered the Board of Trade to increase (or reduce) fares or to vary stages. No two stages forming a section were to aggregate less than half a mile. These provisions were, however, of little use to the company in its existing predicament, as they were not due to take effect until six months after the end of the war which, officially, did not take place until 21 August 1921.

By the end of 1918 the company was in danger of being forced to cease operations and suspend services. Many other undertakings with statutory fixed charges were in similar difficulties. To alleviate this position emergency powers were granted in the Statutory Undertakings (Temporary Increase of Charges) Act, also of 1918, which empowered the Board of Trade to modify such undertakings' charges at their discretion. The company obtained an Order under this Act on 16 December 1918 which went into effect on 1 January 1919, allowing it to charge 1d per mile or part thereof, routes to be divided into half-mile stages, and with workmen's fares at three miles for a penny. This effectively allowed the company to take immediate advantage of the fares provisions in its 1918 Act.

From 1 January 1919 also, the general conditions of issue were to be the same on all three tramway companies to facilitate joint publicity. Workmen's fares were now available on cars scheduled to complete their journeys before 8a.m.; dogs were carried on the upper deck (at the discretion of the conductor) free of charge, while luggage was only charged for if it had to be carried on the front platform of a car.

At the February 1919 directors' meeting the accountant stressed the necessity for a further fares increase and it was agreed that the chairman and managing director should once again see Sir William Marwood at the Board of Trade to impress upon him the urgent need for this. The parties met on 1 March and after hearing the company's case, the outcome was confirmation of the earlier ordinary fare of 1d per mile, but with a reduction of the mileage allowed for the workmen's one penny fare from three to two miles, to be effective from 13 April

Costs continued to increase through 1919 and into 1920, by which time the newly-created Ministry of Transport had taken over the responsibilities for tramways from the Board of Trade on 1 January 1920. In November 1919 the company had taken the radical step of submitting a Bill for the 1920 Session which sought, *inter alia*, powers to amend its 1918 Act which allowed one penny a mile for ordinary passengers and three miles for 1d for workmen, to become effective from six months after the (official) end of the war. The new Bill sought a minimum fare of 2d a mile, the complete abolition of workmen's fares and the deletion of the restriction upon implementation of the fares provisions of the LUT 1918 Act.

These proposals raised a storm of protest from local authorities, trades unions and other interested parties, resulting in the withdrawal of the Bill. The Minister of Transport, reporting to Parliament upon the Bill in July 1920, commented that "the fixing of any new permanent fare scales might best be postponed pending settlement of future general transport arrangements for London".

Meanwhile, the tramway industry had pressed for further legislation covering the special circumstances of fares regulation, which resulted in the passing of the Tramways (Temporary Increase of Charges) Act on 20 April 1920. This Act empowered the Minister of Transport to make Orders varying fares after taking the advice of an advisory committee which in turn could, at its discretion, hold an inquiry into any application. The Minister, in an urgent case, had the power to make an Interim Order of up to a 100% increase on existing statutory fares to remain in force for not more than six months and the matter to be referred to a Tramways Charges Advisory Committee.

Under this legislation the LUT was granted an Interim Order on 20 May 1920, allowing the original statutory ordinary fares to be increased by 100%, but existing fares to be increased by only 50% and workmen's fares to remain unchanged. The new rates, introduced on 1 June, allowed one mile (two stages) for 1½d, up to 5½ miles (11 stages) for 6d and 1d per mile thereafter.

In July 1920 the company applied for an Order confirming these fares with some variations. This was referred to the Advisory Committee, who held an inquiry into it on 5 and 11 October. This application was also opposed by almost all local authorities, trades unions and many other bodies, such as the Middle Class Union and various local trade associations. Some of the local authorities demanded the introduction of "2d All-The-Way" fares at certain times as introduced on the London County Council system, which was successfully opposed by the company.

The application, which succeeded, also asked for continuation of the ordinary fares authorised in the May 1920 Interim Order, with workmen's fares remaining at 2d return minimum on all cars completing their journeys before 8a.m. Child fares were confirmed at 1d for the 1½d and 2d stages; 3d for 5d and 6d stages and so on through the range.

Recognising that these sharp increases might inhibit pleasure riding, the Company introduced cheap returns on the Tooting-Hampton Court route in December 1920 at the rate of 9d, 1s and 1s.3d for single journeys of 6d, 8d and 9d, and extended these to the Teddington route in 1921, but they were withdrawn in 1922. They also found that the 1½d minimum adult fare was driving short-distance traffic away, for a 1d fare for one half-mile stage was introduced by the three LST companies on 1 December 1921. The previous range of transfers was continued, but whereas the 1919 numerical tickets showed these by a code based on the initials of the destination, the 1920 and later issues used the initials A, B, C and D.

Although the longest route (Uxbridge) had 24 stages, the new set of numerical tickets, introduced with the Interim Order of 20 May 1920, had stage numbers from 1 to 30, possibly so that each number occurred once only on each depot's routes. This 1920 numerical set had a short life, being replaced by separate numerical-stage tickets for each depot, with 24 or 26 stages and a depot code; A for Acton; C for Chiswick; F for Fulwell; HL for Hanwell; HW for Hounslow. Hillingdon (Hayes) depot was already closed (to be eventually leased away). Ticket colours were the same as those for the 1919 set, but the conditions of issue, previously printed on the front, were transferred to the reverse, displacing the advertisements.

The December 1920 increase brought workmen's fares into line with those of the MET. Workmen's single tickets disappeared, and return tickets were introduced at single fare for the return journey (minimum 2d), being sold on cars scheduled to complete their journeys by 8a.m. The return half could be used at any time of the day, being surrendered against the issue of a workmen's exchange ticket. The return tickets were in the same colours as adult singles, but bore a red "X" overprint, while the exchange tickets were of salmon colour. During the 1½d minimum fare period the ticket colour was white, the 1d child ticket being sage green, but this was changed in 1921 to adult and child 1d tickets being white and 1½d white with pink side stripes.

At the commencement of the post-war fare increases the company changed from using geographical style to numerical stage tickets. This reduced production costs by allowing the use of a standard printing block, and would also reduce the time taken to implement changes. To help the staff, the stage numbers were printed on fare tables displayed inside the cars, and were also shown on circular white metal plates fixed to traction poles at the fare stage points. These remained a feature of the LUT (and the other two LST tramway companies), and were also continued in the Kingston area in 1931 with the conversion to trolleybus working, where the stage numbers were incorporated in the design of the stop signs.

Two sets of numerical tickets were initially produced, one for the Uxbridge route with stage numbers from 1 to 24, and one for the other routes with stage numbers from 1 to 20, plus some code letters at the foot to indicate transfers. The fare values, from 1d to 10d, were shown by overprints. A.W.McCall recorded the colours as being 1d white, 2d buff, 3d pink, 4d green, 5d flame red, 6d blue, 7d brown, 8d lilac, 9d yellow and 10d grey.

From 2 May 1922 the LCC took over operation of the Tooting-Wimbledon section with their services 2 and 4 from central London. The Council charged 5d for the Embankment-Wimbledon journey and 2d for Tooting Broadway-Wimbledon (four stages) to which end they abolished their own stage point at Longley Road. The LUT Wimbledon-Hampton Court fare remained at 6d, but without a return facility. Wimbledon was included in the 2d All The Way cheap mid-day fare available on LCC cars on Monday to Friday, but this did not apply to the Summerstown branch, which was still worked by the LUT with a single car at fares of 1d and 1½d.

From 1923 to 1933

The 1920 Order was due to expire on 14 February 1923, but the company obtained a Temporary Increase of Charges Order which would have enabled it to keep its fares unchanged until 31 March 1924. However, the LGOC, in response to independent bus competition made a general fares reduction on 1 January 1923, giving two stages for each penny and, under the terns of the pooling agreement, the three tramway companies had to follow suit. The result was a new and simpler fare scale, which lasted for the rest of the LUT's separate existence. Two stages were now allowed for 1d, four for 2d, six for 3d and two for each further penny up to a maximum of 24 stages for one shilling. One 1½d fare survived, on the Haydon's Road route with its three stages. Only three values of workmen's return tickets were now issued, at 2d, 4d and 6d, plus the exchange ticket.

When the first LUT one-man car entered service between Richmond Park Gates and Tolworth in 1922 it was fitted with American "Automaticket" ticket-issuing machines of the type then coming into use at central London tube stations and in common use in cinema box-offices. The pre-printed coloured strip tickets were folded zig-zag fashion in a magazine below the issuing slot. Five sets of buttons enabled the motorman to issue tickets singly or in twos, threes, fours or fives. Tickets were delivered to the passengers from a slot in the front of the machine.

The "Automaticket" machines were short-lived and were replaced by another American-made machine manufactured and marketed as the "Shanklin Rapid Transfer System" by the Shanklin Equipment Company, of Springfield, Massachusetts. This machine issued paper tickets 7¾in. long by 2in. wide, with provision for displaying and recording day, month, time of issue and fare category, but without geographical stages. Unlike its predecessor, the "Shanklin" machine was easily portable and only one per car was required, the motorman detaching it from a fixed pedestal and transferring it to the other end of the car when reversing.

When LCC cars began to run through to Hampton Court at weekends, the fares collected were divided according to the mileage worked, the Council deducting its working costs before paying the balance over to the company. A new set of long geographical tickets was produced by the LCC for use on Clapham Depot routes 2-4, 6, 8 and 10, showing on the reverse all stages from Wimbledon Station to Hampton Court, for use "When Working to Hampton Court". The LCC also created a set of purely theoretical stage numbers extending its own (1-17) Embankment-Wimbledon series from Wimbledon Station (17) to Hampton Court (29). These bore no relationship to the LUT stage numbers, which were in ascending order eastbound up to 31 (Wimbledon Station). The LCC tickets included provision for transfers at Hampton Court to "The Karsino" and Hampton Hill (Uxbridge Road).

In 1926 the standard LUT numerical-stage tickets were redesigned to again release the backs for commercial advertising. The fare stage numbers now occupied the centre of the tickets, with numbers 1-12 or 1-13 downwards on the left and 13-24 or 14-26 upwards on the right, with the company title and conditions of issue vertically on the sides. The depots were shown as ACTON, HNLL (Hanwell), HLOW (Hounslow) and FLWL (Fulwell).

Further minor changes were made two years later. A separate Fulwell set was introduced for the Wimbledon route, with stage numbers from 8 to 31. Workmen's exchange tickets were discontinued, and workmen's returns were cancelled on the return journey, using a small canceller carried on the conductor's punch-holding strap.

The year 1928 also saw the re-introduction of a 9d return facility between Wimbledon and Hampton Court, issued on weekdays only (Saturdays on LCC cars). However, from summer 1929, cheap returns were issued every day on LUT cars on this route, at 3d, 5d, 6d, 7d and 8d, where the respective single fare was 2d, 3d, 4d, 5d or 6d. The tickets, in the same colours as single tickets, were of similar layout to the workmen's returns but worded "Cheap Return Ticket" whereas the 1928 return had carried the title "Ordinary Return Ticket". Through returns were issued at weekends on LCC routes 2 and 4, an example being Embankment-Hampton Court, 1s.4d. At the same time, cheap returns were introduced on route 67, at 8d, 9d, 10d, 11d and 1s where the respective single fare was 6d, 7d, 8d, 9d or 10d, but were not issued on public holidays or before 10a.m. on weekdays.

Other changes in 1928 were a delayed result of the purchase by the LCC of the LUT lines in the Hammersmith area. From 1 May the Shilling All-Day and 2d adult/1d child Cheap Mid-Day fares of the LCC became available on service 26 between Hammersmith and Young's Corner, while the Shilling All-Day ticket was honoured on LUT cars from Hammersmith and Shepherds Bush to Young's Corner and Askew Arms. When LCC/LUT joint working began on 28 November 1928 on service 89, the whole range of LCC concession fares became available on both operators' cars, and LUT conductors carried stocks of those tickets for which there was no LUT equivalent, these being Shilling All-Day; 5d adult; 2d child; 2d adult/1d child Cheap Mid-Day; 5d, 6d and 8d ordinary return and 6d workmen's return. Finally the LCC concessions were extended to the Summerstown route when the Council took over its working on 16 April 1931.

From 1930 cheap return tickets were issued at the same hours on route 7, at 1s, 1s.3d and 1s.6d where the respective single fare was 7d or 8d, 9d or 10d and 11d or 1s. McCall quotes the ticket colours as 1s white with dark blue bars, 1s.3d white with red bars, 1s.6d white with green bars. The Uxbridge route must by now have needed more tickets than the conductors' racks would hold, for it appears that the 11d single (dark red) and 1s single (magenta) were carried only on Sundays and holidays, when there were no workmen's fares. At other times the conductors possibly issued two tickets of lower value to make up the total fare.

A revision of stages took place in January 1930 between Kingston and Malden, requiring the addition of stage number 32 to Fulwell Depot tickets. The Kingston set was again revised when trolleybus operation commenced in 1931, showing stage numbers 13-32 and, from 15 June, an increased range of transfers to eight, resulting probably from changes in service patterns, but reverting to four after 2 September. The cheap return tickets of LUT service 71 continued to be available on its trolleybus successor until September 1950.

After trials by the LGOC, the LUT bought 165 Ticket Issuing Machines (known as TIMs) in October 1932 at £15 each (with 35 more later), and allocated them to the Hounslow and Fulwell services, where they replaced the Bell Punch machines (save in emergencies). The TIM tickets were printed in red on thin white paper and were originally headed "M.E.T., L.U.T. & S.M.T. Cos.". They had a long life, mostly with London Transport, and were not replaced by Gibson machines until 9 April 1953 at Hounslow (Isleworth) and 16 August 1953 at Fulwell.

Together with the issue of the Shilling All-Day ticket, other innovations made by the LCC were a 6d Child All Day ticket available on Saturdays, Sundays and holidays. The first issues were between June and September 1927, and from 1 April to 30 September in subsequent years up to 1930, with an extended issue on Saturdays and Sundays during October of each year. Coupled with this was a 4d ticket for scholars up to the age of 16 years, issued as an experiment during the autumn term of 1930. The arrangement was made permanent on 16 December and continued throughout the following years, with a 6d All Day ticket on issue for children under 14 years of age when the 4d ticket was not available. The pupil ticket could be used for unlimited travel between 7.30a.m. and 5.30p.m. on Mondays to Fridays during school term-time, but in 1932 the limit was extended to 6p.m. Both values were printed on one ticket, the 6d on one side, the 4d on the other.

A 6d Evening Tourist ticket was made available as a daily issue from 26 April 1932, entitling the holder to unlimited travel on the system between 6p.m. and midnight. With all these facilities, the area of availability included the lines in Hammersmith and Wimbledon previously owned by the LUT and on cars of both undertakings, as well as in East and West Ham, Leyton and Walthamstow. From 1 June 1932 it was extended to include the Croydon tramways area.

Following the formation of the LPTB, all were retained for a time, although changes were subsequently made, particularly to the 6d Evening ticket, which was withdrawn as from 8 October 1933, but reinstated at a later date.

Through Bookings with the Underground Railways

From the opening date of the Piccadilly "tube" on 15 December 1906, through bookings were available between LUT trams and the Piccadilly and District Railways via Hammersmith. At first these tickets were issued from any fare stage on the Hampton Court, Hounslow and Uxbridge routes to any station as far as Whitechapel and Finsbury Park, at the sum of the two ordinary fares, but some bookings were rarely used. From 1 July 1912 those in least demand were withdrawn, the surviving LUT points of origin being Turnham Green Church, Gunnersbury Station, Brentford (Half Acre), Hampton Court, Acton (Birch Grove), Ealing Broadway and Hanwell Broadway, passengers changing to the trains at Hammersmith or Ealing Common stations.

From 1 February 1914 bookings were instituted from Brentford and Hanwell on route 55, changing to District line train at Boston Manor, and from Acton (Birch Grove), Acton Vale and Young's Corner to stations as far as Liverpool Street on the Central London tube railway, changing at Shepherds Bush. To cater for these the Bell Punch Company produced a range of Duplex tickets. These were twice as wide and half as thick as a normal ticket, and when folded down the centre perforation would fit into a normal Bell Punch. Tickets of this type were punched twice, once each for the tram and train journey, and the counterfoil was kept by the conductor and served later to apportion the revenue. There were also Duplex exchange tickets for issue on the trams in exchange for a railway-issue card ticket for a through journey.

These facilities were withdrawn by 1918, but most were reinstated by 1922, allowing transfer from tram to train (and vice-versa) at Hammersmith, Shepherds Bush, Ealing Common, Boston Manor or Chiswick Park. The tram issues were now standard size Bell Punch tickets in the same colours as tram singles, and the railway exchange ticket issued on the trams was of a similarly-sized salmon-colour with a green stripe.

With the change to the use of Ticket Issuing Machines in 1932 at Fulwell and Hounslow depots, tickets from these were also issued for through bookings, continuing their use on the replacement trolleybus services, until the facility was finally withdrawn by London Transport on 29 September 1942.

From 1922-23, tram/railway season tickets were issued for many through journeys, passengers changing at Hammersmith, Shepherds Bush or Ealing Common. These were issued for periods of one or three months, with weekly tickets also from April 1928. These had to be purchased at the changing-station or at Oxford Circus station, and lasted well into the London Transport era.

Credits

One of the earlier published references on LUT fares and tickets which has been studied were the notes contained in an appendix contributed by the late Albert W.McCall to Geoffrey Wilson's 1971 book on the London United Tramways, now out of print. The text of these notes was later revised and condensed by Mr.McCall to be used as part of Appendices 1 and 2 of the 1981 book "London's Trams & Trolleybuses" by John R.Day, published by London Transport. Messrs.S.H.Hughes, the late W.J.Wyse and G.L.Gundry also assisted by contributing material during the period that information was being gathered for this work.

For LCC fares policy affecting the LUT, the indispensable sources are "Idealism and Competition" and "The Tramways of Wandsworth & Battersea", both by the late Charles S.Dunbar. Other sources used have included the notes of F.Merton Atkins, O.J.Morris and K.H.Koop, the LUT, UERL and L&ST minute books at the Greater London Record Office, historical material at the National Tramway Museum, the George White Papers at Bristol Record Office and the 1913, 1914 and the 1920 to 1932 issues of the L&ST Tramways Map and Guide.

Finally, the results of subsequent considerable research undertaken by the Rev.P.S.G.Lidgett, custodian of the Omnibus Society Ticket Collection, have been made available and included, and he has also kindly checked through this text,

SUBSEQUENT CHANGES TO UXBRIDGE ROAD SERVICE
(Similar arrangements applied to all other routes)

FARETABLES LUT FROM MAY 1920
Shepherds Bush-Uxbridge
Shepherds Bush
1   Bloemfontein Road
1   1   Askew Arms
1½ 1   1   Birkbeck Road
2   1½ 1   1   Gunnersbury Lane
3   2   1½ 1   1   Ealing Common Station
3   3   2   1½ 1   1   Ealing Broadway
4   3   3   2   1½ 1   1   Northfield Avenue
4   4   3   3   2   1½ 1   1   Hanwell Broadway
5   4   4   3   3   2   1½ 1   1   Asylum Gates
5   5   4   4   3   3   2   1½ 1   1   Dormers Wells Road
6   5   5   4   4   3   3   2   1½ 1   1   Southall Town Hall
6   6   5   5   4   4   3   3   2   1½ 1   1   Beresford Road
7   6   6   5   5   4   4   3   3   2   1½ 1   1   Yeading Lane
7   7   6   6   5   5   4   4   3   3   2   1½ 1   1   Adam & Eve
8   7   7   6   6   5   5   4   4   3   3   2   1½ 1   1   Hayes Post Office
8   8   7   7   6   6   5   5   4   4   3   3   2   1½ 1   1   Whiteley's Corner
9   8   8   7   7   6   6   5   5   4   4   3   3   2   1½ 1   1   Hillingdon Church
9   9   8   8   7   7   6   6   5   5   4   4   3   3   2   1½ 1   1   The Greenway
10 9   9   8   8   7   7   6   6   5   5   4   4   3   3   2   1½ 1   1   St.Andrew's Church
10 10 9   9   8   8   7   7   6   6   5   5   4   4   3   3   2   1½ 1   1   Uxbridge'

FROM INTERIM ORDER MAY 1920 (Applied Later) (Probably 6. Dec. 1920)
(Note that there were no penny fares)
Shepherds Bush-Uxbridge
Shepherds Bush
1½ Bloemfontein Road
1½ 1½ Askew Arms
2   1½ 1½ Birkbeck Road
3   2   1½ 1½ Gunnersbury Lane
3   3   2   1½ 1½ Ealing Common Station
4   3   3   2   1½ 1½ Ealing Broadway
4   4   3   3   2   1½ 1½ Northfield Avenue
5   4   4   3   3   2   1½ 1½ Hanwell Broadway
5   5   4   4   3   3   2   1½ 1½ Asylum Gates
6   5   5   4   4   3   3   2   1½ 1½ Dormers Wells Road
6   6   5   5   4   4   3   3   2   1½ 1½ Southall Town Hall
7   6   6   5   5   4   4   3   3   2   1½ 1½ Beresford Road
7   7   6   6   5   5   4   4   3   3   2   1½ 1½ Yeading Lane
8   7   7   6   6   5   5   4   4   3   3   2   1½ 1½ Adam & Eve
8   8   7   7   6   6   5   5   4   4   3   3   2   1½ 1½ Hayes Post Office
9   8   8   7   7   6   6   5   5   4   4   3   3   2   1½ 1½ Whiteley's Corner
9   9   8   8   7   7   6   6   5   5   4   4   3   3   2   1½ 1½ Hillingdon Church
10 9   9   8   8   7   7   6   6   5   5   4   4   3   3   2   1½ 1½ The Greenway
10 10 9   9   8   8   7   7   6   6   5   5   4   4   3   3   2   1½ 1½ St.Andrew's Church
10 10 10 9   9   8   8   7   7   6   6   5   5   4   4   3   3   2   1½ 1½ Uxbridge

FROM 12 DECEMBER 1920
(Note that a single stage was given for one penny!)
Shepherds Bush-Uxbridge
Shepherds Bush
 1 Bloemfontein Road
1½ 1 Askew Arms
 2 1½ 1 Birkbeck Road
 3   2 1½ 1 Gunnersbury Lane
 3   3   2 1½ 1 Ealing Common Station
 4   3   3   2 1½ 1 Ealing Broadway
 4   4   3   3   2 1½ 1 Northfield Avenue
 5   4   4   3   3   2 1½ 1 Hanwell Broadway
 5   5   4   4   3   3   2 1½ 1 Asylum Gates
 6   5   5   4   4   3   3   2 1½ 1 Dormers Wells Road
 6   6   5   5   4   4   3   3   2 1½ 1 Southall Town Hall
 7   6   6   5   5   4   4   3   3   2 1½ 1 Beresford Road
 7   7   6   6   5   5   4   4   3   3   2 1½ 1 Yeading Lane
 8   7   7   6   6   5   5   4   4   3   3   2 1½ 1 Adam & Eve
 8   8   7   7   6   6   5   5   4   4   3   3   2 1½ 1 Hayes Post Office
 9   8   8   7   7   6   6   5   5   4   4   3   3   2 1½ 1 Whiteley's Corner
 9   9   8   8   7   7   6   6   5   5   4   4   3   3   2 1½ 1 Hillingdon Church
10   9   9   8   8   7   7   6   6   5   5   4   4   3   3   2 1½ 1 The Greenway
10 10   9   9   8   8   7   7   6   6   5   5   4   4   3   3   2 1½ 1 St.Andrew's Church
10 10 10   9   9   8   8   7   7   6   6   5   5   4   4   3   3   2 1½ 1 Uxbridge

1921 AND AFTER (As the result of the Nov. 1920 Order being applied)
Shepherds Bush-Uxbridge
Shepherds Bush
 1 Bloemfontein Road
 1   1 Askew Road
 2   1   1 King's Arms
 2   2   1   1 Acton Library/Horn Lane
 3   2   2   1   1 Twyford Avenue
 3   3   2   2   1   1 Ealing Common Station/Hanger Lane
 4   3   3   2   2   1   1 Christ Church/Ealing Broadway
 4   4   3   3   2   2   1   1 St. Leonard's Road
 5   4   4   3   3   2   2   1   1 Melbourne Avenue
 5   5   4   4   3   3   2   2   1   1 Hanwell Broadway
 6   5   5   4   4   3   3   2   2   1   1 Asylum Gates
 6   6   5   5   4   4   3   3   2   2   1   1 Dormers Wells Road
 7   6   6   5   5   4   4   3   3   2   2   1   1 Trinity Road
 7   7   6   6   5   5   4   4   3   3   2   2   1   1 Southall Town Hall
 8   7   7   6   6   5   5   4   4   3   3   2   2   1   1 Hayes Brickfields
 8   8   7   7   6   6   5   5   4   4   3   3   2   2   1   1 Yeading Lane
 9   8   8   7   7   6   6   5   5   4   4   3   3   2   2   1   1 Adam & Eve
 9   9   8   8   7   7   6   6   5   5   4   4   3   3   2   2   1   1 Hayes Park
10   9   9   8   8   7   7   6   6   5   5   4   4   3   3   2   2   1   1 Hayes Boundary
10 10   9   9   8   8   7   7   6   6   5   5   4   4   3   3   2   2   1   1 Heath Boys' School
11 10 10   9   9   8   8   7   7   6   6   5   5   4   4   3   3   2   2   1   1 Hillingdon Church
11 11 10 10   9   9   8   8   7   7   6   6   5   5   4   4   3   3   2   2   1   1 The Greenway
1/- 11 11 10 10   9   9   8   8   7   7   6   6   5   5   4   4   3   3   2   2   1   1 St.Andrew's Ch.
1/- 1/- 11 11 10 10   9   9   8   8   7   7   6   6   5   5   4   4   3   3   2   2   1   1 Uxbridge

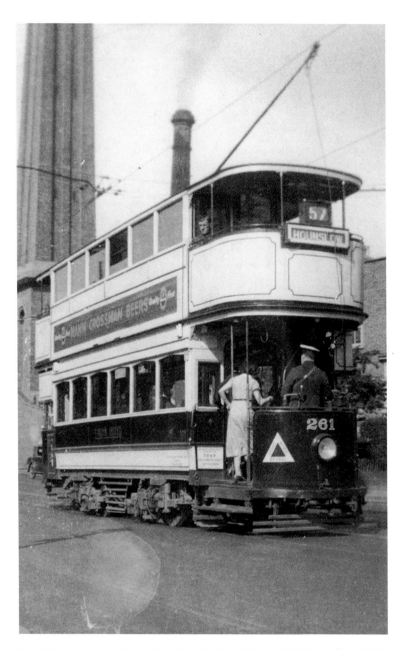

Five WT type cars created from a Type U and four Type W cars in 1928-9 were fitted with the latest electrical equipment, improved seating and lighting. They worked mainly on the the Shepherds BushHounslow route. No.261 halts for a passenger at Kew Bridge pumping station. (Photo M.J.O'Connor. Courtesy National Tramway Museum)

NEW
THROUGH
BOOKINGS

TRAM AND RAIL
VIA HAMMERSMITH

STAGE POINTS.	SLOANE SQUARE.	VICTORIA	ST. JAMES' PARK	WEST- MINSTER	CHARING CROSS	TEMPLE
	d.	d.	d.	d.	d.	d.
ASKEW ARMS	5	5	6	6	6	6
HORN LANE	6	6	7	7	7	7
HANWELL B'WAY	8	8	8	8	8	9
YOUNG'S CORNER	5	5	6	6	6	6
TURNHAM GREEN CHURCH	5	6	6	7	7	7
KEW BRIDGE	6	7	7	7	7	8
BRENTFORD STN.	8	8	8	8	8	9

FROM MARCH 1st.

1922

479

LONDON UNITED TRAMWAYS

TO AND FROM

CHISWICK SPORTS TO-DAY

ALIGHT AT

TURNHAM GREEN CHURCH

TRAMWAYS

1922

'Postage Stamp' receipt

Early 'Route Coded' tickets

c1902-3

481

Early 'Route Coded' tickets

c1902-3

482

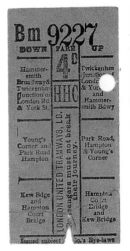

Early 'Route Coded' tickets

c1902-3

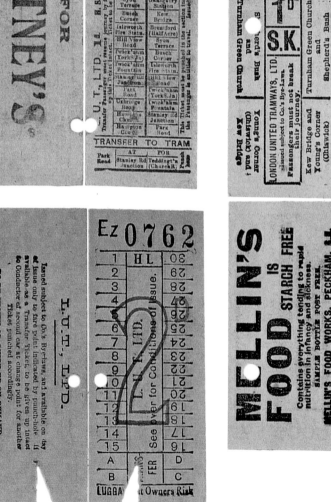

Advertising on tickets

Exchange &
Through tickets

'Shanklin' ticket (right)

1915
'Duplex' type
Through ticket

A 04350
'Automaticket'

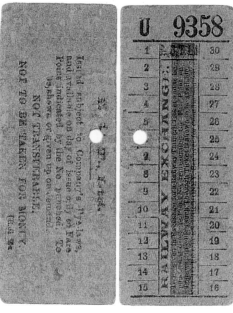

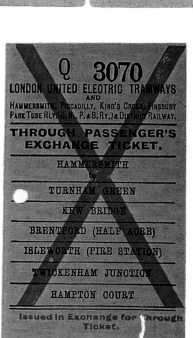

Exchange
Through tickets

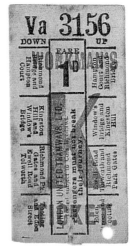

**Workman
Single & Return
Tickets**

488

**Cheap Fare
Exchange**

**Workman
Return
Tickets**

489

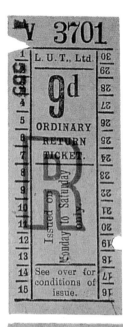

Selection of Returns

490

Df 6230
LONDON

Tc 5822
LONDON

Qd 0426
TOOTING

'Deaf & Dumb'

With Farestage Names

B 1505
UXBRIDGE
LUGGAGE at Owners' Risk

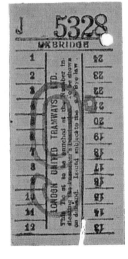

J 5328
UXBRIDGE

Ct 0160
UXBRIDGE

1915 Series

1915 Series

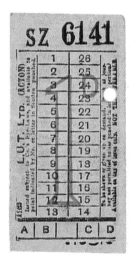

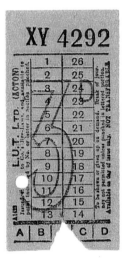

From 1926

Depot Name shown on ticket

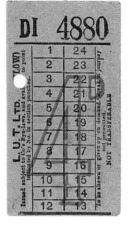
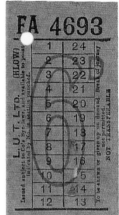

From 1926 Depot Name shown

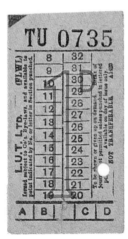

	Lc 9903	
DOWN	FARE D 1½	UP
The Downs		Summerstown
Raynes Park Stn.		Queen's Road
Waterworks Corner	London United Tramways, Ltd.	Kingston Hill
Langley Road		Richmnd Pk. Gates
Tolworth		Eden Street Junction
Dittons		

	H 1901	
DOWN	FARE 3D	UP
Surbiton Park Terrace		Richmond Bridge
Surbiton Station	London United Tramways, Ltd.	Twickenham (York St Junct'n)
Waterworks Corner		Twickenham Green
The Dittons		Stanley Rd Junc.
		Depot

	P 4401	
DOWN	Fare 3½	UP
Surbiton Station		Richmond Bridge
Waterworks Corner	London United Tramways, Ltd.	Twickenham (York St Junc.)
The Dittons		Twickenham Green

1910-14   With Farestages Named

	Gz 4804	
DOWN	Fare 1D	UP
Wimbledon Stn.		Summerstown
The Downs		Queen's Road
Raynes Park Stn.		Latimer Road
Surbiton Station	London United Tramways, Ltd.	Richmnd Pk. Gates
Waterworks Corner		Kingston Hill
Langley Road		Eden St. Junction
Tolworth		Surbiton Terrace
Dittons		

	Za 1343	
DOWN	FARE D 1½	UP
The Downs		Tooting
Raynes Park Stn.		Wandle Bridge
New Malden (Police Stn)		Latimer Road
Wellington Crescent	London United Tramways, Ltd.	Wimbledon Station
Kingston Boundary		The Downs
Park St tion		Raynes Park Stn.
Home Park Gate		New Malden (Police Stn)
Garden Gates		Wellington Crescent
Hampton Court		Kingston Boundary

	A 9502	
DOWN	FARE D 2½	UP
Hampt'n Wick Station	London United Tramways, Ltd.	Richmond Bridge
Kingston (Eden St)		Twicken'm Junction

494

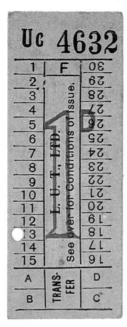
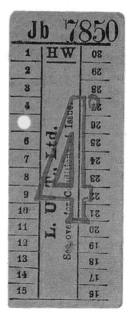

c1920-23 'Deaf & Dumb' Series

LCC   1928-31

c1903 Single

CHAPTER TWENTY-SEVEN

STAFF AND WORKING CONDITIONS

One of the first major changes instituted by Clifton Robinson upon taking over the old West Metropolitan Tramways undertaking was the issue of a staff rule book in the summer of 1894. Entitled "Rules and Regulations for the General Guidance of the Employees of the London United Tramways Limited", it was a handsomely-bound booklet in stiff crocodile-skin finish covers, printed by Edward Everard of Bristol, one of the first directors of the new London United company. This, in its opening paragraphs emphasised the importance of strict adherence to the rules and regulations in order to secure efficiency of working, realisation of the conpany's revenue, the provision of good service to the travelling public and the comfort and well-being of the men employed.

The book incorporated a form of application for employment and a form of contract; the application form made it clear that only men of strict temperate habits would be considered for any post and character references from past employers dating from the previous five or more years were required. The application form also asked of any applicant if he had at any time been employed in a public house.

Men were employed on a seven-days-per-week basis. Depot and other indoor staff were expected to be ready to perform any duty asked of them in the event of emergencies, such as snowstorms or accidents, and all staff were required to reside near the depot from which they were working. Every employee was expected to "render his service to the Company with zeal, discretion and fidelity", and to abstain from smoking, improper language and misconduct. The partaking of intoxicating liquor while on duty was punishable by instant dismissal.

These rules insisted that all staff should do their utmost to promote the well-being of the company by adopting a courteous and obliging attitude to passengers. Conductors were enjoined to assist elderly persons, ladies and children in boarding and alighting from the cars, to announce distinctly the names of the principal stopping places and to ensure that cars ran on time.

The importance of ensuring that all fares were collected was stressed. Conductors on the horse cars initially used an early form of Bell Punch with which to validate tickets, which was attached to a chain and worn round the neck. When not in use the punch was carried either in the cash bag or in a pocket. The later pattern Bell Punch also went into use during the horse tram period, suspended from a leather holding strap slung over the conductor's shoulder. Tickets dropped on the cars by passengers had to be collected and torn in half lengthways.

Drivers, working under the direction of the conductors, were also instructed to pay close attention to the wishes of the travelling public, keeping a vigilant lookout for intending passengers and avoiding talking to passengers in the saloon. Horse-tram drivers were asked to drive at a steady pace with taut reins and with the right hand on the brake handle at all times, but stopping the car with the reins rather than the brake. On starting from a stop, horses were not allowed to trot until the car had moved at least 20 feet, and except in emergency a car was not to be stopped in less than 20 feet.

Inspectors were responsible for working the route or routes under their charge, the conduct of their subordinates, cleanliness, satisfactory lighting and running order of the cars under their charge and a strict adherence to the rules. In addition to ensuring good timekeeping, inspectors' duties also included checking, each day, the condition of cars running on their routes and entering in their report books any defects found, and in no circumstances allowing a car to run with a defect. Breakdowns or accidents in their area were to be attended to at once with all necessary equipment, and every effort made to arrange for speedy resumption of traffic. Other duties of inspectors included the examination and checking of tickets and waybills, reporting irregularities in the issue of tickets and dealing with refusals to show a ticket or pay a fare.

Timekeepers were employed at strategic points and at the depots, whose duties were self-explanatory. They had some disciplinary powers, chief of which was authority to suspend drivers or conductors who were under the influence of drink while on duty. They were empowered to immediately remove such a man from the car, suspend him and at once report the matter to the superintendent, who alone had powers of dismissal. That such occurrences occasionally took place is evident from entries in a surviving company "Punishment Book" of 1907.

A new rule book was issued in April 1901 when electric trams were introduced. This devoted little space to the working of electric cars and is noteworthy in stating that the electric brake should be used as the service brake and the handbrake for emergency stops. Later these instructions were reversed.

Discipline, especially during Clifton Robinson's time as managing director and engineer, was rigidly enforced. An example was the Easter 1909 strike of platform staff, mainly over trades union recognition, but there were also complaints over working conditions and rates of pay. Trades Union representatives asked Robinson to meet a deputation to discuss these grievances. Platform staff pay at this time averaged six shillings per day for a 63-hour six-day week. The men also wished to discuss maintenance of the cars' braking systems.

Clifton Robinson refused to meet the union officials, saying that he would meet a deputation of 20 of the men. This was not accepted, and John Burns, a prominent trade union official, addressed the men at Fulwell Depot on Easter Sunday. An immediate strike was called for Bank Holiday Monday and pickets were posted at Hanwell and Chiswick depots. The Hanwell men were offered an additional day's pay to take out the Fulwell cars. Many Hanwell men accepted Robinson's offer and there were angry scenes when several cars carrying strike breakers from Hanwell arrived at Fulwell. Stones were thrown and several car windows were broken.

Robinson remained adamant that he would not concede to the strikers' demands and all were dismissed, some being replaced from the many unemployed of the day. Every man in the conpany's employ was called upon to sign a bond of loyalty and those who refused were dismissed. While he would not reinstate a striker, Robinson undertook to use his influence to help them obtain other employment. He defended his stand by saying that the men had set out deliberately to disrupt the company's all-important Bank Holiday Monday traffic, something that he and his directors could not overlook.

The strikers' demands had been for shorter hours, higher pay, additional holiday pay and improved pay arrangements for spare men. They had also complained about the cars' brakes and threatened to take their case on this point to the Board of Trade, asking for every car to be fitted with magnetic track brakes.

Numerous meetings were held in the LUT area calling for reinstatement of the strikers and consideration of their demands. Local feelings had run high. On 7 April 1909 Robinson wrote to the men who had remained loyal, thanking them for their help in maintaining services and saying that every man could rely upon full and sympathetic consideration of any matter brought fairly to his notice in which the comfort and wellbeing of the staff was concerned. A copy of this letter was sent to John Burns, who on 4 April had asked Robinson to meet a deputation of the men. Robinson agreed to do this in his letter, but letters of dismissal were sent to the strikers on 12 April.

On 26 April 1909 Robinson reported to his fellow directors that four hundred crew members went on strike on Easter Monday, mainly at Fulwell and Hounbslow depots. He had managed to run services "without serious interrruption" and was rapidly filling the vacancies caused by the abstentions. Services had been reorganised and cars were running normally over the whole system.

Working conditions for the platform staff were eased somewhat after the strike and some slight improvements were made to pay. On 1 November 1911, Albert Stanley, who had succeeded Robinson as managing director in January 1910 told the directors that uniformed staff would be granted paid holidays. The general manager, Z.E.Knapp, proposed five days paid holiday per year for all uniformed staff. After discussion, Stanley suggested seven days paid annual leave be granted to motormen, conductors, ticket checkers, timekeepers and regulators, to which the directors agreed.

The 1909 strike adversely affected the company's relations with the Metropolitan Police. They had accepted LUT, LCC and MET engineers' reports on motormen's competence without enforcing the normal police tests of their ability when relicensing them. Accusations during the strike of poor instruction caused the police to insist that their own officers should test LUT drivers. The company was advised that "recent events have made the Commissioner think it advisable to alter this practice in regard to the LUT". The arrangements covering MET and LCC men were allowed to stand.

By this time the administration of the company was more closely integrated with that of the UERL and staff conditions generally underwent numerous minor improvements. The later merger in the London & Suburban Traction Company brought the three tramway companies still closer together with respect to operational and working conditions, and a rule book common to all three was issued.

On 14 May 1915 London County Council tramways motormen and conductors went on strike after their demand for a 15% wages increase was refused. This took place at a critical phase of the Great War and brought the Metropolitan Electric Tramways into the dispute, car crews working on LCC through routes turning their cars at the Middlesex and London county boundaries. Some crews at Edmonton MET depot, which served several munitions factories in the outer north London area also stopped work in sympathy with the LCC men, but the LCC strike had practically no effect on LUT services. James Devonshire, the LUT and MET managing director told his directors that strike demands would be strongly resisted and little, if any disruption was caused to the LUT services. The LCC and MET strikers returned to work on 30 May 1915.

After the LUT, MET and SMET were amalgamated with the London and Suburban Traction Company, the rules and regulations of all three were combined in a new rule book consisting of sections common to all three systems, and with other sections covering matters applicable only to one or other of the three undertakings.

From about June 1918 a bonus points system operated as an incentive to motormen and conductors to reduce traffic accidents. Men were engaged initially as conductors, being promoted to driving duties as vacancies arose, subject to passing a competence examination. Upon appointment, a conductor was issued with a card credited with 60 "bonus points". Each point was valued at one shilling

WE ARE A HAPPY FAMILY—AND A BIG ONE.

Three Type T cars conveyed the Hounslow Depot staff over the MET system to Barnet for their annual outing to Folly Farm at Hadley Wood in 1925. (Courtesy G.L.Gundry)

Two car crews change duties at Hanwell Depot, an extension of their normal duty from Hammersmith to Acton. Car 259, classified W2 is one of the small number in the "all-red" 1928 livery. (Hugh Nicol. Courtesy National Tramway Museum)

and each year an agreed number of points was added. An infringement of the rules, such as early running, uncollected fares or a dewirement carried a deduction of points. Upon passing as a motorman, a conductor would be issued with a motorman's card.

Conversely, an action benefitting the company, such as helping to clear an obstruction on the track or reporting damaged overhead carried bonus points, which could be cashed from time to time, but 60 points always had to be held in credit. A man who ran out of points was automatically dismissed. In 1925 a conductor who lost his employment on this account was reduced to singing in the street to make a living!

From 29 March 1920 tramwaymen were granted a three shillings per week wages increase for all those over 18 years of age, and from August 1921 a wages agreement of 16 June became operative, whereby reductions of and additions to wages at the rate of one shilling a week for each point variation either way in the cost of living figures above or below 135% over the cost of living figure for August 1914 were made. From February 1922 wages were reduced by three shillings per week under this agreement. A further reduction in August 1923 of one shilling a week was reinstated from the first week in November.

Meanwhile, the National Joint Industrial Council for the tramways industry adopted the principle of a 48-hour week, which the LUT directors agreed to on 31 March 1922. It was this that formed the basis of an ongoing agreement between the unions and employers which remained largely unchanged throughout the remainder of the existence of the company.

However, following the end of the Great War, tramwaymen had suffered wage reductions and pay had lagged behind that in other comparable industries. There was unrest among the men who felt that they were being unfairly treated. Another grievance was the introduction of new motors, resulting in faster journeys causing stress for motormen and for conductors experienceing difficulty in collecting all fares in the time allowed. Accordingly, on 19 December 1923 the Transport & Geberal Workers Union submitted a claim for an eight shillings a week increase for its tramway members in the Metropolitan area. The employers flatly stated that they were in no position to accede to this claim.

The company said that the tramway industry could not bear any additional wage burden and must be self-supporting. They held to this position and on 13 March 1924 the union called a strike to commence on 15 March. The employees offered to submit their claim to arbitration and the strike was postponed until 22 March. At the root of the dispute was the inability of tramway employers to consider the claim, owing to the position in which they were placed by unregulated omnibus competition. This they recognised, and called for legislation to place passenger transport in the Metropolis on a properly regulated footing in the interest of all parties, including the public.

At a Court of Inquiry into the dispute, Lord Ashfield expressed his support for the establishment of an overall regulatory authority for London passenger traffic. He also offered to limit the numbers of LGOC buses running on tramway routes, and also recognised that the tramways were an indispensable part of the London passenger transport system.

The 1924 London Traffic Act went some way to relieveing the tramways' difficulties, but had fallen short of establishing the much-wanted traffic regulatory body; meanwhile, agreement was reached on an increase of one penny an hour for tramwaymen as from 1 May 1924, and the men returned to work on 31 March. The London General Omnibus Company's staff enjoyed higher wage rates than their tramway counterparts and although not making any claim, they had stopped work in support of the men, ensuring maximum effectiveness of the tramwaymens' action.

Hanwell Depot Tug-of-War team was established in the early years and took prizes against teams all over the country. They won the Clifton Robinson Challenge Cup and medals in 1904-5.
(Courtesy David Bowater)

L.V.T.
HANWELL & ACTON
CLUBS & INSTITUTES.
"IN MEMORIAM"

To those of our colleagues who made
the Supreme Sacrifice in the
GREAT WAR 1914-1918

ANSELL. V.	EVANS. S.F.	LEVETT.W.
BANKS.F.E.	FINNEY.C.H	LYONS.S.
BROWN.J.F.	FITCH. A.S.	NORRIS.H.
CANNON.J.C.	FULLER.S.G.	PHIPPS.A.P.
CHALLIS.J.A.	GOODE. A.G.	RICHARDS.F.
CLIFFORD.W.R.	JEFFERIES.W.T.	SMITH.W.A.
COLLINS.E.	KING.H.	SNOOK.A.S.
DEACON.H.J.	KYTE.A.A.	SPIERS.J.W.
DONEGAN.A.	LAMBERT.C.	THEYS.A.W.
ESSEX.A.J.	LAYTON.C.F.	UNDERHILL.G.T.
	LEAN.G.J.	

"MEMORIA IN ETERNA"

Memorial tablets naming staff members lost in the Great War were erected at the depots subsequent to 1920. These were usually of stone but the example at Hanwell was of polished wood and included names of staff members who had been based at Acton. Hanwell depot, later garage, closed in March 1993.

(Photo courtesy David Bowater)

A General Strike of employees in many industries occurred in May 1926, which created a virtually complete stoppage of all public transport throughout the Kingdom. The LUT, along with all other London tramways, was affected almost totally, despite the activities of a few people to provide some sort of service. This is more fully described elsewhere.

Financial results in 1931 were poor, and in accordance with an agreement between the tramway employers and the unions, a temporary reduction in wages of one shilling a week was imposed in September 1932 which remained in force until April 1933.

Other Activities

An early innovation by Clifton Robinson was the establishment of staff recreational facilities. The company encouraged participation in team games and sports, and the various LUT depots had teams which competed among themselves and against other local sides. The J.Clifton Robinson Tug-of-War team of Hanwell Depot in particular, visited venues all over the country and built up an impressive record of successes. Cricket also played an important part in these activities, the Garrick Cricket Club having as its president Clifton Robinson and vice-presidents W.G.Verdon Smith, C.R.Holmes and Clifton Robinson Jnr, with other senior LUT men in the positions of patrons and officers.

Indoor pursuits were also encouraged, and the superintendent at Acton Depot, Henry Balfe, gave regular concerts and recitals which were well received. An annual event was the visit to Garrick's Villa at Hampton of the wives and children of the staff of each depot. On these occasions several trams conveyed the parties to and from the Villa, where entertainments were provided, while Lady Robinson presented gifts to the children.

From 1914 onwards, the UERL group of companies issued a staff magazine under the title of "T-O-T" (Train-Omnibus-Tram)and in the post-war years staff welfare facilities were developed, together with improved working conditions generally. Recreational activities of every kind were encouraged, the various companies within the group establishing their own playing fields with regular inter-company fixtures and competitions with outside organisations. A rifle range was installed at Acton depot during Robinson's regime and later a commodious billiards room was provided at the rear of Hounslow depot.

On a more sombre note and following the end of the Great War, memorial tablets, many of which were made of stone, commemmorating staff members lost in action were erected at almost all UERL depots. One, at Hanwell Depot was however, made of polished timber and was unveiled by C.J.Spencer on 21 October 1923. It bore the names of staff from both Hanwell and Acton Depots. On this occasion the MET Band was in attendance and all chief officers of the company were present.

CHAPTER TWENTY-EIGHT

PUBLICITY AND ADVERTISING

As tramcars had large plain external surfaces, especially upon the upper deck side and end panels, they provided useful advertising space for many national and local retail and other businesses. Inside the lower saloons of the cars the quarter-lights and, additionally, the tops of side windows, could be used to display a considerable number of advertising slips or "transparencies", all of which provided a useful source of income for the tramway undertakings.

Horse trams, being more localised than their electric successors tended to carry displays by purely local advertisers such as theatres, department stores and other retail concerns. They did, however, attract a considerable amount of custom from manufacturers of household products, such as "Hudson's Soap", "Zebra Grate Polish", "Gospo Cleaning Powder", to name but a few.

This tradition was at first continued on the electric trams, but as many electric systems expanded to cover much wider areas than their predecessors, national advertisers of a variety of products and services began to take space on the generally larger cars. Advertising contractors, such as J.W.Courtenay Ltd. handled much of the advertising work on public transport, while some larger undertakings had their own "in-house" advertising departments. Among London tramway managers it was held that the revenue from advertising in and on a car covered the cost of its annual repainting.

When the majority interest in the LUT passed from the White family of Bristol to the UERL associates in 1902, the new management was advised by American business consultants to let advertising spaces on the cars. On 3 November 1904 a seven-year contract, to run from 1 January 1905 was let to Albert Pole & Son, a Bristol advertising agency, covering spaces in and on the cars, for £27.10s. per annum per car, "except on open or summer cars which might later be introduced". The contract stipulated the use of "glass tablets" inside on the upper part of the twelve saloon windows, with paper displays or metal plates outside on the two upper deck side panels and the four end panels. Poles' first payment to the company on 6 February 1906 amounted to £1,031.5s.

Poles' contract was terminated on 31 December 1910 for unstated reasons, to be replaced by one awarded to Willing and Co.Ltd, which was to run for a period of five years as from 1 January 1911. Its terms were that 65% of gross advertising receipts be paid to the company with a minimum annual payment of £7,500, and an additional payment of gross annual receipts above £10,500.

The onset of the Great War in 1914 seriously affected advertising revenue, and on 14 October of that year the LUT directors agreed to a temporary suspension of minimum payments by Willing, subject to their paying the company 80% of advertising receipts. On 12 May 1915 it was agreed that Willing should pay the company the minimum annual rent of £7,500 less 20% as from 1 July. However, advertising revenue continued to decline and Willings' contract was terminated, possibly by mutual consent, on 31 December 1916. On the following day the UERL advertising department took responsibility for advertising on the LUT cars for a flat fee of £300 per annum.

Hillingdon (later Hayes) Depot had four tracks and accommodated 20 cars. Planned extensions beyond Uxbridge did not materialise and by 1923 it had been leased away. Car 109 was photographed there in 1909, and shows typical advertisements of the period.

(Courtesy London Borough of Ealing Libraries)

Efforts were made after the Great War to clear arrears of routine maintenance. Cars were turned out from the Fulwell shops once again resplendent in red and white livery. During the course of this process, blue cars were repainted red.

(Courtesy London Transport Museum U2762)

The largest available spaces on a tramcar were the upper-deck decency panels (known as "wholesides"). On the LUT Surrey lines an early and short-lived example was placed by W.G.Smith's Soap Works of Kingston, reading "USE VOLVOLUTUM SOAP", apparently in light blue or green lettering on white. On the same car a balcony panel displayed "BRANDS' ESSENCE" in dark red or brown. Another early "wholeside" on Surrey cars was for "Kempthorne & Phillips, House Furnishers, George Street, Richmond", while the end panels on some cars showed "JOHN BULL, Edited by Horatio Bottomley - One Penny" and "Pennington, Tailor and Clothier, Clarence Street, Kingston", in black on white enamelled plates.

On the Middlesex lines prominent local "wholesides" were an early display for "Wm. PERRING & Co. House Furnishers, 253-255 High Street, Acton" and another for their Chiswick branch at 94-100 High Road. From just before the start of the Great War few local advertisers were booking "wholesides" and by the early 1920s they became the preserve of national concerns. Prominent among these were the many large breweries, manufacturers of nationally-known products such as Mazawattee Tea, Lipton's Tea and Boar's Head Tobacco. Local theatres, chiefly the King's and the Lyric in Hammersmith and the Wimbledon Theatre kept up the tradition of a weekly change of programme and remained among the few local concerns taking up "wholeside" space.

An interesting sidelight upon changes in public taste down the years is the proliferation of advertisements on "wholesides" for cocoa. Prior to the Great War colourful "streamers" for Van Houten's, Fry's, Rowntree's, Bensdorp's and Cadbury's "Bournville" Cocoa were always in sight. The product is rarely advertised at the present day.

"Feltham" type car No.370 heads through Ealing Broadway on its way to Shepherds Bush. Advertising on these cars was at first confined to the main "wholeside" display and one smaller panel on either side.　　　　　　　　　(Courtesy London Transport Museum U8156)

507

Smaller spaces, the balcony ends of the Type T cars and the "large and small" end panels, together with the small rounded corner panels on the rear nearside ends of the open-top Type W cars, continued to be taken up by concerns such as the Singer Sewing Machine Company, the makers of "Swan Vesta" Matches, Borwick's Baking Powder and Mellin's Food (for invalids). A long-surviving advertiser on the outside end panels was Charles Baker & Co., outfitters with branches in Hammersmith and other west London suburbs.

Colourful "glass tablets", shaped to fit the arched tops of the saloon windows inside the cars, praised the virtues of such diverse products as Bosendorffer Pianos, Hall's Wine, O.K.Sauce and various patent medicines, as well as local shops and the ubiquitous Tramcar and Omnibus Scripture Text Mission. During the Great War the LST companies' cars carried transparencies in the end bulkhead windows showing a swastika! A series of photographs was taken showing this feature, which had been adopted as a "good luck" symbol by the wartime National Savings Committee.

Other internal advertising consisted of small transparencies at the bottom of each glass panel in the twin saloon doors, up to the Great War devoted to Lipton's Tea and thereafter to Borwick's Baking Powder. Frames in the bulkhead panels were reserved for a faretable at one end and company publicity at the other, usually covering terms for hire of private cars and announcements for events such as sporting occasions or the British Empire Exhibition of 1924-25. The "glass tablets" in the saloon windows, by their nature were liable to breakage and not easily removed when necessary. They were comparativelt short-lived and gave way to coloured paper "transparencies" of rectangular form which had a number of advantages over the glass panels.

Dash side panels were used by various concerns from newspapers to building societies, and also by the undertaking itself to publicise events on its routes, service alterations and publicity slogans such as the early 1920s "Don't Tramp It, Tram It" poster. The companies' publicity department produced a large number of these double crown size posters featuring attractions, such as Kew Gardens, all over their system, which frequently appeared on the dash side panels. Another of these panels appeared on the staircase landings from 1909.

The Type UCC "Feltham" cars of 1931, after trials with a "wholeside" streamer along the upper deck sides flanked on either side by a small "corner" display, carried two slightly shorter but deeper "streamers" per side, displaying national products such as "Black & White Whisky", "Maple & Co. Furnishers", "Bovril", &c. No other advertisements were carried externally, while internally faretables and company announcements were shown in dedicated panels. No window transparencies appeared on these cars.

TRAFFIC ACCIDENTS

The LUT system, while not penetrating Central London, did include many miles of busy roads in West London and the LUT cars inevitably had their share of accidents. Compared with other vehicles, the tramcar's share in serious accidents was small, thanks in part to its fast-acting electric brakes and automatic lifeguards. This is borne out by the Metropolitan Police road accident statistics for a typical three-month period (1 April to 30 June 1925), during which fatalities attributed by the police to the following types of vehicle were:-

Trade Vehicles	72	Horsed Vehicles	16
Private Cars	60	Pedal Cycles	7
Motor Buses	39	Tramcars	6
Motor Cycles	20	Taxicabs	5

At this time the London tramways carried about one-third of the road passenger traffic, and were thus about three times safer than the motor omnibus. The LUT had fewer steep gradients than some other London tramways, but had a greater proportion of narrow roads where the tracks ran closer to the kerb.

At first, unfamiliarity with the new electric trams and their tracks, particularly on the part of cyclists, resulted in an upsurge of accidents from 4 April 1901 when the first electric trams commenced to run. Among these were collisions with an omnibus at Shepherds Bush, a coal cart in Acton and a brougham at Ealing Common. A fatal accident in High Road, Chiswick on 22 April 1903 involved a car fitted with the Wood lifeguard described in Volume One, but without central side-guards (or "dog gates"). The cyclist was riding alongside the tram, skidded and was thrown under the car. This and a similar accidemt later in Hounslow involving a boy holding on to the side of a car who fell between the bogies resulted in the fitting of dog gates and an improved form of lifeguard to all the cars.

The May, 1904 issue of *The Tramway and Railway World* reported a court case involving collision between an LUT tram and an LGOC horse bus, with accusations of reckless driving on the part of the drivers concerned. However, the first accident to attract widespread press comment occurred on the evening of Monday 26 December 1904 on the single line at Hillingdon Hill. A car from Uxbridge collided with a trap, blocking the line. A car from London waiting to descend the hill was struck in the rear by the next tram and propelled down hill, colliding with three cars waiting at the bottom of the gradient, with the result that one car was derailed and several passengers and one of the motormen were injured. The line was not cleared until the following morning.

An embarrassing incident, mentioned again, although already described in Chapter 8 (Volume 1), occurred during the ceremonial opening of the Kingston Hill route on 1 March 1906, in the presence of the Mayor of Kingston. As car 320 descended the hill a Hodgsons' Brewery dray proceeding uphill swerved and caught the front of the tram. Sir Clifton Robinson, riding on the front platform, was thrown into the road, suffering bruises and a sprained ankle which, however, did not deter him from speaking at the subsequent ceremonial luncheon.

Kingston Hill was the scene of another incident on Saturday, 1 September 1917 at 8.25a.m. Car No.156 left Kingston Hill terminus for the Dittons, carrying one passenger. A continuous drizzle ensured that the track was in a most unfavourable state, and the car began to gather speed, the motorman endeavouring to check its descent by sanding the rails and using the hand and rheostatic brakes, finally reversing the motors, all of which failed to check the car's increasing speed. It passed through the first two loops on the hill and derailed at the trailing points at the entrance to the third single track section.

The car, having attained a very high speed, said by an eye witness "to be fifty miles an hour", swung across the road and felled a large lime tree. It then struck a traction pole, which was bent at an acute angle. The top deck and one side of the body was torn away, the other side collapsing onto the floor of the lower deck. Despite the heavy impact the car did not overturn. The motorman was thrown onto the road as was the conductress, while the sole passenger lay in the wreckage, severely injured and surrounded by fallen overhead wire and other items.

Major Pringle, Chief Inspecting Officer of the Board of Trade arrived at the scene shortly after mid-day and examined the car and its brakes and the track. After this detailed examination he reported, on the same day, to the BoT. He found the brakes and sanding gear and the flanges of the car's wheels in a satisfactory condition. He recommended an 8mile/h. speed limit for downhill journeys from the terminus at the top of Kingston Hill to Brunswick Road with compulsory stops before entering the Kingston Hill loops. The BoT issued a regulation to this effect on 19 September 1919. This, the most spectacular accident

Car No.171 of Type W derailed outside the Recreation Ground in Haydon's Road, Wimbledon. This incident occurred during the period between 1914 and 1916.

(Courtesy Merton Library)

A length of steel girder seems to have penetrated the top-deck of No.84 in High Road, Chiswick on an unknown date. The breakdown gang appear to be having difficulty in extricating it from its unlikely resting place.   (Courtesy London Transport Museum U15640)

to occur on the system could easily have been attended by loss of life or at least many serious injuries had it taken place at a busier time of the day.

By 1918 worn track resulted in a crop of accidents. On 21 April a car derailed and overturned in High Street, Brentford. On 16 August a defective trolley brought down the overhead wires in Brentford and further derailments occurred in Brentford in October and December and in Hammersmith in December. The worst incident in the year was in November when two cars collided at the commencement of the single line on the Kingston-Malden route at Cambridge Road and twelve passengers were hurt, three of them seriously.

Further derailments occurred during 1919 on the worn track in Brentford, some of which caused cars to overturn and in October a car collided with a steamroller. Elsewhere on the system a car collided with a steam wagon in Acton in May 1919, while three passengers were slightly injured in December when two cars collided in Surbiton.

As the track reconstruction programme proceeded from the early 1920s derailments became less frequent, but a serious accident took place on 16 August 1923 when a tram and an omnibus collided in High Road, Chiswick, injuring several bus passengers, of whom two later died. Car No.33 was badly damaged in an accident at New Malden in 1924, and was eventually scrapped at Fulwell Depot in 1929 together with 26 others, most of which had been out of service for many years. By this time space at the depot was soon to be required for fitting out the Feltham type trams then shortly to be built by the Union Construction & Finance Co.

Finally, on Sunday 24 July 1927 a head-on collision occurred between a tram and an omnibus at Hampton Wick and 20 passengers were injured. The driver of the bus had attempted to pass the tram on the offside and both vehicles were severely damaged, the top deck of the car being totally wrecked.

CHAPTER TWENTY-NINE

OMNIBUS & RAILWAY COMPETITION

The Omnibuses

Throughout its existence the London United Tramways shared many of its routes with omnibus services, some of which had a long history. The original 1856 horse bus services of the London General Omnibus Company (after buying out the previous operators) included those between Kew Bridge and The Bank, and between Acton ("Princess Victoria" Tavern) and London Bridge. An LGOC depot and stables was opened at Turnham Green in 1899. By 1901 the Uxbridge Road service had been extended to Ealing, but a further extension to Hanwell was withdrawn after the electric trams started. From 1889 the West London Omnibus Company ran horse buses between Chiswick ("Pack Horse & Talbot") and Kensington Church via Hammersmith.

Elsewhere in the LUT area, the principal horse bus route was that of the London & Suburban Omnibus Company between Kew Bridge and Kingston via Richmond, which parallelled the LUT Kew and Richmond horse tramway. From April to October 1905 and again in summer 1906 the route was worked by Leyland/Crossley motor buses, extended in 1906 to Surbiton, but mechanical difficulties twice forced a return to the use of horses. The separate Kingston-Surbiton-Esher horse buses were withdrawn in 1906 even though the new electric trams did not go beyond the Dittons. The horse bus company had charged twopence to Surbiton, the LUT one penny.

By 1908 the LUT management was feeling the effects of competition from LGOC motor buses on the Uxbridge Road route and to a lesser extent the Hounslow route. Edgar Speyer noted that the LUT was restricted to an average speed over the system as a whole of 8½ mile/h. The LGOC had 129 buses working on the Shepherds Bush-Ealing and Shepherds Bush-Turnham Green sections alone, running at minimum speeds of 12 mile/h, and some reaching between 15 and 20 mile/h. Authorised speeds for the LUT were 7.6 mile/h. on the Shepherds Bush-Ealing section and 8½ mile/h. between Shepherds Bush and Turnham Green. For the LGOC the authorised speed over both sections was 12 mile/h.

Speyer stigmatised the competition as unfair and referred to the obligations upon the LUT to carry workmen at uneconomic fares; to pay wayleaves to the local authorities; and to observe compulsory stops at numerous points. Conversely, the buses were "free of the road"; were at liberty to vary their operations; whilst their activities destroyed attempts at co-ordination of interests such as through bookings between the tramways and the tubes. This heralded a conflict between the tramways and bus interests which was only partly resolved when the LGOC became part of the Underground Group in 1912.

The March 1911 LGOC map showed two services entering the LUT area; 12, Turnham Green-Goldhawk Road-London Bridge and 17, Ealing-Acton-West Ham. Service 12 was extended to Peckham in May and worked jointly with Thomas Tilling Ltd. LGOC policy, as later defined by Frank Pick, was to run the buses "about a mile to a mile-and-a-half over the tramways, so that people had not to change from bus to tram when they were going for a short ride". Put another way by the LUT Chairman, C.J.Cater Scott, the buses on these shared sections did not pay, but diverted traffic from the trams. The sections concerned were among the busier LUT routes and their receipts were needed to support the rest of the system. Motor bus competition was a recurring theme in LUT annual reports from 1908 onwards.

In 1912, the LGOC announced its intention to extend its operations to a 15-mile radius from Charing Cross. Fortunately for the trams, both the LUT and LGOC had now become members of the Underground Group, restricting competition and coming to an agreement on fares. Agreement was also reached to abandon the Kew-Richmond horse tramway for which purpose the LGOC had extended the Highgate-Turnham Green service 27 to Twickenham via Hammersmith, Kew Bridge and Richmond. Between Richmond Bridge and Twickenham these buses took traffic from the LUT trams on service 69, and were partly responsible for its demise in 1924. The LGOC shared the 27 route with the London Central Motor Omnibus Co. Ltd. (successors to the London & Suburban Omnibus Company), but the Central was sold to the LGOC in February 1926 and absorbed in January 1928. The LGOC had opened its own Twickenham garage near Richmond Bridge in March 1912.

In December 1912 the LGOC opened a garage at Hounslow, reached by service 37A from Richmond and serving as a base for long routes to Egham and Windsor (also Maidenhead on summer Sundays). When in 1922 the trams were cut back from Hounslow Heath to Hounslow "The Bell", service 37A was extended to replace them. At Merton, the enforced change between LUT and LCC trams at the county boundary at Longley Road could be avoided by using LGOC service 32, successor to Thomas Tilling's Clapham-Wimbledon horse buses. On summer Sundays this same road saw the Clarkson steam buses of the National Steam Car Company working between Peckham and Hampton Court ("Cardinal Wolsey") via Brixton, Tooting, Wimbledon and Kingston. Other Sunday workings to Hampton Court were by LGOC 18 and 23 from Aldwych, the 18 via Kew and Bushy Park, the 23 via Putney, Richmond and Kingston. Without these special workings, some at least of their passengers would have travelled to Hampton Court by tram.

The onset of competition from newly-formed independent bus operators during 1922 forced a change in the LUT/LGOC fares agreement. The LGOC made a general reduction in fares from 1 January 1923 and the LUT followed suite from 15 February, abolishing the 1½d fare and lengthening the penny stage, with a resulting drop in LUT revenue. The privately-owned buses were establishing themselves on the LUT trunk route 7, Uxbridge-Southall-Ealing-Shepherds Bush, and there was a lesser influx of competition on the Hounslow routes.

In the early 1920s, LUT route 7, worked by the then-leisurely T and U-type cars, took 81 minutes for the whole journey, through rapidly-growing areas such as Hanwell and Southall. This offered an opportunity with great potential which the independent bus operators from 1923 onwards were not slow to seize. The pioneer on the Uxbridge Road was the already well-established Cambrian Coaching & Transport Company, which by mid-1924 had built up a bus fleet operating some 30 to 40 schedules daily. The bulk of these worked the 17 (Southall-Liverpool Street), with some journeys between Hayes and Uxbridge. Under the numbering scheme introduced by Supt.Alfred Bassom of Scotland Yard, these became 286, Southall-Liverpool Street and 268, Uxbridge-Liverpool Street from 1 December 1924.

The LGOC responded by strengthening its own Ealing service from 4 to 2½ minutes, and projecting the service first to Hanwell, and then to Southall. To quote Frank Pick's own words, reported in the *Electric Railway & Tramway Journal* for 11 April 1924, this was done "not because it was wanted in the public interest, but because, if the trams were to be robbed of this traffic, and were to have competition, they might just as well have our competition as anyone else's." Realising too late that the trams were the principal victims of this policy, the LGOC took some of the buses off, to the advantage of the private bus operators and the continued detriment of the tramways.

The "rich pickings" apparently available attracted numerous, but mainly one-bus concerns, until in mid-1924 there were as many as twelve operators, apart from Cambrian and the LGOC with their frequent services to London on route 17. These "rich pickings" then began to disappear in a welter of unregulated competition, again hitting the trams hard.

In 1924 the London Traffic Act was passed, giving the Minister of Transport power to restrict the number of buses working on given routes or along certain "restricted streets", many of them tram routes. The Act came into force on 1 February 1925, and the Uxbridge Road was inevitably an early subject for a ministerial order. On 11 January 1926 the LGOC assumed operating control of the Cambrian fleet and lost no time in overhauling its schedules, including a significant reduction of the Uxbridge Road services. After various revisions, a stable weekday pattern emerged as from 26 July 1926 when 18 buses (as against 30 or more previously) worked mainly on route 185 (formerly 286, Southall-Liverpool Street) and ten buses worked 291 (Hounslow Heath-Liverpool Street) instead of 18 under Cambrian control. Service 291 conflicted with the LUT route 57 between Hounslow and Isleworth.

The others mostly sold out or faded away, except for Cornelius Beatty, who claimed that the Minister of Transport was not authorised by the Act to consider the financial position of the tramways. His summons had been chosen as a test case from more than 50 issued against the LGOC and the independent bus operators, and the case (which went to appeal) lasted until May 1927. Meanwhile, Beatty continued to run his one bus and became something of a national hero. He lost his case, but a later Order allowed him to resume service on the Uxbridge Road, such was the power of public opinion.

Improvement to the tramcar fleet commenced as from February 1923, as is described in detail elsewhere in this volume. This resulted in speedier services being introduced, again, mainly on the Uxbridge Road route, which in turn allowed cars to be released so that an augmented service could be provided to meet the competition; every ten minutes from and to Uxbridge and at about 2½-minute intervals from and to Southall on the run to Shepherds Bush. As a result, tram passengers on this route in 1928 exceeded for the first time the total carried in 1922. The introduction of the "Feltham" type cars in 1931 gave the Uxbridge Road what was possibly one of the fastest services in London over such a distance.

The wholly independent bus route 526 (North Finchley-Wandsworth Bridge), increased the difficulties for the trams between Acton and Shepherds Bush, but this service, with 16 operators, was the subject of ministerial paring down.

Workings to Hampton Court were entirely different in character, being mainly weekend journeys, particularly on summer Sundays, to which the Restricted Streets Orders did not apply. The exempted days were Sundays, Good Friday, Easter Saturday and all Bank Holidays, plus Saturdays from 12 noon in Richmond and Kingston only. In the days before private car ownership became widespread, it was evidently thought that at weekends and holidays there was enough traffic for all when the weather was fine, and judging from contemporary photographs this was evidently the case. But the presence at some periods of up to 15 operators, plus the LGOC, must have affected the trams' takings.

The ultimate destinations of the independents' weekend services, some ephemeral, some lasting, directly reached a large part of London, to Strand

IF THERE WERE NO TRAMS WOULD YOU BE AS WELL SERVED ?

1926

(Aldwych), Liverpool Street, Aldgate, Hornsey Rise, Hadley Highstone, Leyton, Stoke Newington, East Ham and Peckham, comparing favourably with the trams' hour or more to reach Hammersmith or Shepherds Bush. By 1928, when the LGOC or the London Public Omnibus Company had absorbed most of the smaller operators, the regular services to Hampton Court were in the hands of the LGOC and Premier (daily), joined by Chocolate Express on Sundays with its service 330 to and from Strand.

The Railways

The area served by the LUT lay between two of the earliest main line railways, the Great Western of 1835 from Paddington to Bristol and the London & Southampton of 1838-40 which passed one mile south of Kingston. Between these was the London & South Western Railway line opened in 1846 from Battersea (Clapham Junction) to Richmond, extended in 1849 to Windsor, and its loop line through Hounslow, opened in 1849-50. The year 1849 also saw the opening of the LSWR branch to Hampton Court. At the inner edge of the future LUT territory, the West London Railway was opened in 1844 from Willesden to Chelsea Dock and extended across the Thames to join the LSWR at Clapham Junction in 1863.

The county town of Kingston-upon-Thames had no railway until the LSWR opened its branch from Twickenham through Teddington to Kingston on 1 July 1863, which stimulated villa development along its route. The Shepperton branch opened in 1864, and the Kingston loop was completed with the opening of the Kingston-Malden line on 1 January 1869.

Several rival schemes existed in the 1860s for additional railways to Richmond. To keep control of this area, the LSWR produced a plan for a rather circuitous line from Kensington to Richmond, which was opened on 1 January 1869 from the West London Railway near Addison Road via Hammersmith, Turnham Green and Kew Gardens, with through trains from Waterloo and Ludgate Hill. Between Gunnersbury and Richmond they shared tracks with North London Railway trains from Broad Street, and later with GWR and Metropolitan trains which joined the line at Hammersmith (Grove Road, later renamed The Grove).

Of much more significance was a short link with the District Railway at Hammersmith, which from 1877 allowed District trains to run to Richmond, and from 1879 to Ealing Broadway. The LSWR trains through Turnham Green then became a minority on their own line, outnumbered by those of the other companies. The pattern was completed with the opening of the branch from Mill Hill Park (now Acton Town) to Hounslow High Street in 1883 and to Hounslow Barracks in 1884, more centrally placed than the LSWR station.

The West Metropolitan horse tramway through Chiswick therefore faced railway competition from the start, with a quite frequent steam train service running on a viaduct within sight of the tramway. The arrival of the LUT electric trams in 1901-2 redressed the balance, with frequent services, lower fares and competitive journey times to central London via Shepherds Bush and the Central London Railway (the "Twopenny Tube"). The LUT Hounslow line in particular attracted much traffic from both the District and the LSWR, despite a fare reduction by the District Railway.

Competition from the LUT electric trams was rightly feared. In June 1899 Sir Sam Fay of the LSWR estimated that his company would lose up to 2 million passengers a year if the LUT Twickenham and Hampton Court lines were built, and a one-third drop in LSWR Staines traffic if the LUT built its proposed line to Staines. The LSWR also predicted loss of traffic worth £6,000 a year to the LUT Wimbledon lines. These fears were proved correct in 1902-3 when the LSWR lost two-thirds of its local traffic to the trams between Kew Bridge, Brentford, Isleworth and Hounslow, with receipts down from £1,516 to £524.

The new (1902) American owners of the District Railway quickly decided to electrify their system, and in 1903 reached agreement with the LSWR for the electrification of the shared section from Hammersmith to Richmond. Electric working began with District trains to Richmond, Ealing, South Harrow and Hounslow in 1905, and traffic grew to an extent which required the laying of two extra tracks between Hammersmith (Studland Street Junction) and Turnham Green in 1911, and the opening of a new station at Stamford Brook in 1912. The District Railway and the LUT were by 1905 in common ownership, and it was evidently thought inappropriate to publicise the switch of traffic from tram to electric train, but it is significant that the best years for the LUT were those before the District Railway was electrified.

Uxbridge welcomed the trams, as it had only a GWR branch line, but the position was complicated by the almost simultaneous arrival in 1904 of the Metropolitan Railway from Harrow. District Railway trains began to share this line in 1910. Ten years later, the extension of the Central London Railway tube trains to Ealing Broadway in August 1920 must have reduced the numbers changing from train to tram at Ealing Common and Shepherds Bush.

LUT competition was certainly an important factor in the LSWR 1912 decision to electrify its inner surburban lines on the 600-volt third-rail system, starting with East Putney and the Kingston loop. Electric trains worked the "Kingston Roundabout" and Shepperton services from 30 January 1916, with a ten-minute headway on the shared section, followed by the Hounslow loop on 12 March and the Hampton Court branch on 18 June. At a time when wartime traffic was bringing increased receipts to almost all of the country's tramways, the LUT lost ridership to the LSWR, whose suburban traffic rose from 23 million in 1915 to 29 million in 1916, 33 million in 1917, 40 million in 1918 and 48 million in 1919. The effect on LUT finances is described in other parts of this book.

GIVE THE TRAMS FAIR PLAY AND THEY WILL GIVE YOU FARE VALUE

1926

517

CHAPTER THIRTY

THE LONDON PASSENGER TRANSPORT BOARD

From the time of the Royal Commission on London Traffic in 1904 the regulation of transport services in the capital was a frequent topic for debate in Parliament and the Press. By 1919 the growth of traffic congestion, coupled with a deterioration of services led to the establishment of a House of Commons Select Committee on passenger transport in the metropolitan area. The Committee took particular notice of the large number of organisations involved in the provision of public transport, especially with regard to tramways, the establishment and subsequent workings of which were subject to the whims of numerous official, semi-official and private bodies.

The Committee's report to the House of Commons was published on 25 July 1919. Evidence submitted on behalf of all the main providers of services in the capital led the Select Committee to recommend "... the immediate creation of a Supreme Greater London Traffic Authority ... not as a step which may be taken when opportunity offers, but as a vital measure of the most immediate necessity." By September 1919 a Ministry of Transport had been formed, and its first Minister, Sir Eric Geddes told Parliament that a Bill to create such an authority was in the course of preparation. There was considerable opposition to the Select Committee's recommendations and the Bill was not presented.

In 1923 another Bill was being drafted which, it was stated, would also contain a provision to establish a Traffic Board. This section, however, did not materialise, the Bill being passed and known as the London Traffic Act, 1924. This empowered the Minister of Transport to restrict unreasonable competition by omnibuses over certain tramway routes.

After a further four years, in November 1928, Bills to provide for the co-ordination of London passenger traffic were deposited by the London County Council and the London Electric Railway Company as an associate of the UERL, both of which largely followed the recommendations of the 1919 Select Committee. The two Bills passed a third reading in the House of Lords and were about to be returned to the Commons when a general election was called. A Labour government was returned, resulting in Herbert Morrison, a leading London Labour politician becoming Minister of Transport.

The two Bills were rejected by the new government, and the LCC, dissatisfied with the way in which the matter had been handled, introduced a further Bill in 1929 which, however, did not proceed. Instead, the government introduced its own London Passenger Transport Bill in the 1930 Session, but before any further progress could be made, another general election occurred in 1931, resulting in the Conservative party being in the majority. They allowed the Bill to proceed, but with some changes with regard to the intending authority's controlling body, and in the proposed compensation terms for the owners of undertakings acquired by the new Board.

By mid-1932 the London Passenger Transport Bill was still being delayed due to the political situation then prevailing, in part brought about by there being two parliamentary changes in as many years. This resulted in the Bill being carried forward into the 1933 Session. On 6 April it was in the House of Lords and about to be returned to the Commons for approval of the Lords' amendments, which took place four days later, on 10 April. After further discussion and agreement, the Bill was passed and received Royal Assent on 13 April as the London Passenger Transport Act, 1933. The lengthy passage through Parliament and the ensuing delays resulted in Vesting Day for the new Board, originally planned to take place on 1 April 1932, being postponed.

On 1 July 1933 the London United Tramways undertaking passed into the ownership of the company's Parliamentary and other powers the new Board assumed control of 29.05 miles of tramway route, 18 miles of trolleybus route, the four operating depots at Acton, Hanwell, Fulwell and Hounslow, together with the permanent way depot and stores at Brentford. The depot at Hillingdon, leased away in 1921 to a manufacturing company also passed to the new owners, as did traffic offices and a tower wagon shed at Kingston. Sub-stations at Wimbledon, Kingston, New Malden, Chiswick and Southall also passed to the new owners as did those at the four operating depots.

The new Board also took possession of 150 trams, 61 trolleybuses and a variety of works and departmental vehicles. These included a bogie stores van, three permanent way scrubber cars and a double-deck passenger car retained for various duties at Hanwell Depot. In addition a number of lorries, two "Foden" steam wagons and several tower wagons (including at least one which was still horse-drawn) completed the moveable assets transferred to the LPTB.

Of the 61 trolleybuses transferred to the Board the experimental front-entrance vehicle No. 61 had not become the property of the LUT by Vesting Day. Consequently the Board became responsible for payment to its builders, as it did for payments under hire-purchase agreements covering the acquisition of the 46 "Feltham" trams and trolleybuses Nos. 1-60.

C.J.Spencer resigned his post as general manager of the three former company systems and on 1 October took up the post of resident director of the North Metropolitan Electric Power Supply Company, which came under the control of the Underground Group in 1913 but which the LPTB was unable to acquire. The new Board divided the London complex of tramways into two administrative areas, South-east and Central and North and West, the former covering the London County Council system and the smaller municipally-owned systems of East Ham, West Ham, Walthamstow, Leyton, Bexley, Erith and Croydon. and the latter the three ex-LST systems. Both areas came under the control of Theodore Eastaway Thomas, erstwhile tramways manager of the London County Council, who had commenced his career with the LUT under James Clifton Robinson.

Of the 150 trams taken over by the LPTB 46 were the "Feltham" type, new in 1931. Nine Type W open-top cars of 1902-3, 45 top-covered Type U cars, nine cars partially rebuilt in the 1920s, the 40 Type T open-balcony cars of 1905-6 and the 1927 experimental car "Poppy", which survived to be renumbered into the LPTB scheme. However, one of the nine Type W cars, No. 183 was scrapped at Fulwell Depot for an unknown reason before its new number could be applied.

Following the change of ownership services over the former LUT lines continued with few alterations; meanwhile, the success of the trolleybus conversions in Surrey encouraged the new Board to embark upon a wholesale conversion of the remaining tramway routes. An Act was gained on 31 July 1934 empowering the LPTB to convert the remaining LUT ;ines and the whole of the former MET system in north and north-west London. The first of these conversions took place on 27 October 1935, when tram route 57 Shepherds Bush-Hounslow (The Bell) became trolleybus 657, extended at Hounslow to Wellington

The solitary Type XU car 247 became 2411 in the LPTB renumbering scheme. In this view it is seen departing from Hampton Court for Hammersmith on service 67.

(Hugh Nicol. Courtesy National Tramway Museum)

No.288 of Type U2 was renumbered 2405 by the LPTB and transferred to the MET lines radiating from Paddington. The LUT partially reconstructed the car in 1928, reposting the body, fitting new seating in the lower saloon and installing new electrical equipment.

(Photographer unknown)

Road. On the same day the Hammersmith-Hampton Court via Hampton tram service 67 was replaced by trolleybus 667.

On 5 April 1936 the 89 tram service between Acton Depot and Hammersmith with weekday extensions to Putney was partially replaced by trolleybus 660, Acton Depot-Hammersmith. The trolleybus wiring was taken round the interior of the depot to provide a turning circle pending the later extension of this route via Acton Market Place and over the ex-MET system to North Finchley, Acton Depot then becoming non-operational. Trolleybuses approaching Acton and Hammersmith from the north used the link via King Street, Acton, which for the first time was authorised for passenger-carrying vehicles. Westward from Hammersmith trolleybuses approached Horn Lane via the narrow Market Place.

Conversion of the 12.65-mile Uxbridge Road tram route 7 was completed between Acton and Uxbridge and opened for service 607 trolleybuses on 15 November 1936, followed on 13 December by the 2.25-mile Brentford-Hanwell route via Boston Road. This was the last section of ex-LUT route to be worked with trams and its closure marked the end of nearly 35 years of electric tramway operation by the LUT and its successors.

APPENDIX 8

DIRECTORATE & CHIEF OFFICERS
LONDON UNITED TRAMWAYS LIMITED

Chairman

1894-1901   Sir George White

Managing Director & Chief Engineer

1894-1901   James Clifton Robinson

Directors

1894-1901	Edward Everard
1894-1901	Hugh C.Godfray
1894-1901	William George Verdon Smith
1894-1901	Samuel White

Secretary

1894-1895	James Clifton Robinson (*pro tem*)
1895-1901	Samuel White

LONDON UNITED ELECTRIC TRAMWAYS (1901) LIMITED

(Later reverted to LONDON UNITED TRAMWAYS LIMITED)

Chairman

1901-1903	Sir George White
1903-1905	Charles Tyson Yerkes
1905-1912	C.J.Cater Scott
1912-1925	Wm.M.Acworth (knighted 1921)
1925-1929	H.A.Vernet (Deputy Chairman 1929-33)
1929-1933	Lord Ashfield of Southwell (formerly Sir .A.H.Stanley)

Mananging Director

1901-1910	James Clifton Robinson (knighted 1905)
1910-1912	Albert H.Stanley
1912-1919	James Devonshire
1919-1929	W.C.Burton
1929-1933	Frank Pick

Directors

1901-1903	Edward Everard
1901-1903	Hugh C.Godfray
1901-1905	Samuel White
1903-1905	Walter Abbott (Deputy Chairman 1905-06)
1903-1905	Charles A.Spofford
1905-1913	W.H.Brown
1907-1918	Sydney G.Holland (Viscount Knutsford 1914)
1908-1910	James Russell Chapman
1913-1918	Felix V.Schuster
1912-1916	Albert H.Stanley (knighted 1914)
1916-1925	H.A.Vernet
1916-1919	William Corwin Burton
1919-1930	George Balfour
1919-1920	Sir Lewis Coward
1919-1933	C.G.Tegetmeier
1919-1933	James Devonshire (knighted 1920)
1921-1933	R.H.Montgomery

Secretary
1901-1912	W.G.Verdon Smith
1912-1920	Arthur Lea Barber
1920-1924	Evelyn Boys (and Treasurer)
1924-1929	A.C.Ingram
1929-1933	J.C.Mitchell

Chief Officers

General Manager
1901-1910	James Clifton Robinson (and Engineer)
1910-1913	Zac Ellis Knapp (and Engineer)
1913-1918	Arthur Henry Pott (and Engineer)
1918-1933	Christopher John Spencer (Manager 1918-1921)

Chief Engineer & Deputy General Manager
(Deputy Manager 1918-1921)
1918-1933	Archibald Victor Mason

LONDON & SUBURBAN TRACTION COMPANY LIMITED

Chairman
1913	Emil Garcke (*pro tem*)
1913-1919	C.B.Stuart-Wortley (Lord Stuart of Wortley from 1916) (Deputy Chairman 1919-26)
1919-1933	Lord Ashfield of Southwell (formerly Sir .A.H.Stanley)

Directors
1912-1925	W.M.Acworth (knighted 1921)
1912-1930	Emil Garcke
1912-1933	E.R.Soames
1912-1916	Albert H.Stanley (knighted 1914)
1913-1933	C.G.Tegetmeier
1916-1919	W.C.Burton
1925-1929	H.A.Vernet (Deputy Chairman 1929-1933)
1921-1933	Sir James Devonshire (Managing Director 1912-21)
1929-1933	Frank Pick (Managing Director)

Secretary
1912-1921	Arthur Lea Barber
1921-1933	Evelyn Boys (and Treasurer)

APPENDIX 9

LONDON UNITED TRAMWAYS CAR DIMENSIONS

Car Type	Length overall (ft in)	Length over pillars (ft in)	Width overall (ft in)	Width over sills (ft in)	Height inside lower saloon (ft in)	Height inside upper saloon (ft in)	Height over trolley plank (ft in)	Seats lower/upper saloon	Pivotal Centres (ft in)	Wheelbase Truck (ft in)	Wheelbase Total (ft in)
Z O/T	34 7½	21 11½	7 3	6 0	6 9		(a)(b)	30/39	13 0	4 6	14 7
Y C/T	34 7½	21 11½	7 1	6 0	6 9	6 0	(a)(b)	30/39	13 0	4 6	14 7
X O/T	34 7½	21 11½	7 0	6 0	6 9		(a)(b)	30/39	13 0	4 6	14 6
W O/T	34 7½	21 11½	7 0	6 0	6 9		(a)(b)	30/39	13 6	4 0	14 6
U O/T	34 7½	21 11½	7 1	6 0	6 9		(a)(b)	30/39	13 6	4 0	14 6
XU C/T	35 1½	21 11½	7 1	6 0	6 9	6 0	(a)(b)	30/39	13 6	4 0	14 6
U/2 C/T	34 7½	21 11½	7 1	6 0	6 9	6 0	15 9¾	30/38	13 6	4 0	14 6
WT O/B	35 1½	21 11½	7 1	6 2	6 9	6 0½	15 9¾	30/44	13 6	4 0	14 6
T O/B	34 7½	21 11½	7 2	-	6 3¾	6 0½	15 9¾	27/44	13 4	4 0	14 6
P § F/E	36 1	21 8	6 9	-	6 0½	6 0½	14 10	28/36	13 0	4 6	14 6
S/1 S/D	33 10	25 0	7 0	6 0	7 6		10 8	36 ◆		4 0	14 6
S/2 S/D	34 7½	21 11½	7 0	6 0	6 9		-	32	13 6	4 0	14 6
UCC F/E	40 3¾#	-	7 1¾	-	6 2¾	5 11	15 2½	22/42	13 8 ▲	4 6	16 6

Type U No.300 seating: lower saloon 30; upper 36
Type U/2 Nos.155 and 199 seating; lower saloon 30; upper 38
No.288 seating, lower saloon 27 (part tranverse); upper 38
Reposted with flat-top windows and plain arch ceiling lower saloon
Type T No.307 top deck seating upholstered, accommodating 40
Type T Drawing states "Overall width not to exceed 7ft 2in"

O/T = open top deck
C/T = covered top deck
O/B = open balcony top deck
F/E = full enclosed top deck
S/D = single deck car

Notes:

* Cars with internal trolley masts:-
    (a) Height to top of trolley mast   15ft 5½in
    (b) Height to base of trolley mast   9ft 11½in

§ Experimental car: "Poppy"

Variations in documentation describing overall length of Type UCC cars.
  Possibly due to changes made to fender mechanisms.
    (a) 40ft 3¾in   (b) 40ft 6in   (c) 40ft 10in

▲ UCC cars: Distance between pivotal centres 13ft 8in

◆ Type S1 car. Seating capacity later reduced to 30

APPENDIX 10

LONDON UNITED TRAMWAYS
PASSENGER CAR FLEET & ELECTRICAL EQUIPMENTS AS AT 31.12.31

LUT type	Car numbers	Type details All double-deck bogie	Year Built	Year Rebuilt	Trucks	Motors	Controllers	Notes
W	165, 173, 182, 183, 185, 200, 240, 254, 259	Uncanopied open-top	1902-3		Brill 22E	MV104 2x50hp	WH 90M	a
U	151, 154, 158, 204, 205, 210, 212, 224, 235, 236, 250, 251, 255, 262, 265-274, 276-279, 281-287, 290-297, 299-300	Uncanopied top-covered	1902-3	1910-11	Brill 22E	MV104 2x50hp	WH 90M	b
U/2	155, 159	Uncanopied top-covered	1902-3	1928	Brill 22E	GECWT28KL 2x50hp	BTH B49	c
U/2	288	Uncanopied top-covered	1902-3	1928	Brill 22E	GECWT28KL 2x50hp	BTH B49	d
XU	247	Uncanopied top-covered	1901	1927	Brill 22E	MV104 2x50hp	WH 90M	e
T	301-340	Top-covered open balcony	1906	--	Brill 22E	GECWT28KL 2x50hp	WH 90M	f
WT	157, 161, 211, 243, 261	Top-covered open balcony	1902-3	1928	Brill 22E	GECWT28KL 2x50hp	BTH B49	g
Exp.	350 "Poppy"	Enclosed top-covered	1927	--	Hendon Maximum Traction	BTH510AS 2x50hp	BTH B49	
UCC	351-395 "Feltham"	Totally enclosed	1930-1	--	EE Maximum Traction	GECWT29P1 2x70hp	GEC KB5	
UCC	396 Experimental "Feltham"	Totally enclosed	1930-1	--	Special Equal-Wheel	EEDK131 2x70hp	EE CDB2 Form 5	

(a) Some cars on this batch fitted with BTH lineswitch gear by 1931.
(b) Nos.265-274 and 276-300 fitted with top-covers in 1910-11. Others fitted between 1925 and 1930 with covers removed from scrapped Type U and Y cars.
(c) Partially rebuilt at Chiswick workshops. 90° turn stairs replaced original. Lineswitch gear fitted in 1928.
(d) Similar to (c) but body re-posted. Flat-top windows with opening quarter-lights and 90° turn stairs replaced original. 2 and 1 transverse seating for 27 fitted in lower saloon, 38 in upper saloon.
(e) Body and underframe ex-Type X No.117 nominally scrapped in 1923. New top cover to old pattern fitted and platforms lengthened to 6ft. Car had BTH lineswitch gear for a time. Fleet No.247 taken from a type W car which had suffered an unknown fate c1923 and was not listed as sold or scrapped.
(f) Re-seated and generally refurbished in 1925, re-motored in 1928. No.307 balcony seats removed, reducing total seating to 67.
(g) No.261 ex-type U top cover lengthened to form open balcony. Others ex-type W with entirely new open-balcony top-covers.

APPENDIX 11

RENUMBERING OF LUT TRAMCARS INTO L.T. FLEET AND WITHDRAWAL DETAILS

The following table gives details of car renumbering by LPTB, together with the disposal dates. With regard to scrapping arrangements, after each car was taken out of service and delicensed, it would be stored at some convenient point until it was either broken up or sold.

Due to the complexities involved in the process, whereby many cars were disposed of before they were written off, while with others the opposite process applied, the actual scrapping month and year is shown where known, but where it is not, use has been made of the write-off or delicensing date, whichever was recorded.

Codes used for disposal sites:-

BH	Brixton Hill Depot
CA	Clapham Depot
FW	Fulwell Depot
HP	Hampstead Depot
HN	Hendon Depot
MI	Mitcham (Croydon, Aurelia Road) Depot
PN	Penhall Road Yard, Charlton
PY	Purley Depot
SL	Sold to Leeds City Tramways

Sub references:-

(a)	Scrapped 10/35
(b)	Derelict as at 1.7.33
(c)	Scrapped 4/36
(d)	Scrapped 3/35
(e)	Scrapped 6/36
(f)	Body sold 11/35
(g)	Damaged by fire
(h)	Scrapped 12/49
(j)	Collision 5/47
(k)	Damaged by fire Trucks sold to Leeds

LUT No.	LPTB No.	LUT Type	Disposal Date	Scrap Point	LUT No.	LPTB No.	LUT Type	Disposal Date	Scrap Point
151	2358	U	8/36	HN	313	2329	T	12/36	MI
154	2359	U	5/36	HN	314	2330	T	12/36	MI
155	2403	U/2	8/36	HN	315	2331	T	12/36	MI
157	2406	WT	8/36	HN	316	2332	T	6/36	HN
158	2360	U	7/36	HN	317	2333	T	12/36	MI
161	2407	WT	8/36	HN	318	2334	T	10/36	HN
165	2522	W	11/35	HP	319	2335	T	12/36	MI
173	2523	W	8/35	HP(a)	320	2336	T	8/36	HN
182	2524	W	8/35	HP(a)	321	2337	T	8/36	HN
183	--	W	5/34	FW(b)	322	2338	T	6/36	HN
185	2525	W	8/35	HP(a)	323	2339	T	7/36	HN
199	2404	U/2	8/36	HN(a)	324	2340	T	8/36	HN
200	2526	W	8/35	HP(a)	325	2341	T	8/36	HN
204	2361	U	7/36	HN	326	2342	T	7/36	HN
205	2362	U	7/36	HN	327	2343	T	8/36	HN
210	2363	U	8/36	HN	328	2344	T	8/36	HN
211	2408	WT	8/36	HN	329	2345	T	8/36	HN
212	2364	U	8/36	HN	330	2346	T	8/36	HN
224	2365	U	8/36	HN	331	2347	T	8/36	HN
235	2365	U	7/36	HN	332	2348	T	8/36	HN
236	2367	U	7/36	HN	333	2349	T	12/36	MI
240	2527	W	8/35	HP(a)	334	2350	T	12/36	MI
243	2409	WT	8/36	HN	335	2351	T	12/36	MI

LUT No.	LPTB No.	LUT Type	Disposal Date	Scrap Point	LUT No.	LPTB No.	LUT Type	Disposal Date	Scrap Point
247	2411	XU	8/36	HN	336	2352	T	12/36	MI
250	2368	U	7/36	HN	337	2353	T	12/36	MI
251	2369	U	7/36	HN	338	2354	T	8/36	HN
254	2528	W	8/35	HP(a)	339	2355	T	12/36	MI
255	2370	U	8/35	HP(a)	340	2356	T	8/36	HN
259	2529	W	11/35	HP	350	2317	Poppy	9/35	(f)
261	2410	WT	8/36	HN	351	2120	UCC	4/51	SL
262	2371	U	7/36	HN	352	2121	UCC	4/51	SL
265	2372	U	7/36	HN	353	2122	UCC	5/47	BH(j)
266	2373	U	7/36	HN	354	2123	UCC	4/51	SL
267	2374	U	7/36	HN	355	2124	UCC	4/51	SL
268	2375	U	7/36	HN	356	2125	UCC	4/51	SL
269	2376	U	7/36	HN	357	2126	UCC	4/51	SL
270	2377	U	7/36	HN	358	2127	UCC	4/51	SL
271	2378	U	7/36	HN	359	2128	UCC	4/51	SL
272	2379	U	7/36	HN	360	2129	UCC	4/51	SL
273	2380	U	7/36	HN	361	2130	UCC	4/49	PY(g)
274	2381	U	8/36	HN	362	2131	UCC	4/51	SL
276	2382	U	8/36	HN	363	2132	UCC	4/51	SL
277	2383	U	7/36	HN	364	2133	UCC	4/51	SL
278	2384	U	4/36	HN(c)	365	2134	UCC	4/51	SL
279	2385	U	7/36	HN	366	2135	UCC	4/51	SL
281	2386	U	2/35	FW(d)	367	2136	UCC	4/51	SL
282	2387	U	8/36	HN	368	2137	UCC	2/51	SL
283	2388	U	4/36	HN(c)	369	2138	UCC	4/51	SL
284	2389	U	7/36	HN	370	2139	UCC	2/51	SL(g)
285	2390	U	7/36	HN	371	2140	UCC	4/51	SL
286	2391	U	7/36	HN	372	2141	UCC	4/51	SL
287	2392	U	7/36	HN	373	2142	UCC	4/51	SL
288	2405	U/2	8/36	HN	374	2143	UCC	4/51	SL
290	2393	U	8/36	HN	375	2144	UCC	11/50	PN(k)
291	2394	U	7/36	HN	376	2145	UCC	4/51	SL
292	2395	U	7/36	HN	377	2146	UCC	4/51	SL
293	2396	U	8/36	HN	378	2147	UCC	4/51	SL
294	2397	U	7/36	HN	379	2148	UCC	4/51	SL
295	2398	U	7/36	HN	380	2149	UCC	4/51	SL
296	2399	U	6/36	HN	381	2150	UCC	4/51	SL
297	2400	U	7/36	HN	382	2151	UCC	4/51	SL
299	2401	U	5/36	HN	383	2152	UCC	4/51	SL
300	2402	U	8/36	HN	384	2153	UCC	4/51	SL
301	2318	T	4/36	HN(e)	385	2154	UCC	4/51	SL
302	2319	T	8/36	HN	386	2155	UCC	4/51	SL
303	2320	T	8/36	HN	387	2156	UCC	4/51	SL
304	2321	T	8/36	HN	388	2157	UCC	4/51	SL
305	2322	T	8/36	HN	389	2158	UCC	4/51	SL
306	2323	T	8/36	HN	390	2159	UCC	4/51	SL
307	2357	T	12/36	MI	391	2160	UCC	4/51	SL
308	2324	T	12/36	MI	392	2161	UCC	4/51	SL
309	2325	T	12/36	MI	393	2162	UCC	11/50	PN(k)
310	2326	T	12/36	MI	394	2163	UCC	4/49	PY(h)
311	2327	T	12/36	MI	395	2164	UCC	4/51	SL
312	2328	T	12/36	MI	396	2165	UCC	9/49	PY(h)

APPENDIX 12
LONDON UNITED TRAMWAYS ANNUAL STATISTICS

YEAR	TRAFFIC RECEIPTS £	WORKING COSTS £	PASSENGERS CARRIED	CAR MLES RUN	NUMBER OF CARS	ROUTE MILES OPEN mls; ch.	NOTES
Year To 30 June							
1894	West Metropolitan Tramways In Hands Of Receiver, No Return Submitted						
1895	Nil Return Submitted by W.M.T. to 30.6.1895 No Details						
1896	37,404	27,140	7,026,200	844,000	49H	9 04	1
1897	42,244	31,490	8,079,936	998,393	49H	9 04	
1898	45,411	35,456	8,656,353	1,032,195	59H	9 04	
1899	25,239	18,956	4,740,589	559,986	59H	9 04	
1900	54,369	41,098	10,500,427	1,807,225	59H	9 04	
1901	60,664	42,812	11,710,336	1,355,073	59H	9 19	
1902	No Return of Traffic Received						
Year To 31 December							
1903	280,241	176,391	45,293,473	6,977,512	300E/10H	30 42	2, 1
1904	296,235	176,188	48,126,727	7,141,374	300E/10H	30 42	
1905	301,350	175,314	49,137,139	7,319,460	340E/10H	30 42	
1906	327,896	189,919	55,555,281	7,760,529	340E/10H	48 77	
1907	345,570	214,672	58,725,980	8,618,045	340E/10H	55 34	
1908	348,390	220,232	59,255,819	8,752,252	340E/10H	55 34	
1909	318,226	226,567	55,550,807	8,458,805	340E/10H	55 34	
1910	333,659	234,210	60,132,451	8,772,522	340E/10H	55 34	
1911	343,987	219,033	62,437,128	9,265,142	340E/9H	55 34	
1912	332,016	223,655	61,139,285	9,474,504	340E	53 61	2
1913	328,543	229,143	62,645,125	9,407,226	340	53 61	
1914	316,838	230,582	61,433,783	8,996,801	338	53 61	
1915	318,741	234,256	63,145,226	7,744,894	338	53 61	
1916	322,171	268,266	65,734,446	7,494,898	338	53 61	
1917	345,092	290,396	68,668,035	6,563,541	338	53 61	
1918	No Return of Traffic Received						
1919	488,964	486,322	70,628,244	6,565,979	225	53 61	
1920	523,300	470,429	66,970,416	5,925,461	225	53 61	
1921	575,837	460,252	62,716,404	5,857,139	225	53 61	
1922	506,716	313,439	59,225,226	6,020,368	225	53 48	
1923	425,996	367,822	59,682,942	6,194,107	225	53 31	
1924	404,492	379,241	58,335,461	6,226,704	225	45 68	
1925	374,284	360,551	56,294,247	6,282,550	214	45 68	
1926	390,894	363,698	58,719,273	6,019,658	214	45 68	
1927	412,213	367,786	63,229,345	6,424,755	214	45 68	
1928	453,447	392,456	68,424,601	6,666,663	210	45 67	
1929	469,194	403,197	71,500,297	6,993,542	150	45 66	
1930	465,978	415,558	71,361,575	7,241,149	150	45 66	
1931	464,962*	405,290*	71,508,568*	6,207,135§	150	29 31	3, 8
				1,048,839#	24t/b	17 26	4, 6, 8
1932	475,257*	402,196*	71,249,056*	5,214,484§	150 ‡	29 31 †	3, 7
				2,449,017#	60t/b	17 24 †	4, 6
1933	Half Year Only to 30 June						
	321,447*	277,598*	35,799,763*	2,655,500e	150 ‡	29 05 †	5, 7, 9
				1,108,125e	60t/b	17 24 †	5, 6, 9

1.	H = Horse-drawn tramcars	6.	t/b = Trolleybus
2.	E = Electric tramcars	7.	‡ = Including cars stored prior to disposal
3.	§ = Tramcar mileage	8.	† = Ultimate mileage
4.	# = Trolleybus mileage	9.	e = estimated
5.	* = Tram & Trolleybus		

Vol. 1, Pages 1-288.   Vol. 2, Pages 289-528.